MW00827295

Ceramic theory and cultural process

NEW STUDIES IN ARCHAEOLOGY

Series editors

Colin Renfrew, *University of Cambridge*
Jeremy Sabloff, *University of Pittsburgh*

Titles in the series include:

Ceramic Theory and Cultural Process

DEAN E. ARNOLD

Professor of Anthropology
Wheaton College
Wheaton, Illinois

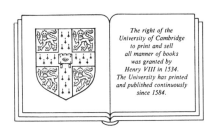

The right of the
University of Cambridge
to print and sell
all manner of books
was granted by
Henry VIII in 1534.
The University has printed
and published continuously
since 1584.

CAMBRIDGE UNIVERSITY PRESS
CAMBRIDGE
NEW YORK   NEW ROCHELLE
MELBOURNE   SYDNEY

Published by the Press Syndicate of the University of Cambridge
The Pitt Building, Trumpington Street, Cambridge CB2 1RP
32 East 57th Street, New York, NY 10022, USA
10 Stamford Road, Oakleigh, Melbourne 3166, Australia

© Cambridge University Press 1985

First published 1985

First paperback edition 1988

Printed in Great Britain at the University Press, Cambridge

Library of Congress catalogue card number: 83-23223

British Library cataloguing in publication data
Arnold, Dean E.
Ceramic theory and cultural process. –
(New studies in archaeology)
1. Pottery   2. Archaeology – Methodology
I. Title II. Series
930.1′028   CC79.5.P6

ISBN 0 521 25262 8 hard covers
ISBN 0 521 27259 9 paperback

LU

CONTENTS

TO JUNE...

whose patience, love, support and commitment
made it possible...

Preface

The idea for this book came from two sources: my own research and a frustration with the existing published accounts of ethnographic ceramics. My own field work on contemporary ceramics in Mexico, Peru and Guatemala revealed a number of similarities between the populations of these communities and in the ecology, production and organization of the craft of these areas even though there were also great differences. My frustration developed over the lack of generalizations and theory about the massive literature on ethnographic ceramics. With the exception of Nicklin (1971; 1979) who reviewed some of this material, no attempt has been made to synthesize this literature and apply it to archaeology.

Unfortunately, the paradigms used in the collection of these ethnographic data have limited their application to archaeology. Often, however, there are great 'gems' of data or insight which are very *apropos* to archaeology, but which lurk beneath a mass of seemingly irrelevant detail. Nevertheless, the paradigms used to collect much of the data limit any future questions that can be asked of them and thus more research needs to be done on ethnographic ceramics using new paradigms.

The lack of synthesis in the literature led to the development of two papers which attempted to formulate some generalizations about ceramics. After I had delivered one of these papers at the Annual Conference of the Archaeology Association of the University of Calgary (Arnold, 1976), my colleague, Dr Scott Raymond, made a casual remark that a cybernetic model like that used by Flannery (1968a) might provide a useful way to tie the generalizations together. It was this suggestion that was the stimulus for the organization of this book.

The work which follows is first of all a synthesis of much of the ethnographic literature on ceramics. More material could be added, but it is not likely that my synthesis would change significantly except to provide broader support for the generalizations. Secondarily, the work presents a set of generalizations described as feedback mechanisms which stimulate or prevent ceramic production. Each mechanism is explained showing why such relationships exist. The thesis of this book is that there are certain universal processes involving ceramics that are tied to ecological, cultural or chemical factors. These processes occur in societies around the world and can provide a solid empirical (as opposed to speculative) base for interpreting ancient ceramics. On a more modest scale, the book presents cross-cultural regularities which relate ceramics to environmental and non-ceramic cultural phenomena. In presenting these regularities, the book shows why these regularities exist. Equally importantly, however, the book presents the regularities in wider explanatory framework in cultural evolution by answering the question why does pottery making develop in an area and why does it evolve into a full-time craft? Thus, the book attempts to explain why these regularities successfully retrodict evolution of ceramic specialization in the past.

Any book requires the help of a great number of individuals and organizations. First and foremost, the Wheaton College Alumni Association and the Norris M. Aldeen Fund administered by the Office of the Vice President of Academic Affairs of Wheaton College provided the funds for three summers of writing and research which made the preparation of this manuscript possible. I am grateful to Dr Donald Mitchell, former Vice-President of Academic Affairs of Wheaton College, Dr Ward Kriegbaum, current Vice-President of Academic Affairs of Wheaton College, Mr Lee Pfund, Director of the Alumni Association, and Dr William Henning, Dean of Arts and Sciences, in making these funds available to me. Dr W. Arthur White (Illinois State Geological Survey), Gilbert Prost, Dr John Thatcher, Dr Carol Mackey, Dr Teresa Topic, Patsy Adams, Dr Michael Moseley (Field Museum of Natural History), Dr Ronald Weber (Field Museum of Natural History) and Dr Paul Powlison provided unpublished data used in various portions of the manuscript. I also wish to express my appreciation to the reference section of the Wheaton College Library particularly Ivy Olson, June Weitting, Dan Bowell and Jonathan Lauer who searched for and obtained on interlibrary loan many obscure sources that were used in this project. Their help in verifying references and sources is gratefully acknowledged. Pauline Roloeffs and Greg Dolezal did much of the typing of various versions of the manuscript in preparation for machine processing. Rich Nickel, Randy Birkey and Jim Markle drafted the illustrations new to this volume. Alva Stefler of the Art Department of Wheaton College prepared many of the high contrast stats for publication. The Data Processing Department of Wheaton College (Wendy Liles, Charlie Reitsma, Jeff Smallwood, Daniel Taylor and Larry Swanson) provided much help and many hours of work in facilitating the many computer processed drafts of the manuscript and preparing the final electronic version on magnetic tape. Dr Robert Feldman (Field Museum of Natural History), Dr Ronald Weber (Field Museum of Natural History), Dr Bee Lan Wang (Wheaton College), Dr James Rogers (Wheaton College), Dr David L. Browman (Washington University), Dr C. Stephen Evans (Wheaton College), Dr Paul DeVries

(Wheaton College), Dr James Yost (Summer Institute of Linguistics), Dr Joseph Spradley (Wheaton College), Prof. Al Hoerth (Wheaton College), Dr James Hoffmeier (Wheaton College), Dr William Henning (Wheaton College) and Dan Olson (Wheaton College) read various portions of the manuscript at various stages and made many helpful comments. Three anonymous reviewers of the manuscript provided many helpful comments and criticisms. I am indebted to the individuals (and organizations) who gave their permission to reprint many of the drawings and photographs that were used in this volume. In addition, Todd Swentek, Susan Warkentein, and Sheryl Fetzer helped in various ways in the preparation of the manuscript. Linda Smith, Sharon Warnock, David Harrell, John Page, Conrad Kanagy, Karen Fischer and my father, Eldon Arnold, put in many hours of work helping prepare the index. Dr Zondra Lindblade, Chair of the Department of Sociology and Anthropology, was very patient with me in shifting or postponing some of my department responsibilities so that I could finish the final draft of the manuscript. Many others have helped in various ways and my failure to mention them here reveals more a lapse of my memory over the years that this manuscript has been in process than my lack of appreciation for their help. My beloved uncle, Harvey E. Marquette, died suddenly as the final version of this manuscript was nearing completion. His lifetime in education was a source of constant inspiration and encouragement to me and others. He will be greatly missed. My parents, Eldon and Reva Arnold, provided much encouragement throughout my academic career and for this project since its inception. Finally, to my wife, June, to whom this work is dedicated, I want to express my deep love and appreciation. Her encouragement and help and willingness to accept my procrastination during my dedication to this task have been instrumental in the completion of this book over the several years that it has been in process. Without her, there would be no book.

1
Introduction

Ceramics are one of the tangible products of man's culture. Their relatively widespread manufacture among cultures of the world, their relatively imperishable quality, their persistence through time and their almost universal presence have made them a very important tool for the archaeologist in his study of the past.

Traditionally, the most widespread use of ceramics by archaeologists lies in formulating typologies which form the basis of chronologies (Willey and Sabloff, 1980:143). In their simplest form, these chronologies are a temporal sequence of types, but more importantly, they are believed to reflect culture historical relationships through time and are based on the similarities and differences between types, styles or attributes that are relatively contiguous in time and/or space (e.g. Egloff, 1972:148ff). This belief rests on a number of assumptions. First and foremost, archaeologists believe that ceramics can reflect the culture of a people such that the main forces of cultural change that affect a society are reflected in their ceramics (Grieder, 1975:850-1). Secondly, typological or attribute similarities are believed to be the result of cultural contact or diffusion; people in one area acquire pots or the ideas of how to make and decorate them by trade, exchange, migration or conquest (MacNeish, Peterson and Flannery, 1970). Conversely, differences in types, attributes or style indicate the lack of such cultural contact and diffusion. Thirdly, except for differences in available resources, the environment is a neutral variable not appreciably affecting the similarities and differences in ceramics. At best, archaeologists recognize the occurrence of clay deposits as an environmental requisite affecting the presence of pottery making communities, but beyond this factor, there are few statements which shed light on the relationship of ceramics to the environment.

The main problem with these assumptions is that the evidence from historical documents and archaeology does not support the relationship of ceramics and political, social or cultural history. Adams (1979), for example, showed that Nubian ceramics could not be related to political, religious, social or cultural history of the area. Tschopik (1950) noted

1

little change in Aymara pottery from the Precolumbian pottery of the Titicaca Basin in Peru up to the present even after the Inca and Spanish conquests and four hundred years of massive acculturation. Similarly, ceramic acculturation to Spanish domination in the valley of Mexico was gradual during the Colonial period and only began 150 years after the conquest (Charlton, 1976b).

Another problem is that archaeologists know little about how ceramics articulate with the rest of culture. Since the 1960s, archaeology has heightened its concern for relating ceramics to other aspects of the cultural system such as kinship and social structure (e.g. Deetz, 1965; Longacre, 1970; Hill, 1970), but there are few ethnographic data to show that such a relationship is justified (Allen and Richardson, 1971; Stanislawski and Stanislawski, 1978). In some cases, the degree of social interaction may be a more valid goal of reconstruction (see Friedrich, 1970). Most recently, however, Plog (1980) has contested this approach.

Certainly, if archaeologists are concerned with generalizations and explanations of culture history and process, an empirical understanding of the relationship of ceramics, environment and culture should be foundational. Thus, as attractive as these assumptions about the interpretive significance of the sequence of ceramic types are for the interpretation of the past, it remains to be demonstrated that ceramic classifications and chronologies do more than group ceramic assemblages in space and time.

Another important use of ceramics by the archaeologist consists of seeing them as one kind of craft specialization. Not only is the role of craft specialization important in the development of civilization, but craft products also provide the archaeologist with his largest share of data about ancient cultures in the form of pottery, stone, metals and textiles. These crafts have been studied from technological, artistic and historical points of view. But, even though the archaeologist depends on these craft data for his interpretations and inferences, little is known ethnographically about the ecology of craft specialization, particularly the relationship of the craft to the environment on the one hand and to culture on the other.

Although an ecological perspective has been important in studies of the evolution of civilization, there has been no corresponding interest in the ecology of crafts. Traditionally, this topic has been of marginal interest to cultural anthropologists. Although important to archaeologists, ceramics, like most crafts, have been largely ignored by most cultural anthropologists as apparently irrelevant and uninteresting (George Foster (1948; 1955; 1960a; 1960b; 1965; 1967; Foster, assisted by Ospina, 1948) and Ruben Reina (Reina and Hill, 1978) are exceptions). Some have written descriptive articles on ceramics, but such studies have tended to focus more on the particularistic details of technique than the relationships of ceramics with the environment and non-ceramic aspects of culture.

Towards a ceramic theory

In recent years archaeologists have become increasingly aware of their conceptual approaches to the past through the influence of the philosophy of science. Thomas Kuhn (1962) demonstrated that all science is based on unstated assumptions (called paradigms) about the nature of the world and the way that world must be approached through science. Kuhn argued that the history of science was not the accumulation of facts about the universe, but rather a radically changing set of perspectives for viewing that universe. The history of astronomy, for example, was not just the accumulation of data about the stars and the planets, but, more significantly, involved the revolutionary changes like those which occurred as a result of Galileo's and Copernicus' proposal that the sun rather than the earth was the center of the solar system. Similar revolutionary changes have occurred in other sciences. The history of science has thus been a set of scientific revolutions in which the prevailing conceptual framework has changed radically and set each discipline on a new course.

Kuhn's notions about the history of science create two problematic implications for scientific investigation. First, there is the belief that Kuhn's scheme is too relativistic since paradigms have changed greatly in the past for seemingly irrational and random reasons. Are paradigms merely conventionally accepted ways of looking at the universe? Or, are they justifiable and based on rational criteria? Paradigms are never merely arbitrary, but are also abstractions which inform one of the ways in which the tangible world actually exists and works. If paradigms were completely arbitrary, science would be analogous to the changing fashions of Madison Avenue, and Feyerabend's (Broad, 1979) belief that science is merely propaganda would be justified. There is a sense in which science is a product of western values such as the desire to understand and manipulate the universe, but even though the values of science are western, its paradigms go beyond the perspective of a single culture. Rather, science aims at truth value; it attempts to discover the patterns and processes of the external physical world. Science is not just what is going on in scholars' heads or that which is reflected in scientific books and journals. Either scientific paradigms are sharpening an understanding of 'truth' about the natural world or they are totally culture bound and relativistic—mere propaganda, as Feyerabend (Broad, 1979) proposes. If one rejects the skeptical view of Feyerabend, the history of science is thus the evolution of paradigms which progressively describe in a more complete way what actually occurs in the physical, objective world.

The second problematic implication of Kuhn's ideas is the question of the absolute or relative existence of scientific 'facts'. Here, the truth value of facts is not in question, but whether 'facts' have an absolute existence by themselves or exist only in relation to a particular paradigm. Philosopher of science Norwood Russell Hanson (1958) has shown that data about the world do not come to the scientific investigator uninterpreted; there are no 'pure' facts. Rather, all data are theory-laden. In order to be known, all 'data' are approached in some paradigmatic and theoretical framework, whether they are expressed or not. No matter how 'raw' and 'atheoretical' data may seem, they are still affected by certain *a priori* paradigmatic and theoretical considerations such as what is important and why, the methods and units used to collect the data and finally the data's ultimate significance. Thus, a paradigm will affect all levels of inquiry from large scale problem orientation to description and explanation.

There was a time in American anthropology, for example, when data collecting was the primary goal of the field. The result was an eclectic 'butterfly collecting' of miscellaneous ethnographic data. Although this period of American anthropology provided a great deal of information about the peoples of the world, it left anthropology with the erroneous notion that theory construction came *after* data collection rather than before it. If one makes the erroneous claim that data are non-theoretical, then the paradigmatic and theoretical considerations are still present and still affect the data, but they are unrecognized and unexpressed. Thus, all data exist within some paradigmatic framework whether this framework is explicit or not. Data, then, should be informed by paradigmatic and theoretical considerations.

Paradigms of ceramic study

The importance of paradigms in science means that ceramic studies in anthropology are no less affected by paradigmatic considerations than the other sciences. One of the most important of these is the atomistic/analytic/mechanistic paradigm. This paradigm has its roots in Newtonian physics, which conceives of the world as made up of units which are acted upon by forces. The goal of science is then to break up phenomena into units, isolate them and then determine the forces that are acting upon the units. The notion of scientific 'laws' has come out of this tradition and these 'laws' are mono-causal statements which express a presumably universal relationship of a force acting upon a particular analytical unit.

This paradigm expresses itself in ceramic studies as an emphasis on classification. The basic units of study are potsherds (or less frequently entire vessels) which are broken up into attributes and then clustered and reassembled as abstract 'types' which are acted upon by the forces of culture process or culture history. Classic statements of this are Gifford

(1960), Rouse (1960), Whallon (1972) and Smith, Willey and Gifford (1960).

There are several problems with this paradigm. First, potsherds are not cultural units of behavior. They are only arbitrary divisions of such units. When a vessel is broken, the behaviorally significant unit in the culture (the vessel shape) is fragmented. Not only is the shape of the vessel often lost, but much of the information communicated in the design is lost as well.

Like all cultural behavior, the behavior used in the production and decoration of pottery is structured; behaviorally meaningful units are structured into higher level patterns and sequences. Like language, it is not the units themselves that carry information, but rather the way these units are structured relative to one another. Basic sounds in language, for example, are patterned into sequences and it is the sound sequences that carry information, not the sounds themselves. Similarly, in pottery studies, it is not the attributes (whether technological or decorative) that carry information, but the way these attributes are patterned on a particular vessel shape. By focusing on a potsherd rather than a whole vessel, the basic unit of cultural behavior (the vessel shape) and the structure of the other cultural units on it are missed. Ascertaining behavioral structure from potsherds, rather than the structure on the vessel shape, and attempting to derive culturally meaningful information from them is like shredding a dictionary and trying to reconstruct its organization without reconstructing the pages.

A second problem with the analytical paradigm in ceramic studies is that arbitrary units of cultural behavior make ceramic analyses difficult to relate to other aspects of culture. Although such analyses may provide classificatory criteria which have heuristic value in formulating chronologies, they produce a lot of behavioral 'noise' which has no cultural significance apart from the ceramics themselves. Indeed, ethnoarchaeological work by David and Hennig (1972) suggests that great detail is not necessary in ceramic classification in order to ascertain accurately the cultural behavior that produced it; it is possible to over-classify pottery.

The point is not that classificatory schemes are unimportant or not useful, but that the analytical paradigm that has dominated ceramic studies in archaeology has greatly limited the kinds of questions that can be answered by ceramic data.

Other paradigmatic notions which affect ceramic studies came out of American anthropology in the 1920s and 1930s. The first of these was mentalism or 'the native's point of view'–a perspective which dominated anthropological thought in the final decade of the nineteenth and early twentieth centuries in reaction to the materialism of nineteenth-century anthropological thought.

Mentalism brought two important analogies to ceramic studies—one from psychological anthropology and one from linguistics. With the former, the concern with the natives' point of view found its fullest expression in the Culture and Personality school which developed in the late 1920s. One of the most important concepts of this school was the importance of enculturation in molding the human personality. American anthropology in general and the Culture and Personality School in particular argued for the total plasticity of the human personality and its ability to be molded into any shape during the process of enculturation (Hatch, 1973b:88-91). This notion developed in reaction to Freud's idea of a basic universal human nature called the 'libido' and his universal developmental stages (oral, anal and genital) which were presumably common to all mankind. The plastic human personality was thus a convenient analogy to use for the plastic clay in the potter's hands which he could mold into virtually any shape. This plasticity is one common theme between Bunzel's (1929) *The Pueblo potter* and Benedict's *Patterns of culture* (1934). Benedict argued that the personality was plastic while Bunzel argued that it was the clay that was plastic. Both argued that it was tradition that shaped the plastic raw material (whether clay or personality) and accounted for the great diversity of cultural practices on the one hand and kinds of vessel shapes on the other. Bunzel expresses it as follows:

Owing to the plastic nature of the material, almost any conceivable form is possible. Setting aside modelling in the round as outside the scope of the present investigation, and confining ourselves to practicable utensils, we find even in these an enormous range of possibilities. In aboriginal North America, pottery is made entirely by hand, so that there is not even the limitation to circular forms which is inevitable where pottery is turned on the wheel. Square, box-like vessels can be made and are, in fact, still made in some places. An endless variety of curvilinear forms are possible. Futhermore, there are no definite limits to the size of vessels that can be made of clay. What limits there are, are set by the skill of the potter in mixing her materials, building the vessel and firing it, rather than by the inherent nature of the material. In the larger vessels the difficulty of firing increases out of proportion to the size. Nevertheless, vessels of great size are still made by primitive potters. As the size of the vessel increases beyond a certain point, the range of forms becomes more restricted. (Bunzel, 1929:2)

This same view of ceramics can also be found in descriptions of ceramics in the 1970s.

Clay is the plastic medium, imbued with the quality of instant changeability, and possessing within its formless mass the possibility of an infinite number of designs, both primitive and sophisticated. Damp clay turning on the wheel is brought to its finest purpose by the skilled hand and eye of the potter; the quality and impact of the finished product is dependent solely upon the experience, dexterity, and imagination of the craftsman working within the natural limitations of the material itself. (Bivins, 1972:14)

Another important analogy came from linguistics. In the first half of the twentieth century, linguistics in America was a part of anthropology

(Robins, 1967:207). One of the dominant themes of linguistics during this period was the phoneme. Although grammatical analysis also developed during this time, phonological concerns dominated linguistic theory. This interest goes back into the nineteenth century when phonological analysis, orthography and spelling reforms were the concern of linguistics (Robins, 1967:202-3). During the early third of the twentieth century, phonological studies became the pace-setter of the field (Robins, 1967:204; 1975) and the phoneme was viewed as the basic unit of linguistic description and analysis. In the period between the World Wars, however, linguistics was dominanted by the Prague school which applied Saussurean theory to elaborating the concept of the phoneme (Robins, 1967:204). Speech acts belonged to *parole*, which was later described as speech performance, whereas the phoneme belonged to *langue* or language competence—an abstraction which was the collective knowledge held by the speech community (Robins, 1967:204-5). Earlier, the phoneme had been viewed as a linguistic unit or a class of sounds, and variously as a psychological reality, a physiological entity or merely a descriptive convention (Robins, 1967:204). The Prague school, however, did not treat the phoneme as a transcriptional device or a class of sounds, but rather as a complex psychological unit which was composed of a number of distinctive features which characterized it as a linguistic entity (Robins, 1967:205). Each feature existed in opposition to its absence or to another feature in at least one other phoneme in the language. Phonemes were not all members of one set of contrastive language units, but had different sets of relationships with other phonemes in the language.

The concern for using the phoneme for basic linguistic description and its alleged mental reality influenced four important developments in ceramic studies in archaeology that were in harmony with the mentalism of the Boasian tradition. First of all, the phoneme was used as an analogy for the ceramic type. Since the phoneme was the basic unit of linguistic description, the ceramic type became the basic unit of ceramic description. Secondly, the ceramic type, like the phoneme, had a psychological reality (see Gifford, 1960; Deetz, 1967:45-9) and became the 'mental template' (Deetz, 1967:45-9) or ideal type that a potter had in his mind before he made a pot. Thirdly, the ceramic type was thus seen as the archaeological homologue of the potter's mental template. Fourthly, since the phoneme was composed of features, the ceramic type and the potter's mental template were also composed of features. The potter thus constructed a pot according to an ideal set of attributes that he had in his mind and these features were also characteristic of the archaeologist's ceramic types. In summary, the definition of the potter's mental template and the archaeologist's ceramic type had their origin in this period and these concepts are still important in American archaeology.

In contrast to this view, recent information indicates that knowledge of 'style' that guides the construction of a pot is imbedded in the motor habit patterns rather than in mental templates (Steadman, 1980). Furthermore, work by Kempton (1981) indicates that the way that Mexican potters and non-potters think about pottery does not involve attribute clusters or abstract types. Rather, the 'mental templates' used by potters consist of prototypic visual categories which correspond most closely to a vessel shape.

Even more important than the analogies which early American anthropology supplied for ceramic studies in archaeology was the impact that mentalism had on the lack of generalizaton in archaeological research. Boas not only reacted to nineteenth-century anthropology by emphasizing a mentalistic point of view, but he also reacted to the search for similarities among the world's cultures during the nineteeth century by stressing cultural differences. Nineteenth-century anthropology had used the cultural similarities to develop world-wide generalizations. In reaction to the speculation and lack of good quality ethnographic data during this period, Boas claimed at first that generalizations should follow data collection, but ultimately he abandoned the goal of generalization entirely (Harris, 1968). His concern for mentalism and the native's point of view led to a relativistic approach in which the units of analysis were defined differently in each culture with no cross-cultural standards of comparison. Only relatively recently has this trend begun to change. (Not all mentalistic approaches are relativistic. Current work in linguistic anthropology has focused on cross-cultural generalizations of how and why cultures classify color, plants and animals (Witkowski and Brown, 1977; Brown, 1977).) The impact of this perspective in archaeology thus created a focus on ceramics in particular cultures with little concern for using ceramic similarities to develop cross-cultural generalizations. Although some cross-cultural comparisons were made using widely occurring attributes, types and styles (like the Lapita Ware Horizon in the islands of eastern Melanesia (Golson, 1972:554-7; Specht, 1968; Kennedy, 1981; see also Willey and Sabloff, 1980:173-4) or the Horizon styles of Peru (Willey, 1971:86) in South America, or the evolutionary stages of ceramic development (Willey, 1947)), the concern for generalization in ceramic studies was limited.

Early American anthropology also influenced ceramic studies by generally ignoring the role of the environment as either ubiquitous or benign in its effect on culture. This perspective is clearly reflected in Benedict's *Patterns of culture* (1934:35). Just as Benedict avoided ecological factors as explanations of 'culture' and its effect on the human personality (see Hatch, 1973b:86-8), so archaeologists seem to have avoided ecological factors as explanations of ceramics. The pot, then, was affected more by particularistic historical factors of tradition, aesthetic considerations and, more recently, social structure, than by the environment. Among archaeologists, the environment was viewed as having no significant relationship to ceramics except as providing the necessary raw materials (see Chapter 2). Willey (1947:143), for example, in his discussion of ceramics in the *Handbook of South American Indians* implied that the occurrence of clay conditioned the occurrence of pottery making communities. Similarly, the ecologically oriented report of the Tehuacan Valley project also fails to recognize the articulation of the ceramics with the environment except for resources (MacNeish et al., 1970). Other archaeologists have focused on the articulation of the social structural, ideological and culture historical interrelationships of ceramics with little, if any, recognition of environmental relationships (Deetz, 1965; Longacre, 1970, 1974; Hill, 1970). Thus, because the environment appears to have had an ubiquitous effect on ceramics, it could be discounted. This benign role of the environment is another common element of *Patterns of culture* (Benedict, 1934) and *The Pueblo potter* (Bunzel, 1929).

The tendency to emphasize the culture historical and social significance of ceramics without considering the ecological variables makes Steward's critique of anthropology seem equally appropriate for the archaeologist's approach to ceramics:

...anthropologists have been so pre-occupied with culture and its history that they have accorded environment only a negligible role. (Steward, 1955:35)

Cultural diffusion, of course, always operates, but in view of the seeming importance of ecological adaptations its role in explaining culture has been greatly over-estimated. (Steward, 1955:42)

Although mentalism was a dominant theme in early American anthropology, ecological and materialistic concerns were not dead (see Hatch, 1973a), and the ecological perspective was brought together at mid-century in a unified synthesis including several articles published fifteen years earlier (Steward, 1955). The effect of this ecological perspective on ceramic studies has been limited, however. Steward argued that the aspects of culture most directly affected by the environment constituted the 'culture core', whereas those not so directly affected were the peripheral features and were more affected by tradition. Anthropologists did not view ceramics as part of the core, but rather, by implication, ceramics were one of the numerous peripheral features which Steward argued were more influenced by culture history. This view, of course, is reinforced by the belief in the plasticity of the clay and its response to particularistic cultural forces. Thus, except for the importance of resources, environment is left out of the discussions of ceramics, and such oversight would seem to argue for the perceived unimportant role of environment in ceramic variability. Matson (1965), however, related Steward's work to ceramic studies and emphasized the need to go beyond the ceramics to understand the environment and cultural patterns behind them. To call attention to this approach and show its difference from traditional ceramic studies, Matson referred to his perspective as 'ceramic ecology'. Arnold (1975a) used the approach to describe the pottery making communities of Quinua, Peru, and of the Valley of Guatemala (Arnold, 1978a; 1978b). Kolb (1976) also used this approach in his study of South American ceramic technology and Van der Leeuw (1976) used it to study archaeological pottery of Holland and the Near East. Rice (1981) developed a model of specialized pottery production also using this perspective.

Since early anthropology argued that the effect of the environment was benign, the human personality as well as the ceramics were totally shaped by culture. Ceramics were thus a product of culture in an analytically isolated sense with no environmental relationship except resources. In the Boasian tradition, ceramics were a product of culture more in an ideological sense than an adaptive sense and thus provided cognitive information about a culture (again see the definition of 'type' by Gifford (1960)). It is understandable, then, that this approach led to the classification of ceramics, which were then used for discovering how 'culture' varied in time and space and for reconstructing culturally relative culture histories.

A final important theme of early American anthropology that influenced archaeologists' paradigms of ceramics was the interrelatedness of culture. Culture was viewed as an integrated whole with its parts interacting in such a way that change in one part produced changes in one or more other parts. The history of this concept is somewhat diverse, but can be traced back through the work of Leslie White, Julian Steward, Ruth Benedict, B. Malinowski and Franz Boas in anthropology; but the idea had its more distant origin in the organismic model of society proposed by H. Spencer and later by E. Durkheim in the nineteenth century. Parallel ideas also developed in physics in the nineteenth century with the development of field theory and relativity. Usually, this systemic notion was articulated as 'integration', 'interrelationships' or 'organic whole of interdependency', but there were attendant concepts which have tended to receive the focus in anthropology. These concepts revolved around the other characteristics of the organismic model (or 'body') rather than the notion of the interdependency among the parts (or organs). Thus, each body had a mind or 'collective consciousness' (Durkheim), 'needs' (Malinowski (1944:40)—classic functionalism) and a personality or a psychological 'configuration' (Benedict, 1934). Throughout the history of the discipline, these auxiliary concepts of the organismic analogy have been emphasized, but it is the interrelatedness aspect of the analogy itself (rather than the auxiliary concepts) which was the focus in archaeology. To apply this concept to ceramics, ceramics are interrelated with the rest of culture and can thus provide information about other aspects of culture. This means that the archaeologist who digs up ceramics can potentially infer and reconstruct the non-ceramic aspects of culture. This assumption implies that ceramic changes through time do not reveal merely a change in the technological aspects of ceramics, but a change in the culture as well. More importantly, however, ceramics can be used for synchronic social and cultural reconstruction of ancient societies.

Since the late 1960s, American archaeology has witnessed a shift in perspective away from the traditional concerns of archaeology to what has been called the 'new archaeology' (Klejn, 1977; Martin, 1971; Willey and Sabloff, 1980). This trend parallels recent interest in cultural ecology, generalization, cultural evolution and cultural materialism in cultural anthropology (e.g. Harris, 1968, 1979; see Price, 1982). Although Martin (1971) refers to the development of this new trend as a paradigm shift, it does not have all the characteristics of Kuhn's revolutions. Percival (1976) noted a similar situation in linguistics after the great changes that occurred in that field since the publication of Chomsky's *Syntactic structures* in 1957. Others (Klejn, 1977; Willey and Sabloff, 1980) have reviewed the history of this change in archaeology and its effects, so it will not be reiterated here except to review briefly some of the important themes and note how the new perspectives have changed the effect that early American anthropology has had on ceramic studies in archaeology.

One important theme of the 'new perspective' in archaeology consists of an increased concern for the philosophy of science which emphasizes a materialistic, deductive and generalizing orientation as opposed to the mentalistic, inductive and particularistic perspective that has influenced much of anthropology since Franz Boas. Secondly, there is concern with ecological interactions which serve as a basis for understanding cultural process based on the cultural ecology of Steward (1955). This theme provides the foundation for more cross-cultural generalizations than were possible with the more particularistic notions of culture history in the past. Thirdly, there is an explicit and overriding focus on the interrelatedness of cultural phenomena–particularly in using material culture to infer non-material culture. Fourthly, there is marked concern with the systems paradigm as a holistic conceptual framework to describe the generalizations and as a theoretical base to infer social behavior from the material aspects of culture. The interrelatedness of culture (sometimes called the systemic definition of culture) was a crucial factor in applying systems theory to archaeology because it fit so well with the characteristics of the systems paradigm.

In spite of the revolutionary assumptions and goals of the new orientation, the theory has not penetrated into the assumptions of ceramic description and the 'new' archaeologists are in reality using the 'old' untested assumptions about the relationships between the ceramics and environment and culture. It is indeed ironic in light of the prominent place of ecological studies in contemporary archaeology that some archaeologists search for the social structural relationships with ceramics while ignoring the environmental ones, when ceramics (as part of the technological subsystem) are so closely tied to the environment. This approach seems more akin to the culture and personality theme in anthropology of the 1930s than to ecological anthropology of the 1970s.

Another trend coincidental with the new archaeology is the study of living peoples from an archaeological perspective (ethnoarchaeology or 'living archaeology' (Gould, 1980)). The study of material culture has had a long history in American anthropology (Hatch, 1973a), but the emphasis of ethnoarchaeology is quite different from the more traditional studies of artefact production. Besides ascertaining the relationships of artefacts to the rest of culture, ethnoarchaeology is concerned about artefact patterning, processes of discard and the formation of the archaeological record.

The theoretical perspective of this book

Since paradigms affect all of scientific enterprise from data collection to the significance of the results, any presentation is more comprehensive and clearer if the paradigms are specified before the data are presented. Thus, it is desirable that any theory of ceramics should also specify its conceptual approach. The notion of 'theory' has a variety of meanings in anthropology, varying from more modest conceptual concerns to comparison, generalization and explanation of cultural phenomena.

In recent years, some archaeologists have emphasized the notion of 'prediction' as an important goal of science in general and archaeology in particular (e. g. Thomas, 1974:58-60). As Stephen Toulmin (1961) has pointed out, however, prediction is possible without 'science'. Prediction can be accomplished by the observation of regularities and the projection of these regularities into the future. Toulmin, for example, noted that the ancient Babylonians successfully predicted certain types of celestial phenomena, but they had no science. While the Athenian student of Plato, Eudoxus, first worked out an explanation of planetary motion in principle, it was not until the time of the Helienistic astronomer Ptolemy that the first comprehensive explanation existed concerning why regularities existed in the movement of the stars and the planets. Later, a more comprehensive and accurate explanation was developed by Copernicus and was subsequently elaborated by Newton. It was the Newtonian explanation (based on the Copernican system) which provided the most predictive power and facilitated the discovery of the planets Neptune and Pluto. Thus, Toulmin (1961) argues that science deals with explanation (or what Toulmin calls 'understanding'). It shows 'why' phenomena exist. First, science retrodicts and makes sense of past phenomena by providing coherence. If some regularity in nature is truly understood and properly explained, then prediction should ultimately follow (although not always immediately). Successful retrodiction permits successful prediction of future phenomena and is the ultimate test for any successful explanation. Explanation, however, is the focus, not prediction; prediction follows successful explanation. Prediction without explanation is not science. Thus, in this book, the notion of 'theory' means explanation and indicates *why* some phenomena exist; it 'aims at what Stephen Toulmin called 'understanding'.

The first major theoretical perspective of this book is the systems paradigm (see Doran, 1970). As was stated earlier in this chapter, much of science in general and archaeology in particular operates under the atomistic paradigm which breaks apart data into smaller units and focuses on those units and their inherent characteristics. Causation tends to be linear and mono-causal, with statements of universal applicability (now commonly called 'laws') about forces acting upon these units. The problem with this paradigm is that once a phenomenon is analyzed and taken apart, it is difficult, if not impossible, to reassemble, and one cannot predict the interactions of one unit with the other units (Buckley, 1967). The systems paradigm (often called systems 'theory'), however, provides a different perspective. First, in contrast to the analytical/mechanical paradigm, the systems paradigm is more concerned with relationships between entities than with the entities themselves (Laszlo, 1972). It concerns the principles of organization rather than the intrinsic properties of the units of organization; its focus is on the 'how' of organization more than the 'what'. With its concentration on the principles of organization, systems are thus concerned with wholes. Ludwig Van Bertalanffy (1968), the father of systems theory, called it the science of wholes. Probably the second most important assumption of the systems paradigm is that there are systemic relationships in the world that are so basic that they occur in many different living and non-living phenomena. The principles of organization, then, are translatable into many different disciplines not as analogies, but as isomorphisms. Thirdly, systems are dynamic organisms which can change through time (Buckley, 1967). The 'state' of a system at any given point in time is not just based on the initial conditions, however, but is characterized more by the experiences that come to it (Buckley, 1967). Since any one component is related causally to other components in a given period of time, change in the system will affect any one relationship in several ways (Buckley, 1967:41). Thus, causation in a systems paradigm is not mono-causal, but multi-causal.

The second theoretical approach used in this book is cultural ecology. Originally pioneered by Steward (1955), the cultural ecological approach seeks to generalize about cultural similarities and differences by analyzing the relationships of the technologies of cultures to particular environments. The ecological approach gives methodological priority to working out the relationships of the environment and 'the exploitative or productive technology' (Steward, 1955:40), or, as Steward says, 'the material culture of a society'. More recently, this approach has broadened to embrace demographic factors and has been called cultural materialism (Harris, 1979; Price, 1982). Since ceramics are one kind of material culture and are part of the 'exploitative technology', an ecological approach to ceramics should first analyze the relationship of the ceramics and the environment before examining the relationship of ceramics to the other subsystems of culture like the social and belief subsystems. Indeed, the environmental relationship with ceramics has more potential for generalization at this time than relationships of ceramics to other aspects of culture. Once such relationships are understood, one can then examine how the ideological and social structural subsystems articulate with ceramics.

Since the ecological approach to ceramics is basically etic and thus cross-cultural in nature (see Pike, 1967:37–8; Harris, 1968:568–82), it is possible to compare the ceramic–environmental relationships in many societies and develop a set of generalizations about them which could apply to the past as well as to the present. The assumption is that since cultures have the characteristics of systems, there are certain internal relationships which are isomorphic with other societies around the world. These isomorphic relationships provide the basis for generalizations which can then enable archaeologists to utilize ceramics to interpret the social and cultural behavior of ancient cultural systems without the use of ethnographic analogies.

The final theoretical perspective of this book is ethnoarchaeological. Although anthropologists have studied the ceramics of living people for decades, the study of living peoples from an archaeological perspective has only recently become a popular enterprise among archaeologists. One problem of interpreting ancient ceramics is that very little is known ethnographically about how ceramics articulate with environment and culture. What is needed is a ceramic theory drawn from ethnography which can be applied to the past. Although ethnoarchaeology has seen rapid growth in recent years and has provided a lot of data on material culture from an archaeological perspective, there are a number of limitations to the studies thus far: (1) they are mainly particularistic in character, focusing on specific societies; (2) they are largely eclectic and anecdotal, in the form of cautionary tales; and (3) their application to archaeology is largely through: (a) specific direct historical situations, or (b) hypotheses for further testing rather than more general analogies (Ascher, 1961) or empirically supported universals or generalizations. If archaeologists rely on these approaches as the only applications of the present to the past, however, they are limiting the number of ancient cultures that they interpret because few will have analogies in the ethnographic present. Clearly, ethnoarchaeology does not yet have much generalizing power in cross-cultural situations, and another approach is needed to expand this interpretive tool for use in the past.

This book is one contribution to developing such a theory and is written from an ethnographic perspective. This approach has two advantages: (1) it provides cross-cultural generalizations concerning a series of relationships of ceramics to the environment and the rest of culture that occcur in many societies around the world; and (2) it provides an understanding of these relationships in space before the variable of time is added. The obvious benefit in these advantages is to combine the generalizing power of cultural ecology (and cultural materialism) with ethnoarchaeology with its heretofore particularistic, culturally specific interests and to derive general universal principles which are useful in interpreting ancient ceramics. These generalizations are an attempt to implement what Watson (1973) and Schiffer (1976) call 'law-like generalizations' about the past. Methodologically, this approach is consonant with Schiffer's second strategy of behavioral archaeology that 'pursues general questions in present material culture in order to acquire laws useful for the study of the past' (Schiffer, 1976:5).

Ethnographic generalizations relating ceramics to environment and culture should make it possible to interpret ceramics in a greater number of ancient cultures with greater confidence than was possible through the use of ethnographic analogy alone. Assuming that at least some of the same processes are responsible for ceramic production in the present and in the past, it behooves the archaeologist to discover what these processes actually are.

In addition to explaining why these generalizations exist, the book presents them in a wider explanatory framework in cultural evolution by answering the question 'why does pottery making develop in an area and why does it evolve into a full-time craft?' Thus, the book attempts to explain why these generalizations successfully retrodict the evolution of ceramic specialization in the past. Others will have to determine whether the theory presented here is sufficiently explanatory to be truly predictive.

An introduction to the theory

This book thus applies the generalizing power of a systems approach to ethnoarchaeological data by concentrating on one very small part of material culture–ceramics. In order to interpret the past using archaeological data, it is necessary to develop a theory of material culture and how it relates to behavior, society and culture. Material culture is so vast and complex, however, that generalizations about it based on cross-cultural data are either too overwhelmingly difficult or too trivial for use by the archaeologist. Thus, to make the development of such a theory more realistic and useful, material culture needs to be separated into smaller, more manageable units. Ceramics are one such type of material culture and consist of purposeful creations of potters who use clays to produce objects which are recognized by archaeologists as pottery. Although variable in structure and chemical composition, clays have a similar structure as hydrous aluminium silicates and have the property of plasticity which permits clay to be molded into many different forms and then fixed with the proper amount of heat.

The book will attempt to provide cross-cultural generalizations which can be applied to many different societies in the present and the past. The approach will be to formulate generalizations about the relationship of ceramics to environment and culture from a variety of contemporary societies. The basic assumption is that relationships between the technology (in this case, the ceramics) and the environment must be worked out before ceramics can be related to the rest of culture. In this case, several of the generalizations are developed from the physical and chemical nature of the ceramic raw materials. By deriving generalizations from modern cultures, it is possible to understand and explain how ceramics articulate with the rest of culture and the environment. By applying these generalizations to the past, it is possible to develop a more precise interpretation of how archaeological ceramics relate to an ancient environment and culture.

Culture and the environment constitute the 'system' discussed in this book. Culture is man's extrasomatic adaptation to the environment and consists of an integrated whole composed of mutually interacting subsystems such as the techno-economic, social structural and ideological subsystems. Like all systems, culture has the ontological characteristic that changes in one part of the system will create changes in other parts of the system (Rappaport, 1971; Sharp, 1952).

Ceramics can be conveniently described as a highly specialized part of the techno-economic subsystem of culture–that subsystem which adapts to and modifies the environment for cultural ends. It is not a 'subsystem' of culture with its own boundary maintaining mechanisms, but it does have systemic relationships with the other aspects of culture like the remainder of the techno-economic and the ideological and social structural subsystems. Furthermore, as a part of the larger culture–environment system, ceramics are also systemically tied to the environment.

The interrelationships of ceramics to environment and culture can be described as a channel for the flow of information between parts of the ecosystem—in this case between the environment and human beings. The most basic type of information flow consists of necessities for life-sustaining processes like water, energy and nutrients which move from the environment to human beings to meet their nutritional and caloric needs. Ceramics, in fact, make it possible to increase the flow of biologically required constituents from the environment to humans (see Chapter 6) making it possible for man to adapt to a wider range of environments. Besides water, energy and nutrients, ceramics can also provide a channel for ideological and/or social structural information between members of the society when ceramics reflect mythical themes and/or are used in ritual or in burial. This latter use of ceramics broadens the channel of information flow and represents a more evolved state of ceramics from their strictly utilitarian function as a channel for biological nutrients.

The focus of this book is not so much on the ceramics themselves, but on the way in which pottery production is related to the environment and culture through the local community of potters. Rather than the pottery itself, the focus is on the ceramic producing population which is the interface between culture and the environment on the one hand and the actual pottery on the other. Thus, the book will not deal with pots or potsherds. It will not be concerned with: (1) how to classify pottery; (2) how to use chemical and physical tools to analyze pottery; or (3) how to analyze an ethnographic pottery tradition. The book is less concerned with 'analysis' *per se* and more concerned with the interrelations of populations of potters with their environment and culture. Some 'analysis' is inevitable, but every attempt is made to focus on the relationships instead of the units of analysis.

Systems have a wide variety of properties which are isomorphic and can be applied to any number of disciplines. Of all of these properties, the systemic relationships between ceramics and the environment can be usefully described in terms of a cybernetic perspective. Cybernetics is attractive to biologists and behavioral scientists because it removes the distinction between living and non-living systems and concentrates on the similar properties of both. From a cybernetic perspective, these similar properties consist of goal-directed behavior and the processes of control and communication that permit the system to achieve that goal (Boulanger, 1969). Goal-directed behavior may involve goals as diverse as the maintenance of a certain temperature or a particular width of sheet metal leaving a rolling mill. The processes of control and communication collect information about the difference between the goal and the actual performance of the system and then work to reduce that difference (Miller, Galanter and Primbaum, 1960:42). These processes are called feedback mechanisms and are viewed as mutual causal relationships in which the output of the system affects the input. There are two types of these feedback mechanisms. Regulatory or deviation counteracting feedback (sometimes called negative feedback) are processes which promote equilibrium and counteract deviations from stable situations over long periods of time. They prevent divergence from a prescribed set of boundaries. Positive or deviation amplifying feedback are processes which promote or amplify deviations as the result of some external input into the system that the system can not regulate. These processes cause the system to expand and eventually reach stability at new, more complex levels (Maruyama, 1963). The external inputs into the system that stimulate deviation amplifying feedback are called 'kicks' and redefine the thresholds of the system, forcing the inputs of the system through the threshold of regulatory feedback. Ultimately, these 'kicks' can be a regulated input creating a new parameter of the system. Deviation amplifying mechanisms thus cause disequilibrium and change within the system and are the means by which the system gains information and changes. In some situations, feedback may be both deviation counteracting and deviation amplifying (Maruyama, 1963:178). Flannery (1968b) has effectively used this cybernetic approach to describe and explain the cultural changes leading up to the development of agriculture in Meso-America.

The relevance of this book to archaeology lies in its elucidation and explanation of the universal processes which relate ceramics to the environment and culture. These processes can be viewed as a set of some of the feedback processes that stimulate or limit ceramic production and can aid in interpreting the role of ceramics in the ancient society. All feedback processes should be understood as interacting together. It may appear that explanations for processes in some chapters are mono-causal (like the total negative feedback of weather and climate in the Northwest Coast of North America), but this impression is the result of choosing particular cases to illustrate the feedback mechanisms. Thus, while regulatory feedback may be total on the Northwest Coast of North America, for example, it does not constitute a mono-causal explanation of the lack of pottery there, and other feedback mechanisms operate as well. Each process is clearly interrelated to other processes. The discussion is not meant to be exhaustive of all the relationships that exist, but rather only describes those relationships for which there is sufficient ethnographic data.

The relationships of a population of potters to the environment and culture are viewed as a series of feedback mechanisms following a cybernetic model. These relationships are presented as processes which help explain the evolution of ceramic specialization from non-potters to part-time potters and finally to full-time craft specialists. Part-time potters are those who make pottery for only part of the year (usually seasonally). Full-time potters are those who practice their craft during the entire year. The use of these terms is not distorted to mean that full-time potters are really part-time specialists who work part of the year and make enough pots to support themselves for an entire year. Neither are there heuristic economic tricks used to define part-time potters as full-time potters:

Potters...apparently have no tillable land and therefore they are considered full-time specialists. (Ramírez-Horton, 1981:294; my translation)

Just because contemporary potters have no tillable land, they are not necessarily full-time potters, and may still perform agricultural labor. If potters have no land to work, they may either rent the land of others as tenants or share croppers or become agricultural laborers (Behura, 1978; Voyatzoglou, 1974). Furthermore, it is not likely that potters who work part of the year will make enough money to support themselves for the entire year. Even highly specialized potters (like the itinerant potters of Crete) who work seasonally do not make enough money for a whole year's living expenses (Voyatzoglou, 1974:24). As Chapter 7 indicates, highly evolved and specialized part-time potters may often live on the edges of society both socially and economically.

The presentation is not concerned with the 'event' of the origin of pottery making nor how or why it began. Pottery making most certainly began as a result of diffusion from another culture in space or as a result of an innovation within the culture. Furthermore, the book does not deal with the 'event' of the development of full-time ceramic specialists. Rather, the book explores some of the processes which favored or prevented the origin of pottery making, maintained it once it began and stimulated or prevented its evolution into a full-time craft. The cybernetic approach thus will help explain the pre-industrial evolution of ceramic production. Since cybernetics involves understanding feedback processes, this book will be organized according to the feedback processes that characterize the relationship between ceramics, its cultural context and the environment.

Because this work concerns processes and their interaction, the presentation does not deal with a typological development of the craft through stages nor with levels of socio-cultural integration such as band, tribe, chiefdom, state. Every effort is made to avoid traditional typologies, both social and ceramic. There are two reasons for this approach. First, in order to fully use the methods of cultural ecology, methodological priority must be given to the technological–environmental relationships before relating them to the more complex political and social phenomena. Secondly, these typologies are part of the analytical paradigm and the processes presented here crosscut these 'types'. Nevertheless, the processes described here do not always apply to all societies in the same way, so the application of the processes to synchronic modes or types of production will be described in the conclusion.

2
Resources

The availability and suitability of the resources necessary to make pottery provide the most obvious and most frequently cited factor favoring the development of pottery making. The presence of suitable clay, for example, is often viewed as being the primary environmental factor responsible for the craft (e. g., Linné, 1925:23-6; Oliver, 1967:81, 297; Hogbin, 1951:81; Radcliffe-Brown, 1933:473; Rhodes, 1970:158-64; Solheim, 1952b:2; Tuckson, 1966:9; Nicklin, 1979:441). Conversely, the presumable absence of good quality clay allegedly explains the absence of pottery production (McBryde, 1947:54; Huntingford, 1950:86; Buck, 1938:46).

The minimal resources necessary to make pottery are clay, water and fuel for firing. Temper (or non-plastic material) is not as important as clay because all raw clays usually contain some naturally occuring non-plastics (Shepard, 1956:18). In some cases, enough may be present, so that the potter does not need to add more (Shepard, 1956:24). If the raw clay is too plastic, however, the potter must add some non-plastics to the paste in order to improve workability, counteract shrinkage, facilitate drying (Shepard, 1956:25; Rye, 1976:109) and manipulate firing properties (Rye, 1976:109; Gait, 1897:6). Paints, slips, glazes and materials for tools to form and decorate the pots are not as significant ceramic resources as clays, fuels and water, nor are they as universally important. Paints, slips and glazes are not used universally to decorate pottery, and the materials used for the potter's tools vary widely.

The resource feedback mechanism can be broken down into two parts: (1) the appropriateness or quality of ceramic resources; and (2) their availability as measured in the distance to their source locations. Each of these two aspects can be seen as a feedback mechanism either limiting (negative feedback) or stimulating (positive feedback) ceramic specialization. Readily available ceramic resources, along with those of suitable quality for making pots, provide deviation amplifying feedback for the origin of the craft and its development into a full-time speciality. Conversely, resources of poor quality or those too far from the potter's household provide regulatory feedback for ceramic production and prevent the craft from developing.

The quality of resources

In order to provide positive feedback for the origin and development of pottery making, ceramic materials must be of good quality in order to assure a sturdy product that will not crack and break during drying, firing or use. All apparent ceramic resources may not be of equal quality and thus may not be equally well suited for making pottery.

Clays, particularly, may not have qualities that produce a desirable product. There are many factors that affect the qualities of clays such as mineral composition, degree of crystallinity, plasticity, particle size, and the amount of soluble salts, exchangeable cations and non-plastics present. Clays of the montmorillonite or smectite group, for example, have a crystal structure which expands greatly when hydrated and require greater quantities of water to become plastic than other clay minerals (Shepard, 1956:337; see also Grim, 1962:56-8; Arnold, 1971:30-1). Since all of this water must be lost before firing, montmorillonite also contracts greatly when it is dried. Thus, the greater the amount of water needed for plasticity, the greater the possiblility of shrinkage and cracking of the ceramic product during drying and firing (Grim, 1962:56-8). This characteristic causes pottery made with montmorillonite to sag, crack and break in the drying process. Potters in Ticul, Yucatan, Mexico, for example, recognize this problem and avoid using a montmorillonite clay (except for very small vessels) for this reason (Arnold, 1971:30-1). Similarly, other potters recognize and avoid using poor quality clays. The Chacobo on the Ivon river in northeastern Bolivia avoid using the large deposit of poor quality clay in their village and instead prefer to walk for 15-20 minutes to obtain a suitable clay (Gil Prost, personal communication). Similarly, Amphlett Island potters of Melanesia use local clay for small vessels, but they prefer to import higher quality clay from nearby Fergusson Island for large vessels (Malinowski, 1922:282-8).

Clay quality may be also affected by the non-plastics naturally present or added by the potter. Clays generally contain some naturally occurring non-plastics (Shepard, 1956:18), but potters may need to add non-plastics such as mineral materials (like sand or crushed stone), ground potsherds or organic materials (like crushed bone, shell, straw, grass, chaff, sponge spicules, silicaceous ash (Linné, 1965), manure, crushed reeds, or fluff (Ochsenschlager, 1974b:151) for reasons cited earlier. Generally, the size of non-plastic materials in the paste is important for reducing shrinkage during drying. As the particle size and amount of non-clay minerals decreases, drying becomes more difficult. Since drying involves the escape of moisture from the interior of the ware, the extremely small particles and pore spaces do not permit the water to escape easily. Further, when the particle size decreases, the amount of adsorbing surface causes an increase in the relative amount of water tightly adsorbed. ('Adsorbed water' and 'adsorbing surface' refer to interlayer water which is held directly on the surface of the clay minerals and occurs in a physical state different than liquid water. In contrast to the water held in the pores and on the surfaces and edges of discrete clay minerals, this adsorbed structural water usually requires temperatures approaching 100 degrees Centigrade for its removal (Grim, 1968:234-5).) Satisfactory drying requires uniform drying from all surfaces so that shrinkage will be uniform in all directions (Grim, 1968:82). Non-plastic materials aid this drying process by opening the paste up for more rapid drying. They also reduce the amount of water-adsorbing surfaces and provide a skeletal structure (Grim, 1962:81). Granular particles with a wide size range are the most effective non-plastic additives and the presence of about 25 per cent of these materials in a clay body is generally desirable to prevent excessive shrinkage (Grim, 1962:77).

Potters' perceptions of clay quality, however, may be limited by their experience with their traditional clays. When the community of Yayuvana on Fergusson Island (Melanesia) began to charge a substantial fee for obtaining clay near the community, Amphlett potters began searching for other clay sources and experimenting with the clays from them. Their experimentation revealed a number of inferior clays which caused vessels to break during drying and firing. The main problem with these clays was that they contained significantly less (21-8 per cent) clay than their traditional source (34 per cent). The remainder of the raw clay was made up of sand and silts which acted as non-plastics and there was no need to add any further non-plastics to the clay. Since potters were unfamiliar with the idea of adding non-plastics to the clay to manipulate working, drying and firing properties, their judgement of the experimental clays as inferior was conditioned by their lack of awareness that the properties of 'inferior' clays could be modified with the addition of *any* materials (Lauer, 1974:143-4,158,197-8). In this case, the addition of a clay with more plastic material could have made the inferior clays more workable, but such a concept was completely foreign to the Amphlett potters. The presence of montmorillonite in one of the inferior clays may also have created problems of drying and firing (Lauer, 1974:197-8).

Clay quality may also be related to the utilitarian advantages of the vessel shapes made from it. First, white or pale colored vessels reflect heat in hot climates and this quality of the fired clay (plus its high porosity) makes it well suited for water pots (Rye 1976:113). The heat reflectivity of light-colored vessels is probably one reason why the white, white-slipped and buff-colored water pots of Chinautla, Durazno and Sacojito are so widely distributed and traded over southwestern Guatemala (see Reina, 1960). White or near-white firing clays are unusual among non-industrial and traditional potters, and the widespread distribution and presumable popularity of these vessels suggest the unusually superior quality of these water jars in comparison to jars from other communities.

Second, the quality of materials may be extremely important in the production of cooking pottery. Cooking pots, in contrast to water pots, need to be a dark color in order to retain heat. Carbon staining from cooking fires contributes to heat retention (Rye 1976:113), but a dark colored paste is also important in this regard. The vessel walls should also be relatively impermeable to fluids and the vessels should be resistant to thermal shock (Rye 1976:113). Resistance to thermal shock permits the vessel to withstand repeated cycles of heating and fast cooling without damage (Rye 1976:113; Cardew, 1952:191-2). In contrast to metal, ceramics are not good conductors of heat (Rye 1976:113; Cardew, 1952:191). When a ceramic vessel is heated from below, the outside becomes much hotter than the inside. Since the heated side expands more than the cold side, tensile stresses are produced on the cold side and when these stresses exceed the tensile strength of the ceramic body, a crack occurs on the colder interior side of the vessel (Rye, 1976:113). The liquid inside the vessel may help equalize the strains, but since pottery is a poor conductor of heat, equalization may not occur quickly enough to alleviate cracking (Cardew, 1952:191-2).

The kind of non-plastics used as temper in cooking pottery can affect the resistance to thermal shock. Non-plastics affect the ability of the pot to withstand a very rapid heating and cooling cycle during firing and thus provide the essential physical characteristics of the fired fabric which are best suited for cooking (Rye 1976:109). There are two major variables involved in thermal shock resistance which relate to non-plastic resources (Rye 1976:114). First, porosity contributes to thermal shock resistance by arresting cracks in the vessel walls; when a crack begins, it is stopped when it reaches a large pore. High porosity, however, can contribute to inefficiency in heating. For a given pore size, however, there is a given temperature at which the quantity of heat passing through it by radiation equals the same amount of heat carried by a solid substance occupying the same space (Searle and Grimshaw, 1959:66). In extrapolating these data for the temperature of a cooking fire (300-500 degrees C.), the ideal pore size would be between 7 and 9 mm (Rye 1976:115). Allowing for the highest conceivable temperatures of a cooking fire, Rye (1976:114) says the range of desirable pore size would be larger than 5 mm to smaller than 1 cm. Thus, in this size range, pores provide effective resistance to thermal shock without loss of a pot's cooking efficiency. Potters have achieved the control of the presence of large pores in a pot by using organic tempering materials such as grass, seeds or straw. When these organic materials burn out in the firing they leave pores of appropriate size (Rye, 1976:115).

If inorganic materials are used for temper, a different set of factors affects thermal shock resistance. The non-plastic minerals in the clay should have thermal expansions close to that of the fired clay matrix and their crystal lattice should not change within the range of temperatures used for cooking. If these criteria cannot be met, the amount and particle size of non-plastic mineral inclusions in the paste should be as small as possible (Rye, 1976:114). Ground potsherds made from the same clay as that used for vessels provide an ideal temper when a clay has an insufficient amount of natural mineral inclusions for adequate workability. When fired, the potsherds have the same thermal characteristics as the clay matrix and expand at the same rate. Thus, considerable variability in the amount and particle size of potsherd temper is permissible without risk of cracking. This factor in turn permits considerable latitude in the method of grinding and preparation of temper (Rye 1976:115). Potsherds also have the advantage of being readily available.

When using non-plastic mineral materials as temper, the control of thermal shock resistance becomes more complex. The thermal expansion rates for these mineral materials will profoundly affect the ability of the vessel to withstand thermal shock. Rye (1976:116-18) has summarized and condensed average thermal expansion rates (as volume percent) for several minerals (Figure 2.1). Besides those graphed, Rye (1976:116) says that most feldspars plot between plagioclase and rutile, hornblende is similar to graphite, augite is similar to calcite, and the iron oxides are in the same range as calcium oxide (CaO). As for rocks, Rye (1976:116) summarizes Winkler (1973:47) saying that, in general, the more basic rocks (basalts, grabbos, diorites, etc.) have a much lower expansion rate than the more acidic rocks such as granites. Sedimentary and low grade metamorphic rocks tend to have a very wide range of expansion rates within any rock type. Generally, Rye (1976:116) says that the thermal expansion of rocks tends to be lower than that averaged from the individual minerals of which they are composed, suggesting that the structure is capable of absorbing some of the stresses during the expansion of the individual grains.

The graph (Figure 2.1) of mineral expansion rates thus permits some prediction of the minerals best suited for tempering cooking pots in order to achieve thermal shock resistance. Minerals with the lowest thermal expansions or those with expansions closest to the clay fabric are the most suitable in avoiding stresses during repeated heatings and coolings of the pottery (Rye, 1976:117). Thus, zircon, plagioclase and other feldspars, augite, hornblende and calcite are the most suitable materials. By way of contrast, quartz is unsuitable because of its relatively high thermal expansion (Rye, 1976:118).

Calcite, however, has problems for the traditional potter. At firing

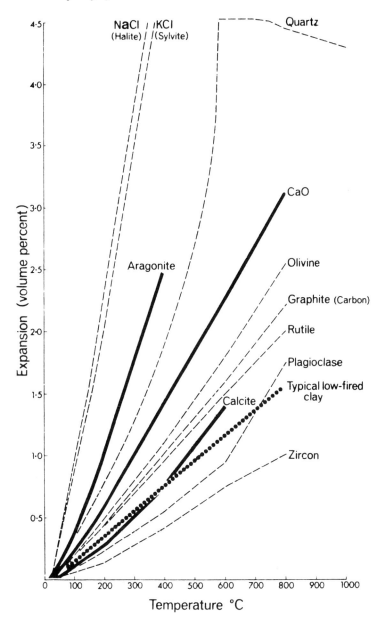

Figure 2.1 Thermal expansion (expressed as volume percent) of some non-plastic materials which commonly occur in ceramic fabrics, plotted against temperature (reprinted from Rye, 1976:117; used by permission of *Archaeology and Physical Anthropology in Oceania*).

temperatures as low as 620 degrees C., calcite decomposes to form calcium oxide and carbon dioxide, and at 900 degrees C., this decomposition becomes very rapid. The decomposition is also affected by the amount of carbon dioxide present during firing. Thus, traditional firing techniques with little control of firing atmosphere could create substantial amounts of calcium oxide in the ware. When cooled, the calcium oxide can combine with water vapor in the air and create calcium hydroxide which occupies considerably more volume in the pottery than the original calcite. The result is spalling at best, or severe cracking and crumbling at worst (Rye, 1976:120-1).

Rye (1976:121-31) found that the addition of salt water to calcite-tempered paste generally has the effect of mitigating the decomposion of calcite during firing by raising the firing temperature at which calcite decomposes (Figures 2.2a-c). Rye (1976:131) speculates that the cause of this phenonemon is that the presence of sodium from the salt water lowers the vitrification temperature of the clay to well within the range of traditional firing methods. Increased vitrification at ordinary firing

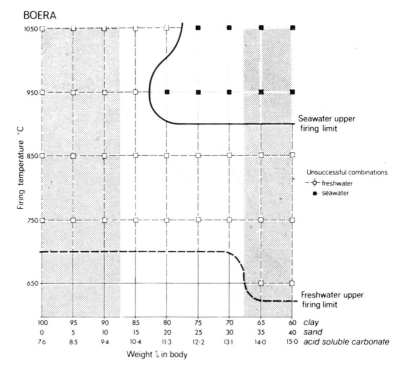

Figure 2.2 a. The effect that firing to various temperatures has on mixtures of Boera (in Melanesia) clay and beach sand (calcite), wetted with either seawater or freshwater. Non-workable mixtures are indicated by shaded areas (reprinted from Rye, 1976:128; used by permission of *Archaeology and Physical Anthropology in Oceania*).

MAILU

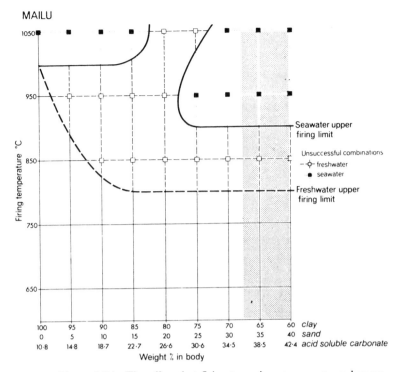

Figure 2.2 b. The effect that firing to various temperatures has on mixtures of Mailu Island (in Melanesia) clay and beach sand (calcite), wetted with either seawater or freshwater. Non-workable mixtures are indicated by shaded areas (reprinted from Rye, 1976:129; used by permission of *Archaeology and Physical Anthropology in Oceania*).

temperatures has two important effects: (1) it produces a stronger fabric more able to resist the hydration of calcium oxide after firing; and (2) it seals some of the pores restricting the access of water to the calcium oxide. Since the salts in solution are carried to the surface and deposited there when the water evaporates, these effects would be greatest on the surface of the vessel.

Although potters may not be able to recognize verbally the superior quality of calcite for cooking pots, there is some evidence that they do so behaviorally. Potters in Ticul, Yucatan, for example, select pure crystalline calcite as a temper for cooking pottery while rejecting a mixture of materials (including crypto-crystalline calcite, dolomite and the clay minerals attapulgite and montmorillonite) for this purpose (Arnold, 1971). This latter material is used only as a temper for non-cooking pottery.

The value of the addition of salt to calcareous clays or tempers has the effect of improving the overall quality of these raw materials in an area of less than desirable clays and tempers. Thus, the beneficial addition of

MOTUPORE

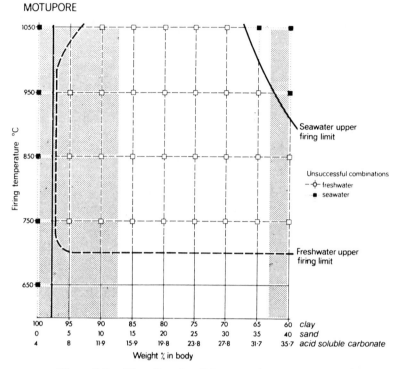

Figure 2.2 c. The effect that firing to various temperatures has on mixtures of Motupore (in Melanesia) clay and beach sand (calcite), wetted with either seawater or freshwater. Non-workable mixtures are indicated by shaded areas (reprinted from Rye, 1976:127; used by permission of *Archaeology and Physical Anthropology in Oceania*).

salt could be obtained from adding sea water to wet clay, using clays naturally containing soluble salts, using tempers containing soluble salts or adding crystalline salt to the plastic clay. The amount of salt necessary to achieve this effect is actually very little. Rye (1976:133) mentions that as little as 1-5 per cent may be sufficient to avoid spalling. There is some ethnographic evidence that these practices do exist. Rye observed that Arab potters (Rye, 1976:125) and potters in some areas of Pakistan (Rye and Evans, 1976:39) add ground salt to their clay body. Rye (1976:122) also argues that the salty taste and consequent existence of sodium chloride in the preferred potters' clay in Ticul, Yucatan (see Arnold, 1971:29-30) reflect a behavioral attempt at counteracting the effect of temper high in calcite in both cooking and non-cooking vessels.

Another effect of the quality of non-plastics on pottery is the relationship between pottery temper and porosity. In hot dry climates, porosity of the paste is an advantage because water can seep through the walls of the vessel. Subsequent evaporation will draw heat out of the contents. This quality of the paste can be manipulated by the addition of non-plastics because an increased amount of non-plastics increases porosity.

The effect of non-plastics on clay quality is also related to the technology used to make pottery. Coarse gritty clay used by many Nigerian potters in hand forming and open firing is well suited to traditional methods of production. If this clay were used for the production of wheel-made pottery it would cut the potter's hands. Thus, clay for wheel-thrown pots must be of a smaller particle size than the clay used for hand forming techniques (Cardew, 1952:195).

Since non-plastics also weaken the body of a vessel, too much may make the paste too friable to provide much strength for the vessel walls and the pottery may fall apart or crack easily (Shepard, 1956:26). Thus, clays with too much non-plastic material are unsuitable for pottery making.

There are other aspects of clay quality that affect the success of pottery making. The adsorbed cations, for example, can affect the amount of shrinkage during drying. Grim (1962:76) points out that montmorillonites containing sodium have the highest drying shrinkage of all the montmorillonites. Conversely, for kaolins and the other clay minerals (except montmorillonite), the amount of shrinkage decreases progressively with adsorbed cations of hydrogen, calcium and potassium with sodium having the least amount of shrinkage (Grim, 1962:76).

In some cases, the potter can improve the quality of his raw materials using a relatively simple technology. Besides the addition of non-plastics, sifting or screening the temper or clay (as in Sind, Pakistan (MacKay, 1930), Moveros, Spain (Cortes, 1958:98); Hamirpur, India (Dobbs, 1897:3) or Quinua, Peru) can remove large non-plastic materials (like rocks and large organic materials) which can cause weakness or cracking during firing. Soaking the clay in water (as in Sind, Pakistan (MacKay, 1930:128), in San Bartolo Coyotepec, Oaxaca (Van de Velde and Van de Velde, 1939:28), or in Ticul, Yucatan (Thompson, 1958:66)), or aging it prior to use (Van de Velde and Van de Velde, 1939:29) can also improve its qualities. Grim (1962:76) points out that allowing the clay to stand in water can improve the strength of the unfired vessel. This 'green strength' is important for the potter because he may have to stack his vessels in storage before and during firing and he cannot risk breakage (Figure 2.3). The green strength of halloysite clays increases sevenfold with soaking, but it increases considerably less with kaolinite and illite. There is no increase in green strength for soaked montmorillonite clays. This increase in green strength is related to the time required for water to penetrate to all the potential surfaces of the clay minerals and for orientation to develop in the adsorbed water (Grim, 1962:76). Other aspects of clay quality like particle size, and the presence of soluble salts and exchangeable cations, can be also affected

Figure 2.3 A stack of unfired vessels in a kiln prior to firing in Ticul, Yucatan. The green strength of pottery is necessary to prevent sagging after forming and to withstand pressures of stacking before and during firing. Green strength can be improved by soaking or aging the clay prior to preparing the paste.

by the technology of the potter – techniques such as soaking the clay and decanting off the water prior to the forming process.

Besides clay and temper, fuel may also have varying qualities which affect firing success. In India, cow dung retains higher temperatures longer during firing than sawdust (Gupta, 1969:18). On the Peruvian Altiplano, llama dung provides superior burning qualities giving a hot, even fire with little smoke and a heat value superior to other types of dung or grass (Winterhalder, Larsen and Thomas, 1974). In Yucatan, Ticul potters are acutely aware of differing qualities of fuel for firing.

Ticul potters carefully select specific varieties of wood for different parts of the firing process in order to achieve a desired effect. For example, potters use undried (or 'green') wood and/or any variety of wood (such as *ha'abin, tsalam, tak'in che'* and *chakah*) that burns with considerable smoke for the initial warming stage of firing because smoke does not damage the pottery at this time. Conversely, only quick-burning, relatively smokeless wood (such as *katsim, peres kuch* and *chukum*) must be used during the last stage of the firing process. If potters use undried or smoke-producing wood during this latter stage, the pots will become black and fire-clouded and will have to be fired again.

In some cases, the quality of fuel varies with firing technique. In Pakistan, Rye and Evans (1976:166) noted that dung is the best fuel for pit firing because it provides the most even heating and the best output of heat. When wood is used and mixed with other fuels, however, high firing losses result due to rapid and uneven heating. For firing in a closed kiln, other types of fuels are preferred. In Bannu, Pakistan, a simple updraft kiln is fired with reeds which burn quickly with a very short flame (Rye and Evans, 1976:166). For more complex kilns that are used to fire glazed pottery, potters prefer wood (such as *Dalbergia sissoo*) which they say burns with a long clear flame as opposed to wood (such as pine) which burns with a short flame (Rye and Evans, 1976:167).

In other cases, the potter appears to have no concern for varying quality of fuel. Key (1968:654) reports that potters in the Wanigela area of Papua New Guinea use anything within reach for firing: coconut husks, coconut palm fronds and other dried scraps of wood from the gardens. In other cases, they use readily available resources such as palm fronds (Lauer, 1973:37; Palmer and Shaw, 1968:57), brush near the gardens (Egloff, 1973:67), dried stalks of tall tropical grass, coconut butts and husk (Palmer and Shaw, 1968:57), or twigs or brush (Voyat-zoglou, 1974:23).

Besides a few general principles, it is not possible to develop a general model on the quality of resources. First, except for some general guidelines for clay minerals, every potential ceramic resource is not appropriate for every local technology. Certain clays of poorer quality such as montmorillonites may be adequate for small items of pottery as in Ticul, Yucatan and in the Amphlett Islands in Melanesia, but unsuitable for larger items (see Arnold, 1971; Malinowski, 1922:283). Similarly, one type of fuel may be appropriate for one type of firing technology, but inappropriate for another. Secondly, since ceramic resources like clays and fuels are diverse and highly variable, extensive testing of and experimentation on local resources are necessary in order to determine their suitability for each local technology. Cardew (1969:255-60), for example, suggests practical guidelines for sampling and testing raw clays and Hill (1975) has provided a practical system of clay evaluation which emphasizes changes in volume and porosity that result from water loss during drying and firing. Thus, it is not possible to provide a generalization that could predict where pottery making could occur based upon the quality of ceramic resources.

In summary, the quality of ceramic resources provides important feedback relationships with pottery production. If the resources are of sufficient quality to make pottery, this quality produces a deviation amplifying effect on ceramic production permitting the craft to originate and to develop into a full-time specialization. Conversely, poor quality resources provide deviation counteracting feedback limiting the initial development of pottery making or preventing its evolution into a full-time craft. In some areas, poor quality resources may be sufficient to fabricate poor quality pottery or small vessels and provide positive feedback for the origin of the craft, but inhibit its evolution into a full-time specialization.

Distance to resources

The second aspect of the resource mechanism concerns the availability of ceramic raw materials as measured in the distance to those resources. The distance of the sources from a potter's house is not random, arbitrary or unimportant but rather provides an important feedback relationship for pottery production. In order for pottery making to originate in a society and develop into a full-time craft, a population must have raw materials available in the vicinity of their work area. Ceramic resources must be close enough to a population of potters in order to be easily exploited. Energy inputs for obtaining resources cannot be excessive to production or the costs of obtaining resources will exceed the economic returns from selling or exchanging pottery.

A close relationship exists between the ability of a population to exploit a resource profitably and the expenditure of energy necessary for this exploitation (Jarman, 1972). Energy expenditure is closely related to the distance to a resource; a population can exploit only resources that exist within a certain distance. Jarman points out that this 'exploitable territory' varies greatly according to a range of complex factors, but:

...behind the apparent variability occasioned by these factors [lies] the existence of a powerful limiting force which restricts the actual range of human behavior to a relatively small area within the theoretical, possible range. (Jarman, 1972:706)

This small area is limited by the friction effect of time and distance on energy expenditure (Clark, 1977:38).

Browman (1976) has utilized an exploitable territory threshold model in his discussion of pastoralism in the Junín region of highland Peru. His model is a generalization about the distance to subsistence resources based on a number of hunting and gathering and agricultural societies which exploit a territory of a given radius. His model (like other spatial theories) is based on the assumption that resource exploitation involves choices which minimize energy and information expenditures or which maximize energy or information returns (Clark, 1977:42; Christenson, 1982; Doxiadis, 1970:393). The following discussion is adapted from Browman (1976).

The cost/returns of exploitable territory for a population can be usefully described as a curve with the cost/returns along the Y-axis and distance to resources along the X-axis (Figure 2.4). The cost curve rises geometrically as distance increases from the habitation site. Distance and associated costs have four major components: (1) geodesic distance, or the straight line distance between two points; (2) pheric distance, or the time necessary to cover the topography; (3) transport costs, such as energy costs which are necessary for the hunter to bring game back to camp, for the agriculturalist to bring field produce back to the settlement, for the peasant to transport goods to market centers or, in this case, for the potter to bring ceramic raw materials from their sources; and (4) the social and psychological costs, like those incurred when the hunter's game or farmer's field are far enough away to require temporary separation from the social community (Browman, 1976).

Browman argues that there is one range where returns increase more rapidly than costs and this distance (up to threshold A on Figure 2.4) is the preferred territory of exploitation. There is a second range where costs rise sharply toward a limit of what is considered a maximum range of exploitation and this limit is threshold B (Figure 2.4). Finally, there is a marginal range where exploitation is considered uneconomic. Except for periods of economic crisis, this area is generally not exploited without modification of the systems of exploitation or the establishment of new

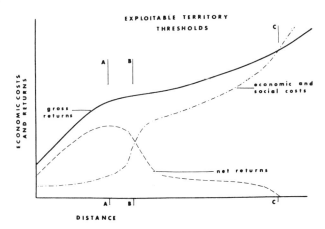

Figure 2.4 An exploitable territory thresholds model (reprinted from Browman, 1976: 470; reproduced by permission of the Society for American Archaeology from *American Antiquity* 41(4):465-77, 1976).

settlements. This distance lies between threshold B and C (Figure 2.4).
Threshold C is the absolute limit of exploitation.

In the model, Browman argues that the form of the curve (Figure 2.4)
will be the same for both mobile and sedentary economies, but numerical
values of the thresholds will be different. In both cases, however, a major
constraint upon the territory that can be effectively exploited is that it
must be close enough to permit a round trip in one day from the
occupation site. In his survey of the literature of hunting and gathering
economies Browman noted that an hour's walk (4-5 km) was the preferred collecting distance for women and a radius of one day's journey (or a
maximum of 35 km) was the maximum hunting distance for men. The
data for agricultural settlements indicated that the threshold distances
to fields were far less than those to subsistence resources exploited in
hunting and gathering economies. In Chisholm's (1968) survey, a distance of 1 km adversely affected the prosperity of the subsistence agriculturalist by causing a decline in returns. At 3-4 km, the costs rose
significantly enough to be oppressive, and beyond 3-4 km, the costs of
cultivation become prohibitive without modification of the settlement or
the system of cultivation. Similar regularities occur in studies of central
place theory where the lowest level agricultural places are spaces with a
maximum exploited distance of 4-6 km radius (or one hour's walking
distance) in the U.S., England (Loesch, 1954; Brush and Bracey, 1955),
Germany (Christaller, 1966), Rhodesia (Roder, 1969) and China (Skinner, 1964). Similarly, archaeological studies indicate that in Roman
Britain (Hodder, 1972) and among the lowland Maya (Hammond,
1972; 1974; Bullard, 1960) the lowest level central place distance is 3-6
km, and in Mesopotamia it is 3-8 km (Adams, 1972). For societies with
shifting cultivation such as in New Guinea (Clarke, 1971) and Amazonia
(Carneiro, 1956), agriculture is impractical much beyond 5 km with a
maximum radius of 7-8 km. In the Petén region of Guatemala, Carter
(1969:36) reports that the fields of the Kekchi are fifteen minutes to more
than an hour's walk away. In summary, fields are maximally exploited
with a one hour radius limit for subsistence agriculture with a geodesic
distance of 3-5 km and a maximum distance of 7-8 km (Browman, 1976;
see also Doxiadis, 1970:395). Morrill (1970) estimates that with modern
transportation this radius is closer to a half-hour maximum.

In cases where societies are semi-sedentary and depend upon hunting
and gathering besides agriculture, the exploitable territory would exceed
that of subsistence agriculturalists and approach the distances for hunting and gathering societies. Among the Akawaio in the Guinanas of the
tropical forest of South America, for example, fields are half to as much
as one day's travel away (Butt, 1977:6). For the Boni (the African Bush
Negroes in the Guinanas) gardens are 0.8-1.6 km from the village because women say that it is hard to transport manioc roots over a greater
distance. Often, however, the Boni will travel as much as 20-30 km away

by canoe, but will still have gardens no more than 1.6 km from the canoe landing site (Butt, 1977:13-16).

Using similar data, several authors (Jarman, 1972; Higgs and Vita-Finzi, 1972; Jarman, Vita-Finzi and Higgs 1972) developed the concept that an archaeological site occupies a position within an exploitable territory and has certain economic possibilities according to its location. In this 'site catchment' model, threshold A is two hours' walking distance for hunting and gathering economies and one hour for subsistence agriculturalists. Similarly, in central place theory, Christaller (1966:159-60) regarded one hour's distance as the basic measure for the establishment of the size of the lowest ranked region, and suggested that the time measure had an important geographical effect in determining the number and distribution of central places.

The exploitable threshold model and ceramic resources

How does the exploitable territory model apply to ceramic resources? What is the exploitable territory for ceramic resources? More specifically, how close must ceramic resources be in order to serve as a deviation amplifying mechanism? Conversely, how distant must they be in order to act as a negative feedback mechanism that will prevent or inhibit ceramic production? The purpose of this section is to develop a general model to determine the size of the exploitable territory around the pottery making community based on ethnographic data.

Since a pottery making population can be viewed as living in the center of an area of ceramic resources, the exploitable territory threshold model can also be applied to the utilization of ceramic resources. The model is based upon the frequency of distances to ceramic resources of a sample of pottery making communities from around the world. Before the model is directly applied to pottery making communities, however, five important qualifications that affect the model must be examined.

First, relatively few data exist on distance to ceramic resources. While construction techniques are often dealt with in excruciating detail, precise location of and distance to ceramic resources is a relatively rare occurrence in the ethnographic literature (Rye and Evans, 1976; DeBoer and Lathrap, 1979; Lackey, 1982 and Lauer, 1974 are notable exceptions). Distances to clay sources are mentioned most frequently, with progressively fewer data existing on distances to temper, slip, paint and fuel resources. Thus, the sample presented here represents the available data.

Secondly, resource threshold distances may be different for sedentary and non-sedentary communities. Ceramic production has been traditionally associated with sedentary agricultural communities. While this generalization will be examined in detail in the chapter on sedentariness (Chapter 5), there is evidence that nomadic, semi-nomadic and semi-sedentary populations do make pottery. Just as Browman (1976) noted greater threshold distances for hunters and gatherers than for subsistence agriculturalists, one would expect the threshold distance to ceramic resources would also be greater among hunters and gatherers. A hunter, for example, finding clay during his hunting trek, may transport it back to the village for his wife to use for making pottery (Gayton, 1929:240). The distance to such a casual source would probably far exceed distances to clay sources of sedentary communities. The data presented here, however, are limited to sedentary and partly sedentary agricultural communities. No data on precise distances to ceramic resources were found among totally non-sedentary groups (i. e. 'nomadic' in Murdock's (1967:51) terminology).

Thirdly, one would expect the different types of ceramic resources to have different threshold values in the model. The most important ceramic resources are suitable clay, water, fuel and temper, depending on whether the clay contains enough naturally occurring non-plastics or not. Of all the ceramic resources, clays and temper are heaviest to transport and are needed more frequently than slips or paints. Furthermore, the ratio (by weight) of clay to finished pottery is greater than that of slips or paints. Water, of course, is equally important, but its importance for human consumption suggests that water sources are probably closer to habitation sites than more specialized ceramic sources and thus, the distance to water sources is not primarily related to the prerequisites of pottery production, but rather to the biological and general subsistence needs of the population. Fuel is important as well, and its use in cooking and heating also suggests that fuel sources (like water sources) are located closer to habitation sites than other more specialized ceramic resources because of their domestic importance apart from pottery production. Potters may, however, use fuel for firing that is not used for domestic purposes. Nevertheless, the ratio of fuel to finished pottery is less than that of clay. Potters may require one fourth to one half the weight of finished pottery for fuel (Rye and Evans, 1976:165).

Fuel resources may be unwanted by-products of subsistence activities and thus be readily available. In Greece, for example, Matson (1972:213) notes that fuel for firing often consists of prunings from olive groves and vineyards. In Spain, fuel consist of prunings from olive orchards and old olive trees (Curtis, 1962:496). In Quinua, Peru, straw from the harvest is occasionally used for firing. In Ticul, Yucatan, Mexico, potters use firewood cut during clearing of land for the swidden cycle. Similarly, potters in Chinautla, Durazno and Sacojito (Guatemala) use by-products of charcoal making such as pine cones, needles and bark obtained from trees cleared from land used for the swidden cycle (Arnold, 1978b). Thus, the importance of clays and tempers and the use of local unwanted by-products of subsistence activities for fuel suggest that these primary ceramic materials probably have similar threshold distances in the model.

Ceramic resources also include glazes, paints and slips in some areas, but these materials are used in smaller quantities relative to clay and tempering materials. Potters need to replenish their supplies of slips and paints less often and can expend more energy per trip to obtain them than clays and temper. Newari potters in the Kathmandu valley in Nepal, for example, obtain clay in the fields near their village, but they travel for two days to obtain a six year supply of slipping material (Birmingham, 1975:380). Similarly, potters in Acatlán, Mexico, obtain enough paint (100 kg) in one trip to the source for almost an entire year's supply using it at a rate of 2 kg per week (Lackey, 1982:58). Thus, the threshold distance for exploiting paint and slip resources would probably be far greater than that for primary resources of clay, temper and fuel.

Other resources such as materials for tools are not as important and can be imported from greater distances. These include such items as: (a) volcanic tuff, slate, or wood for pottery supports; (b) leather for smoothing; (c) a gourd, metal or cane scraper; (d) a stick, stamp or a piece of cane for plastic decoration; (e) a brush, feather or hair for painting; and (f) a fine grain stone for polishing. These are needed even less often then paints or slips and would be expected to have greater threshold distances than the paints. These materials are variable from community to community and since so few data on distance to these resources were available, they are not included in the model.

Fourthly, while most of the available ethnographic data mention geodesic distance, pheric distance is probably a more accurate measure of distance because it includes some correction for the topography and more closely reflects energy costs. In mountains, for example, more walking time is required to traverse a given geodesic distance than for the same distance over plains; one kilometer in a tropical rainforest requires more walking time than one kilometer in a steppe or savannah. Furthermore, straight line distance could give an unrealistic measure of the costs involved. Canoe travel along a meandering river in the tropical forest of South America may occur over a relatively short straight line distance, and thus only the actual distance covered or the amount of time necessary for the trip provide an accurate measure of the distance.

The type of transportation available (pack animals, canoe or motor vehicles as opposed to human carriers) may affect the distances to resources. With transportation, human energy inputs per unit of distance are less than with human carriers and so geodesic distances to ceramic resources can be increased without affecting the time per trip. Transportation such as pack animals would also reduce the overall energy costs by greatly increasing the amount of clay or other ceramic resource obtained. For traditional communities which are land-locked,

the feedback of distance to resources that affected the original development of the craft was probably most often based on energy costs of
human carriers walking, although in some locations in the Old World
and perhaps in the Central Andes, pack animals may have been used
originally. For coastal, riverine or island communities which had ceramic resources located over stretches of water and used canoe transportation, the energy costs were probably the same as for obtaining ceramic
materials on foot, but the distances were greater. A man in a canoe can
probably transport more clay over a greater distance than a man ex-
pending the same amount of energy, but carrying clay on foot. Thus,
ceramic materials obtained by canoe would be further away than resources carried by human carriers, and the amount of energy used to
transport clay a given threshold distance on foot is equal to that necessary to move a greater amount of clay a much greater distance by canoe.
Because of these problems and the relative lack of pheric distances in the
literature, pheric distances to ceramic resources will be described separately from geodesic distances.

Fifthly, the transport costs in terms of energy expended to obtain
ceramic resources is another significant variable. Energy costs are an
effective way to equalize mode of transportation, distance, topography
and time. The threshold distance could be stated in terms of energy
expended in extracting and transporting a unit of clay in a given unit of
time over a given distance. None of the ethnographic literature examined
provided this type of data, however, and distances are usually stated in
terms of geodesic distance. The composite threshold distances in the
model, however, probably represent the upper limit of energy potters
will use to transport a given amount of clay (approximately 25 kg) over
that distance on foot.

Finally, this relationship of the energy limits of a population to the
distance traveled in terms of a cost/benefits model is not affected by
cultural contact, diffusion or other kinds of historical relatedness
(Strauss and Orans, 1975). Thus, energy expenditures, their limits and
their expression in geodesic and pheric distances exist independently of
historical factors and are assumed to apply universally (with the exceptions noted here) to all populations of pre-industrial potters.

A survey of the ethnographic literature for geodesic distance to ceramic resources provided data consisting of distance to clay (Table 2.1),
temper (Table 2.2), and slip and paint (Table 2.3) resources. Distance
to each resource was plotted against the frequency (in percent) of the
sample that occurred at that distance (Figures 2.5 and 2.6). Frequencies
were graphed in units of 1 km, so that the graph at each kilometer unit
represents the percent of the sample that obtains their resources at that
distance.

The geodesic distance to clay resources (N = 111) has a range from
less than 1 km to 50 km (Figure 2.5). The preferred territory of exploita-

Table 2.1 *Distance to clay resources*

Community/Group	Location	Distance (in km) to clay source[1]	Bibliographic source	Type[2]
Chalkis	Greece	10	Matson, 1973:121	T
Eretria	Greece	12	Matson, 1973:124	T
Simbilá	Peru	4	Christensen, 1955:10	T
Guazacapán, Santa Rosa	Guatemala	6.5	Spicknall, 1975:3,32–7	M
Taourirt	Morocco	3	Beckett, 1958:187	T
Texcoco	Mexico	2	Foster, 1955:13	T
Ccaccasiri, Huancavelica	Peru	2.5–3.5	Ravines, 1966:211	TM
Tororapampa Huancavelica	Peru	~1	Ravines, 1963-4	E(TM)
Cotocallao	Ecuador	1	Litto, 1976:112	T
Claros	Colombia	2.5	Litto, 1976:157	T
Otusco	La Libertad, Peru	1.5	Teresa Topic, personal communication	E
Chalky Mount	Barbados	.3–.4	Handler, 1963a:318	T
Bomboret Valley Kafiristan Northwest Frontier Province	Pakistan	.15	Rye and Evans, 1976:9	T
Dir, Northwest Frontier Province –inferior clay	Pakistan	2	Rye and Evans, 1976:20	T
–superior clay		2	Rye and Evans, 1976:20	T
Swat, Northwest Frontier Province	Pakistan	2	Rye and Evans, 1976:28	T
Prang, Northwest Frontier Province	Pakistan	4.5	Rye and Evans, 1976:37	T
Kharmathu, Northwest Frontier Province	Pakistan	5	Rye and Evans, 1976:39	T

Table 2.1 (*Contd.*)

Community/Group	Location	Distance (in km) to clay source[1]	Bibliographic source	Type[2]
Machigenga community unknown	Cuzco, Peru	1	Pat Davis, personal communication	E
Picha		.3	Pat Davis, personal communication	E
Mórrope	Peru	30	Collier, 1959:421	T
Ingalik Eskimo	Alaska	.4	Osgood, 1940:146	T
Bontok Igorot (Bila)	Philippines	3	Solheim and Shuler, 1959:2	T
Bontok Igorot (Bila)	Philippines	4	Solheim and Shuler, 1959:2	T
Ifugao (male tradition)	Philippines	3	Solheim and Shuler, 1959:5	T
Jocotán	Guatemala	14.5	Reina and Hill, 1978:159	T
Mixco	Guatemala	1	Reina and Hill, 1978:42	T
Mixco	Guatemala	<1(.01)	Arnold, 1978b:338	T
La Ciénaga	Guatemala	<1(.01)	Arnold, 1978b:331	T
Papoyán	Colombia	<1(.01)	Whiteford, 1977:202	T
Santa María Chiquimula (white clay)	Guatemala	8.8	Reina and Hill, 1978:70	T
Rabinal	Guatemala	~2	Reina and Hill, 1978:133	T
Zahalte'tik, Chamula/Tzoltzil	Chiapas, Mexico	3	Howry, 1978:242	T
Chacobo	Bolivia	~2	Visit to community	E
Yagua	Peru	1	Paul Powlison, personal communication	E
Culina	Peru	~1	Patsy Adams, personal communication	E

Table 2.1 (*Contd.*)

Community/Group	Location	Distance (in km) to clay source[1]	Bibliographic source	Type[2]
Skala	Greece	3	Matson, 1972:205	T
Peto, Yucatan	Mexico	4	Visit to community	E
Quinua	Peru	.25–2	Arnold, 1975a:188	EM
Raqchi	Peru	1	Visit to community	E
Machacmarca	Peru	1	Visit to community	E
Moro (Yoruba)	Nigeria	4.8	Waldman, 1972:314, 317	M
Abeokuta (Yoruba)	Nigeria	11.9	Waldman, 1972:340	M
Oyo (Yoruba)	Nigeria	6.5	Waldman, 1972:344	M
Acatlán, Puebla	Mexico	5	Foster, 1960b:208	T
Tehran	Iran	.01	Matson, 1974	T
Cairo	Eqypt	25	Matson, 1974	TM
Vounaria	Greece	<1	Matson, 1972:213-14	T
Kombi	Greece	~1	Matson, 1972:222	TM
Petriadhes	Greece	2	Matson, 1972:222	TM
Ticul	Mexico	7	Thompson, 1958:66	T
Lerma	Mexico	.01	Thompson, 1958:65	T
Sacojito	Guatemala	2	Arnold, 1978b:Fig. 1; Rice, 1977:Fig. 2	EM
Durazno cooking pots, water storage jars	Guatemala	.05	Arnold, 1978b:Fig. 1; Rice, 1977:Fig. 2	EM
white-firing clay		.5–2	Arnold, 1978b:Fig. 1; Rice, 1977:Fig. 2	EM
Chinautla white clay	Guatemala	1.5	Arnold, 1978b:Fig. 1	EM

Table 2.1 (*Contd.*)

Community/Group	Location	Distance (in km) to clay source[1]	Bibliographic source	Type[2]
red clay		.02–.35	Arnold, 1978b:Fig. 1; Rice, 1977:Fig. 2	EM
Bailén	Spain	<1	Curtis, 1962:491	T
Tiv	Nigeria			
white clay		24	Bohannan, 1954:40	T
dark clay		24	Bohannan, 1954:40	
Beit Shebab	Lebanon		Hankey, 1968:28	T
source within the village		<1		
alternate source		2		
Andros	Greece	<1	Birmingham, 1967:38	E
Santa Clara	U.S.South-west		LeFree, 1975:7	T
Pit #1		6.1		
Pit #2		6.9		
Bida/Nupe	Nigeria	16.1	Nicholson, 1934:70	T
Use	Nigeria	24	Willet and Connah, 1969:134	T
Ghorepuripet, Poona City	India	4.8	Gupta, 1966:72	T
Shahbaz Ahmed Khel Bannu, Northwest Frontier Province	Pakistan	.15	Rye and Evans, 1976:44	T
Quetta, Baluchistan	Pakistan	5	Rye and Evans, 1976:73	T
Zakhel Bala, Northwest Frontier Province	Pakistan	2.5	Rye and Evans, 1976:73	T
Multan, Panjab	Pakistan	1.1	Rye and Evans, 1976:73	T
San Juan Metepec, State of Mexico	Mexico	7	Whitaker and Whitaker, 1978:88	T

Table 2.1 (*Contd.*)

Community/Group	Location	Distance (in km) to clay source[1]	Bibliographic source	Type[2]
Samachíque	Mexico		Pastron, 1974:104	T
(Tarahumara)				
dark red		10		
red		9		
yellow		3		
black		2		
Buka Island	Melanesia		Specht, 1972:126	M
Malasang		2.6, 3.0		
Hangan		5.2, 6.6		
Lonahan		5.6, 6.6		
Maxcanú	Mexico	19, 22, 50	Thompson, 1958:66	M
Mama	Mexico	2	Thompson, 1958:66	T
Koreaf	Papua New Guinea	1.6	Key, 1968:653	T
Komabun, Rainu Oreresan	Papua New Guinea	4.03	Key, 1968:653	T
Bibil	Papua New Guinea	1	Kakubayashi, 1978:139	T
Dangtalan/Kalinga	Philippines	<1	Longacre, 1981:54	M
San Ildefonso (red clay)	Southwest	<1	Guthe, 1925:20	T
Wanigela (Rainu)	New Guinea	<3	Egloff, 1973:61	T
Buduna	Goodenough Island, Melanesia	2	Lauer, 1974: 12, 58	T
Nasama/Fiji	Oceania			
for jars		<1	Palmer and Shaw, 1968: 50-1	M
for bowls		<2		
Kufr Lebbad	Israel	8	Crowfoot, 1932:183	M

Table 2.1 (*Contd.*)

Community/Group	Location	Distance (in km) to clay source[1]	Bibliographic source	Type[2]
Kikwanauta	Goodenough Island, Melanesia	2	Lauer, 1974:12, 58	M
Vedakala	,,	1	,, ,, ,,	,,
Huneya	,,	1	,, ,, ,,	,,
Monunaoya	,,	<2	Lauer,1974:12, 58	M
	,,	<1	,, ,, ,,	
	,,	<1	,, ,, ,,	,,
Diudiugana	,,	<2	,, ,, ,,	,,
Maiyabu	,,	<1	,, ,, ,,	,,
Waibula	,,	1	,, ,, ,,	,,
Bwaula	,,	4	,, ,, ,,	,,
Yauyaula	,,	2	,, ,, ,,	,,
Manubuleya	,,	<1	,, ,, ,,	,,
Wisalu	,,	<1	,, ,, ,,	,,

Notes

[1] Distance of source from pottery making community. Statements that indicate a source of clay in or very near the potter's yard (e.g. in the courtyard or behind the house) were given a value of <1 km. If distance was not mentioned in a bibliographic source but the description included a place name of the source with a map, the distance from the community to a source was measured using straight line (or geodesic) distance. If the settlement is nucleated, the distance was measured from the center of settlement. If the pottery making community was dispersed, the distance listed was that which most of the people would have to travel. When ranges were given, mean values were used in preparing Figure 2.5. When decimal fractions exist, values are converted into the next highest whole number (i.e. 6.1 becomes <7 km).

[2] This column refers to the type of source of information from which distance to the clay source was obtained. 'T' is a distance mentioned in the text and 'M' represents a distance to a source from a map when place names were given in the text. 'E' is the estimate of a distance based on the author's own experience or the experience of others in the community.

Table 2.2 *Distance to temper resources*

Community/Group	Location	Distance (in km) to temper source[1]	Bibliographic source	Type[2]
Acatlán, Puebla	Mexico	<1	Foster,1960b:208; Lackey,1982:18	T
Yatenga/Mossi	Upper Volta	.01	Hammond, 1966:62	T
Fulani	Cameroun	.01	David and Hennig, 1972:5	T
Lame	Cameroun	.01	David and Hennig, 1972:5	T
Tepekán	Mexico	<1	Thompson, 1958:69 Visit to community	ET
Ticul	Mexico	4	Thompson, 1958:69	T
Mama	Mexico	2	Thompson, 1958:69	T
Uayma	Mexico	.5	Thompson, 1958:69	T
Lerma	Mexico	1	Thompson, 1958:69	T
Moro/Yoruba	Nigeria	.01	Wahlman, 1972:318	T
Simbilá	Peru	4	Christensen, 1955:10	T
Quinua	Peru	.5–1	Arnold, 1975a: Fig. 5 Visit to community	M
Akil	Mexico	.1	Visit to community	E
Pampay, Luricocha	Peru	2	Visit to community	E
Chinautla	Guatemala	.5	Arnold, 1978b:Fig. 1	M
Sacojito	Guatemala	.5–1	Arnold, 1978b:Fig. 1	M
Durazno	Guatemala	1-3	Arnold, 1978b:Fig. 1	M
Guazacapán, Santa Rosa	Guatemala	3.25	Spicknall, 1975	M
Calcapirhua	Bolivia	1	Litto, 1976:59	T
Mbua Province, Vanna Levu Island	Fiji			
red sand		3.2	Roth, 1935:229	T

Table 2.2 (*Contd.*)

Community/Group	Location	Distance (in km) to temper source[1]	Bibliographic source	Type[2]
black sand		24.1	Roth, 1935:229	T
Bomboret Valley, Kafiristan, North-west Frontier Province	Pakistan	.3	Rye and Evans, 1976:10	T
Swat, Northwest Frontier Province	Pakistan	2	Rye and Evans, 1976:28	T
Machigenga	Peru			
Dept of Cuzco, community of Pichu		.1	Pat Davis, personal communication	E
Community unknown		.5	Pat Davis, personal communication	E
Machacmarca	Peru	5	Litto, 1976:30	EM
Ccaccasiri, Huancavelia	Peru	3.5	Ravines, 1966:211	T(M)
Buka Island	Melanesia		Specht, 1972:126	M
Lanahan		8.		
Malasang		5.2		
Hangan		7.4		
Kufr Lebbad	Israel	9	Crowfoot, 1932:183	M

Notes: Table 2.2

[1] See Footnote 1, Table 2.1.

[2] See Footnote 2, Table 2.1.

Table 2.3 *Distance to slip and paint resources*

Community/Group	Location[1]	Distance (in km)[1]	Bibliographic source	Type[2]
Chalkis (white slip)	Greece	46	Matson, 1973:125	T
Simbilá	Peru	100	Christensen, 1955	T
Taourirt	Morocco	3	Beckett, 1958	T
La Chamba (red slip)	Colombia	12	Litto, 1976:152	T
Quinua	Peru			
red paint		19	Arnold, 1972a:859	M
white paint		.5–2.5	Arnold, 1975a:188	M
black paint		1–2.5	Arnold, 1975a:188	M
Chinautla	Guatemala			
white slip or paint		7	Arnold, 1978b:Fig. 1; Rice, 1977	M
red paint		3.5	Arnold, 1978b:Fig. 1; Rice, 1977	M
Durazno	Guatemala			
white slip or paint		2.5–4.6	Arnold, 1978b:Fig. 1; Rice, 1977	M
red paint		.1–2	Arnold, 1978b:Fig. 1; Rice, 1977	M
Chirag Dilli	India			
red paint		8	Gupta, 1969:17	T
white paint		12	Gupta, 1969:17	T
black paint		140	Gupta, 1969:17	T
Kharmathu, Northwest Frontier Province	Pakistan			
(body clay is slip)		5	Rye and Evans, 1976:39-40	T

Table 2.3 (*Contd.*)

Community/Group	Location[1]	Distance (in km)[1]	Bibliographic source	Type[2]
Shahbaz Ahmed Khel and Bannu, Northwest Frontier Province	Pakistan			
black paint		40	Rye and Evans, 1976:46	T
red slip		40	Rye and Evans, 1976:46	T
Shahdarah, Panjab	Pakistan	90[3]	Rye and Evans, 1976:55	M
Shadiwal, Panjab	Pakistan	18[3]	Rye and Evans, 1976:58, 60	T
Zakhel Bala, Northwest Frontier Province	Pakistan			
white slip (1968)		88	Rye and Evans, 1976:77, 81	T
white slip (1971)		240	Rye and Evans, 1976:77, 81	M
blue pigment		240	Rye and Evans, 1976:77, 81	M
green pigment		28	Rye and Evans, 1976:77, 81	T
Hala, Sind	Pakistan	880	Rye and Evans, 1976:109	M
glaze components:				
soda ash	Pakistan	170	Rye and Evans, 1976:110	M
lead glaze	Pakistan	170	Rye and Evans, 1976:110	M
Santa María Chiquimula	Guatemala			
red paint		13[3]	Reina and Hill, 1978:70	M
Tonalá	Mexico			
slip		48	Charlton and Katz, 1979:48	T
Bibil	New Guinea	5	Kakubayashi, 1978:139	T
red slip				

Table 2.3 (*Contd.*)

Community/Group	Location[1]	Distance (in km)[1]	Bibliographic source	Type[2]
Sacojito	Guatemala			
white slip or paint		8	Arnold, 1978b:Fig. 1; Rice, 1977	M
red paint		5	Arnold, 1978b:Fig 1; Rice, 1977	M
Bailén	Spain			
white paint		60	Curtis, 1962:494	T
lead sulfide powder glaze		15	Curtis, 1962:495	T
red ochre (glaze constituent)		40	Curtis, 1962:496	T
Tonalá	Mexico	161	Diaz, 1966:141	T
Acatlán	Puebla	5	Lackey, 1982:18	M

Notes

[1] See Footnote 1, Table 2.1.

[2] See Footnote 2, Table 2.1.

[3] Supplier only; original source unknown.

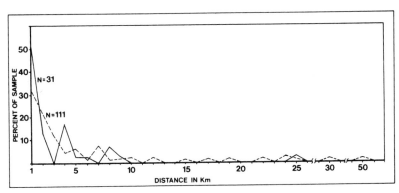

Figure 2.5 Distances to clay and temper sources. The dotted line refers to the distances to clay sources (N=111) and the solid line refers to distances to temper sources (N=31). The data were obtained from Tables 2.1 and 2.2.

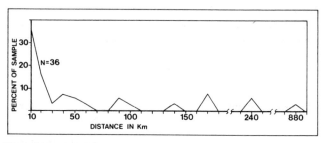

Figure 2.6 Distances to slip, glaze and paint sources. The data were obtained from Table 2.3.

tion (threshold A) probably occurs at 1 km because the largest percentage of the distances in the sample (33 per cent) are 1 km or less. Eighty-four per cent are within 7 km and this distance probably represents the upper limit of the maximum range of exploitation (threshold B).

Pheric distances to clay sources are few and vary greatly. For non-canoe distances, Solheim (1952a:49) mentions that potters on the island of Masbate in the Philippines obtain their clay at a location one day's trip away and obtain enough (10 kg) for at least three days of work. Similarly, one potter in the Chitral Valley in the Northwest Frontier Province of Pakistan makes a full day's journey to obtain clay, going out early in the morning, digging the clay and transporting it back to the village late at night (Rye and Evans, 1976:14, 127). Howry (1978:242) found that all of the six major ceramic producing hamlets in Chamula, Mexico, were located within approximately an hour's walk from sources of clay. The Lame and the Fulani of the Cameroun walk fifteen minutes (probably 1-2 km) from their village to obtain their clay (David and Hennig, 1972:21). Specht (1972:127) notes that the potters of Malasang on Buka Island walk 30-40 minutes to obtain their clay. Conklin (1953:3) notes that among the Buhid people on the island of Mindoro in the Philippines, clay sources are one day's travel away if they walk fast. If the clay sources are more than one full day's travel away, communities generally do not make pottery (Conklin, 1953:10).

The geodesic and pheric canoe distances to clay resources greatly exceed the non-canoe distances. The Motu potters of Manumanu in Papua New Guinea travel approximately 24 kilometers to obtain their clay. The Amphlett Islanders of Melanesia use a traditional clay source one day's journey away by canoe on Fergusson Island (Lauer, 1974:131,143) some 24 kilometers away. They undertake a four day trip to obtain the clay and acquire enough clay (about two tons) to supply one potter for about half a year (Malinowski, 1922:283-4). Recent clay sources that Amphlett potters discovered on their islands are 4 to 11 kilometers away by canoe (Lauer, 1974:131,143). Similarly, natives from the villages of Lababia and Laukana, in the Huon Gulf in New

Table 2.4 *Mean canoe distances to clay sources among Shipibo-Conibo communities with potters*(data from DeBoer and Lathrap, 1979:112-14)

Community	Mean distance (in km) to each clay type			Community mean
	White	Red	Black	(of all clay types in km)
San Francisco	1[1]	1[5]	39[6]	13.8
Iparia[1]	10	- -	30	20
Sonochenea[1]	5	5[1]	- -	5
Shahuaya[1]	25	5	5	11.6
Panaillo	22.5[2]	22.5[2]	5[3]	11.6
Charashmaná	Only one clay used (1)			1

Notes

[1] N=1
[2] N=4
[3] N=5
[4] N=9
[5] N=10
[6] N=13

Guinea, make a two day trip to the Fly Islands (10 km and 22 km away respectively) to obtain clay (Hogbin, 1951:88). In San Jose, in the Department of Peten, Guatemala, Reina and Hill (1978:142) point out that potters travel 2 1/2 hours by canoe (a geodesic distance of 10 km (Reina and Hill, 1978:Map 5)) to obtain their clay. The Shipibo-Conibo of the Peruvian jungle may travel half a day by canoe in order to obtain clay (Lathrap, 1973:171), but different clays used in different communities have different geodesic distances (Table 2.4). An Ecuadorian potter in the tropical forest visited by Litto (1976:210) travels two hours by canoe to dig her clay. (Actually, the Shipibo-Conibo potters may not make a special trip to obtain clays from distant sources, but may acquire them (as well as slips, paints, resins or polishing stones) through trade or when visiting in the vicinity of a distant resource.)

The distances to temper resources are very similar to those of clays except that the sample is smaller (N=31). Distance to temper resources ranges from less than 1 km to 25 km, with the majority of the sample (52 per cent) obtaining their temper at a distance of 1 km or less (Figure 2.5). This 1 km radius is probably the preferred territory of exploitation. Ninety-seven per cent of the sample obtain their temper within 6-9 km, suggesting that this distance constitutes the upper limit of the maximum range of temper exploitation. (Since 88 per cent of the sample occurs at 6

Table 2.5 *Mean canoe distances to glaze, paint and resin sources among Shipibo-Conibo communities with potters* (data from DeBoer and Lathrap, 1969:112-14)

Community (N=1 except as noted)	Mean Distance in km to each paint or resin source				Community mean (in km) for all paint and resin sources
	White	Red	Black	Resin[1]	
San Francisco (N=12)	250	98	190 (N=10)	125 (N=14)	165.75
Iparia	70	70	260+	5	101.25
Sonochenea	85	85	5	5	45
Shahuaya	15	15	175	5	52.5
Panaillo (N=5)	200	200	220	166.25 (N=4)	196.625
Charashmaná	180	100	100	100	100
Paucocha	145	85	165	- -	131.67

Notes

[1] The two resin types were combined since they either came from the same location or had data missing for one type.

km or less, it is possible that 6 km may be the maximum range of exploitation. Since almost all (97 per cent) of the sample occurs within an additional 3 km (in contrast to the clay distances–see Figure 2.5), however, a range of 6-9 km is suggested for the threshold B distance.)

Pheric distances to temper resources are practically non-existent in the literature. Reina and Hill (1978:142) mention that potters of San Jose, Peten, in Guatemala travel half an hour by foot or canoe (a geodesic distance of 3.3 km on the map) to obtain temper (Reina and Hill, 1978:120). Specht (1972:127) notes that the temper source for the village of Malasay on Buka Island in Melanesia is about 60-70 minutes' walk away.

The distance to slip and paint resources (including glazes) are far greater than for clay and temper and harder to interpret (Figure 2.6). The range was so great that the geodesic distances were graphed in 10 km units. The greatest percentage (36 per cent) of communities obtain their slips and paints at a distance of less than 10 km and this range is probably the preferred territory of exploitation. Fifty-seven per cent of the sample obtain their slip resources at 30 km or less. Canoe distances to slip and paint sources are also scanty, but the best data come from DeBoer and Lathrap (1979; see Table 2.5).

Concerning pheric distances to slip and paint resources, Reina and Hill (1978:153) note that San Vicente potters in the Department of Zacapa, Guatemala, walk several hours to a source of steatite (a material consisting mostly of talc which is used like a slip to keep *tortillas* from sticking to the griddles) and spend about a half a day mining and traveling to and from the source.

There are few data on distance to fuel resources. The potters of Quinua, Peru, travel 2-6 km to obtain their fuel for firing. Potters of the Chinautla, Sacojito and Durazno area of Guatemala obtain their fuel (grass and pine bark, needles and cones) from the local forests surrounding these communities. Similarly, Ticul potters obtain their firewood from peasant farmers (*milperos*) who cut it in the forest around the community. Potters in the Temascalcingo area of the State of Mexico obtain their fuel for firing (sawdust) from middlemen who bring it by truck from 26 km away (Papousek, 1974:1027). Potters in Acatlán, Mexico, obtain their fuel (mostly cactus) from 9 km away, a fifteen minute journey by car, but which would take a burro at least 2 hours. Buduna and Kiwananta potters on Goodenough Island in the D'Entre-casteaux Islands use palm fronds of sago and coconut (Lauer, 1974:54) while all of the other potters on Goodenough Island use dry branches or split logs from the nearby forest (Lauer, 1974:61). Both coconut palm fronds and dry wood are used by Amphlett potters (Lauer, 1974:151). Potters in Pucará, Peru, use llama and cow dung (Litto, 1976:36), those in Simbilá, Peru, use straw, animal dung, rags and refuse (Litto, 1976:14) and potters in Chitapampa, Peru, use cow dung or hay for firing (Litto, 1976:22). The Mono and Western Yokuts use wood and oak bark for firing (Gayton, 1929:244). From these and other data, it is clear that fuels used by potters are local materials, but few data exist on precise distance to the resources.

From the limited amount of data, the results are inconclusive as to whether distance to fuel resources is a significant deviation counteract-ing feedback for ceramic production, since potters tend to use local materials. Nicklin (1979:448) in his summary of some of the literature on ceramic resources, concludes that the wide range of adaptations to local fuel supplies for pre-industrial potters suggests that the quantity and quality of fuel available do not impose severe restrictions on the location of pottery making communities. This may be true for non-specialist potters or those in forested areas who are not undergoing population pressure (like those using swidden agriculture). Fuel supplies in these cases may not be a significant deviation counteracting mechanism. Nevertheless, in communities undergoing population pressure (see Chapter 7), fuel supplies may provide considerable deviation counter-acting feedback. Howry (1978:242) found that in Chamula, Mexico, the distances to fuel resources were more crucial than distances to clay sources, and the loss of fuel supplies within a reasonable distance from the potter's house caused changes in the potter's settlement. While distances to clay sources may have been more important as recently as twenty years ago, overgrazing and greater demand for firewood from a growing population have produced deforestation. When the wood supply becomes short, the potters move out of the deforested areas to more wooded and less populated areas and purchase wooded land to ensure adequate fuel supplies for firing.

Shortage of traditional fuel can also create changes in the type of fuel used. Shortage of wood for firing (because of deforestation) around Tonalá, Mexico, has caused potters to expand their range of fuels to include more available materials like scrap wood, dry bushes, branches, cow dung and occasionally sawdust (Diaz, 1966:149). Similarly, shortage of traditional fuel for firing among Acatlán potters has caused a shift towards a new fuel source. Originally wood was used for firing, but when the forests around the village disappeared, potters switched to using two species of cactus. Recently, cactus has had to be transported from increasing distances by burro, and with increasing costs, potters have experimented with other fuels like rubbish, corn stalks and sugar cane. They have discovered that cut up old tires used with cactus cut firing costs since a bag of shredded tires costs one eighth as much as a burro load of cactus (Lackey, 1982:59-60). Thus, among potters in communities undergoing population pressure, the lack of fuel resources may be a significant deviation counteracting feedback mechanism.

Potters may make pottery even though fuel is insufficient or not present. The Daflas villages of north eastern India have a shortage of fuel to fire pottery because of deforestation and sometimes they sell unfired pots to the nearby Apa Tanis. The Apa Tanis transport the pots to the forest belt which divides the Apa Tani territory from that of the Dafla and there they fire the pots before carrying them to their villages (Fürer-Haimendorf, 1962:50).

Some data were located concerning distances of sources for pottery making implements. Potters in Basama in the Sigatoka Valley in Fiji obtain their anvil stones for making pottery from the upper valley 67 km away (Palmer and Shaw, 1968:52). By far the best data on distances to sources of polishing stones (Table 2.6) come from DeBoer and Lathrap (1979). This small amount of data, however, scarcely merits inclusion in the model.

When the threshold model is applied to graphs of the frequencies of the distances that different communities travel to their ceramic resources, the curves for clay and temper are very similar. Threshold A, the preferred territory of exploitation, is 1 km or less for both clay and temper. The greatest percentage of the communities prefer to obtain those resources at this distance because returns increase more rapidly than costs. The dramatic drop in the frequency of communities that travel more than 1 km to clay and temper sources suggests that costs

Table 2.6 *Mean canoe distances to sources of polishing stones among Shipibo-Conibo communities with potters* (data from DeBoer and Lathrap, 1979:112-14)

Community	N =	Mean distance to source for each community (in km)
San Francisco	7	107.1
Iparia	1	150
Sonochenea	1	5
Shahuaya	1	65
Panaillo	4	191.2
Mean distance to source of polishing stones for Shipibo-Conibo communities		105.66

increase rapidly after 1 km and that at greater distances, exploitation of clay and temper resources becomes increasingly less economic. At threshold B, costs rise sharply to the maximum range of exploitation and this ranges from 7 km for clay and 6-9 km for temper. After threshold B, there is a marginal range where exploitation of clay and temper resources is uneconomic, and not exploited without modification of the system of exploitation.

There are a number of pottery making commmunities which have resource distances beyond threshold B, but each represents less than 5 per cent of sample. In most of these cases, modern transportation like railroad, ox cart or truck is used and probably reflects the modification of the original economic system when pottery making began. One way in which this modification occurs is when local supplies of raw materials are exhausted or inaccessible and potters must travel greater distances to obtain them. When the original clay source on the island of Chowra in the Indian Ocean became exhausted, for example, potters had to travel 8 km by sea to a nearby island in order to obtain a suitable supply (Man, 1894:22; MacKenzie, 1949:164; Mathur, 1967:14). A second modification of the system may occur when modern transportation is used to transport ceramic materials. Modern transportation can lengthen the geodesic threshold distances that existed when the pottery making community was established. The pheric distances may remain the same. In both of the Greek communities of Chalkis and Eretria, for example, the distance to clay resources is 10 km and 12 km from the village respectively, but clay is transported to the potters' houses by horse drawn cart and truck (Matson, 1973:121, 124). Similarly, Thompson (1958:66) reports that Maxcanu potters obtained their clay by horse drawn cart or railroad from Becal (19 km away), Tepekán (22 km away) and to a lesser extent Ticul (50 km away).

The distance to glaze, slip and paint resources is far more difficult to integrate into the threshold model because of the smaller sample. Distances to slip, paint and glaze resources (Figure 2.6) have a range of 1 km to 880 km with the largest percentage (36 per cent) of the sample (N=36) obtaining these materials within 10 km. This radius of 10 km is probably the preferred territory of exploitation. Additional thresholds are difficult to determine from the data, although 71 per cent of the sample obtain their slips and paints from no more than 60 km away. Distances to glaze, slip and paint resources are clearly greater than those of clays and tempers.

By applying the results of the ethnographic data and threshold distances to the systems model, it appears that if the distance to primary resources is less than threshold A, the result is deviation amplifying feedback for ceramic production, both for the origin of the craft and its development into full-time specialization. The area between thresholds A and B probably also produces deviation amplifying feedback. Distances greater than threshold B, however, limit or prevent the development of pottery making except in situations where modification of the system has occurred with modern transportation. Even then, however, the absolute upper range of distance to primary ceramic resources indicates that resources that exist farther away serve also to prevent the origin and development of pottery making. Once local resources are exhausted either resources must be brought from farther away than threshold B, or potters must move nearer to a source of supply, or pottery is no longer made. In areas with modern transportation, threshold B can be extended because it may be within the one day maximum time limit necessary to obtain ceramic resources.

The distances for threshold A for clays and temper (1 km) are much less than the maximum threshold distances (3-5 km) noted by Browman for subsistence agricultural communities (Table 2.7). It is not totally clear why this difference exists, but it is probably related to energy costs in that potters always return with some raw materials from their trip to the source area, whereas an agriculturalist does so only at harvest. Thus, because energy costs per trip are higher with potters than with agriculturalists, the distance to ceramic resources is less than that to agricultural resources.

Long distance transportation of primary ceramic materials like clays and tempers is unusual, but it is by no means impossible. Local clays, temper and slips from the pottery making community of Quinua, Peru, are taken 340 km to Lima for use by Quinua potters there. Producing Quinua pottery in Lima brings the manufacture of pottery closer to its market and prevents breakage of the pottery during the 340 km trip over mountainous terrain.

Table 2.7 *Comparison of threshold distances of pottery making and subsistence agricultural communities*

	Distance to resources	
	Threshold A (in km)	Threshold B (in km)
Subsistence agricultural communities' fields	3–5	7–8
Clay	1	7
Temper	1	6–9

The abundance of ceramic resources is also an important feedback consideration. The existence of some ceramic resources within the distances discussed earlier will provide deviation amplifying feedback, but once the craft develops and approaches a full-time speciality, abundant ceramic resources become a significant prerequisite for sustained production. The notion of 'abundance', however, is vague and subjective and is difficult to evaluate and quantify.

While ceramic resources must be generally within the distances suggested by the threshold model in order to provide deviation amplifying feedback for pottery production, the mere existence of high quality ceramic resources within the theshold values in the model is an insufficient single cause for the development of ceramic production. Arnold (1978a) found that areas in the Valley of Guatemala with ceramic resources like clays, temper and fuel do not necessarily co-occur with pottery making communities. Clays occur widely in the area. Volcanic ash from the nearby volcanoes for temper and wood (and forest products) for firing from local pine forests are virtually universal in the region. Thus, the quality, abundance and nearness of ceramic resources alone are not sufficient cause for the development of ceramics because other important feedback relationships are involved in the development of pottery making. These will be discussed in subsequent chapters.

Implications for archaeology

Besides the processual questions, this chapter has important implications for identifying microzonal and long distance distribution of pottery. Firstly, clays do not occur within the distance of threshold B of every population and thus all societies probably do not have the same potential to make pottery.

Secondly, there may be considerable overlap in the exploitable territory of ceramic resources and what appear to be areas of exchange. One of the important problems of local and intra-regional exchange is that of distinguishing zones of resources for production from zones of distribution. This issue is not as significant in long distance trade or in the trade of many non-ceramic artefacts. Resources like obsidian, semi-precious stones or certain lithic artefacts generally have single, discrete sources which are easily identified chemically, geologically and archaeologically as workshop and quarry sites. Furthermore, in long distance ceramic distribution, the distance over which these items are traded is great enough that there is no question that the zone of production is removed from the zone of distribution.

Ceramics, however, have quite a different character. In contrast to lithics, for example, ceramics are compositionally complex–behaviorally as well as chemically and mineralogically. Ceramics contain clay and non-plastics which occur naturally in the clay and also may be added by the potter. Slips and paints may be used for decoration. Ceramics, then, bring together different materials of different compositions from a variety of different sources.

If ancient pottery making communities are closer together than twice the distance of threshold B in the model, they may use identical clay and temper resources, and ceramic distribution, if it occurs at all, can not be determined by paste analysis. Thus, potters in communities less than 12-18 km apart are likely to have resource areas (each with a 6-9 km radius) that overlap, and apparent 'local' distribution may involve using raw materials within a resource area of another community (which may include a different geological area). Conversely, if such pottery making sites are located a greater distance than theshold B for clay and temper, it is not likely that communities used overlapping exploitable resource territories, and mineralogical or trace element analysis of ceramic pastes may be productive for analyzing distribution patterns. Thus, the identification of ceramic distribution is best accomplished when the distance between production centers exceeds 18 km.

Since not all clays may be suitable for use with local technology (e.g. Arnold, 1971), potters could avoid 'local' clays and travel greater distances to obtain suitable clay, and communities could have a resource area with a 25-50 km radius. Thus, intra-regional trade in pottery between communities as much as 50 (for temper) to 100 (for clay) km apart may not be able to be identified from paste analysis alone because of overlapping resource areas. But, although this situation is possible, it is not very probable since the low frequency of these distances in the ethnographic literature suggests that they occur in what Browman calls a marginal range and generally are not exploited except in times of crisis. Nevertheless, since times of increased non-local ceramic distribution co-occur with increased ceramic specialization which in turn results from demographic pressure on agricultural resources (see Chapter 8 and Arnold 1975a; Arnold 1978a), resource distances in the marginal range may prove to be important in defining minimum distribution distances in the past. It is clear, however, that there may be exceptions to this generalization. Donnan (1971) found, for example, that potters in the Callejón de Huaylas in Peru may be itinerant, taking local clays with them into remote areas at greater distances than the threshold model would predict. Palmer and Shaw (1968:59) noted a similar practice in Fiji.

This model also can provide insight into specific archaeological problems of ceramic distribution when the distance to ceramics greatly exceeds the distances in the threshold model. One such problem is the existence of quantities of volcanic ash-tempered pottery in the northern Yucatan Peninsula (Mexico) during the Post-Classic Period (Smith, 1971:269; Shepard, 1952:265). This pottery does not appear to come from a local source since the nearest ash sources are the volcanoes 700 km to the south in highland Guatemala. Rather, Simmons and Brem (1979) argue that the ash was probably imported from this distance for use in pottery of local manufacture.

A distance of 700 km to a temper source is far greater than the present model would predict. While a significant ash fall 700 km from a volcano seems impossible, it can occur. During the eruption of Mount St Helens on May 18, 1980 in the State of Washington, volcanic ash fell 644 km away (Fruchter et al., 1980) at an estimated density of 159 kg. (350 pounds) per acre (*Time Magazine*, 1980:34). Problems caused by ash fall-out occurred at 800 km away (*Facts on File*, 1980) and ash falls were reported from more than 2000 km away (*Chicago Tribune*, 1980:5). Such a movement of wind-born ash is not unusual. Studies of cores and strata of ash falls at Lost Trail Pass Bog in Montana have revealed that windborn volcanic ash desposited there came from Mount Mazama, Oregon, 790 km away, and Glacier Peak, Washington, some 640 km away (Blinman, Mehringer and Sheppard, 1979). Thus, the alternative explanation to imported volcanic ash as a ceramic resource in the northern Yucatan is that potters were exploiting a local, but heretofore undiscovered deposit of volcanic ash for pottery temper.

In some respects, volcanic ash is superior to calcite for temper. The intervening 700 km between the northern Yucatan and highland Guatemala is largely limestone and if limestone is used for temper and is fired at too high a temperature, the calcite in the paste may decompose into calcium oxide and carbon dioxide and then hydrate in the presence of water (or water vapor) and cause spalling. This problem does not exist with ash temper, and if firing temperatures were too high, volcanic ash temper may have been the only alternative to avoid spalling. As was discussed earlier in this chapter, the addition of salt to pottery clay can greatly reduce this problem without the use of volcanic ash. Simmons and Brem (1979) argue that the Maya of the northern Yucatan Peninsula traded salt to the Guatemala highlands in exchange for volcanic ash for tempering pottery. But, why should the highland Maya trade for salt from the Yucatan when salt from the sea water of the Caribbean and Pacific are closer? Furthermore, salt sources are also available along the Chixoy River in extreme northern Alta Verapaz, Guatemala, at Salinas de los Nueve Cerros (Dillon, 1977).

Thirdly, since glazes, paints and slips have the greatest threshold distances in the model, there are two archaeological implications of these distances. Firstly, these materials are likely to be exchanged or traded inter-regionally. Secondly, identical slips, glazes and/or paints may be used by widely separated potting communities that use different pastes. It would not be surprising, for example, to discover that the white slip on the Anasazi White Wares in the U. S. Southwest has one or relatively few source locations and was widely traded throughout the Anasazi area and perhaps elsewhere in the Southwest as well. Although it may be difficult to remove slips and paints from pottery, physico-chemical analysis of them may prove more useful in defining trade connections in the Anasazi area than the analysis of pastes. The electron microprobe provides a good technique for the analysis of slips and paints since so little material (a chip 1 mm square) is necessary for analysis (Nelen and Rye, 1976). Since ceramics are so compositionally complex with the mixture of clay, temper, water and sometimes two or more clays from different locations (as in Manipur and among the potters of the Khasi and Jainita Hills in Assam, India (Gait, 1897:1) and among the Shipibo-Conibo (DeBoer and Lathrap, 1979:118-19)), the analysis of slips, paints and glazes may be as equally indicative of long distance inter-regional contact as the analysis of pastes. In contrast to the analysis of slips, glazes or paints, however, paste analysis (particularly by trace element analysis) may identify general source areas rather than specific source locations.

3
Weather and climate

Weather and climate are both a regulatory and a deviation amplifying mechanism imposed on ceramic production by a combination of the chemical and physical characteristics of the ceramic materials themselves and the yearly pattern of weather and climate. A combination of the unique molecular structure of clay minerals and water gives clay its plastic quality. Water usually occurs in two ways in clays: (1) it physically envelops the clay particles, filling the capillary spaces in between them; and (2) it is bound chemically in the crystal structure of the mineral (Grim, 1968:234; Shepard, 1956:72, 81; Linné, 1925:113; Rye, 1976:111). To transform the plastic clay into a sturdy product that will not revert again to a formless mass with the addition of water, both types of water must be removed from the clay product. First, the capillary water must be lost gradually in order to avoid undue shrinkage and cracking (e. g. Lackey, 1982:110). In pre-industrial societies, this process is achieved by air drying, but some of this water is also eliminated in the early stages of firing (Shepard, 1956:81; Linné, 1925:113; Rye, 1976:111; see Grim, 1968:234-5). The chemically bound water, on the other hand, cannot be lost in air drying and is removed only during firing. This latter process transforms the plastic clay irreversibly into a sturdy product (Shepard, 1956:20; Linné, 1925:113; Rye, 1976:111).

The drying of pottery is a crucial step in pottery production so that the water can evaporate from the clay object. A clay body has to be dried carefully until its shrinkage limit is reached, when it can be dried as rapidly as possible without cracking or warping (W. Arthur White, personal communication). Rate of drying is affected by the permeability, mineralogy, and size and shape of the clay body, but also by temperature, wind velocity and relative humidity in the environment (Shepard, 1956:74; Grim, 1962:75; W. Arthur White, personal communication). Permeability of the clay body is largely affected by the amount of non-plastics in the clay. Mineralogy of the clay also affects the rate of drying in that some clay minerals such as the smectite group, for example, absorb a great deal of water and take longer to dry than clay minerals (like halloysite) that do not absorb so much water (see Grim, 1968:235).

Size and shape of the body affect the drying process in that larger pieces require more time to dry than smaller pieces. For example, W. Arthur White (personal communication) reports that some pieces of china can dry in a couple of hours whereas large sewer pipes may require a week to dry under controlled temperature and relative humidity. The temperature, wind velocity and amount of non-plastics all bear an inverse relationship to the amount of drying time so that as the values of these factors increase, the amount of time necessary to dry pottery decreases correspondingly (see Grim, 1962:81). Conversely, clay with fewer non-plastics and an environment with lower temperatures and wind velocities increase drying time. The relative humidity, on the other hand, has a direct relationship to rate of drying such that increases in relative humidity will increase drying time and decreases in relative humidity will correspondingly decrease it.

The lack of careful attention to drying can produce disastrous results. If the drying process is too rapid, strains may develop which may cause cracking because of uneven drying or excessive shrinkage (Shepard, 1956:72; Linné, 1925:120; e. g. Diaz, 1966:143; Palmer, 1968:75). Drying pottery in the sun or in the wind without turning the vessels can also cause uneven drying with potentially similar results such as warping and cracking (e. g. Lackey, 1982:110). Inadequate drying, on the other hand, may affect firing success because the water trapped in the clay may cause cracking and breakage because of excessive shrinkage or the formation of steam (Shepard, 1956:81; Linné, 1925:113; e. g., Curtis, 1962:493).

Because the environmental variables of temperature, wind velocity and relative humidity affect the drying of pottery, weather and climate can have a profound effect on the success of pottery production, and thus constitute an important feedback mechanism for the craft. There are six major adverse effects of this feedback on pottery making.

First of all, raw material sources may be inaccessible during rainy weather and mining may be dangerous. Among the Shipibo-Conibo of the tropical forest of eastern Peru, in the Bida (Nupe) area in Nigeria and in the state of Orissa, India, clay sources are under water during part or all of the rainy season and thus are inaccessible (DeBoer and Lathrap, 1979:116; Nicholson, 1934:71; Behura, 1978:226). Similarly, in communities where pottery clay is extracted from large underground mines such as those in Ticul (at Hacienda Yo' Kat; Figure 3.1), Yucatan (Arnold and Bohor, 1977) and Chinautla, Guatemala, rainfall causes cave-ins, making clay inaccessible and clay mining dangerous, and potters thus do not mine clay during the rainy season (Reina, 1966:11, 60, 63-4; Reina and Hill, 1978:32; Arnold, 1978b:364-6). In Ticul, Yucatan, where temper is also extracted from underground mines, one potter was reportedly killed when a mine in which he was working collapsed during a rainstorm (Arnold and Bohor, 1977). Reina (1966:63) also noted one casualty in mining clay from the underground

Figure 3.1 View of part of the large subterranean clay mine at Hacienda Yo' Kat, Yucatan, Mexico. Because of the physical and chemical characteristics of clays, digging clay in underground mines like this one is dangerous in the rainy season and mining thus occurs only in the dry season (reprinted from Arnold and Bohor, 1977).

clay mine in Chinaulta, Guatemala, during the years in which he studied the community.

Second, rainy weather can prevent raw ceramic materials from drying properly prior to use, can inhibit sifting, and can thus affect paste quality. In Temascalcingo (Mexico), potters must dry clay in the sun prior to pulverizing it and sifting it into a fine-grained fraction for preparing the paste. Rains and moist weather may prevent the clay from drying adequately, and thus prevent proper pulverization (Whitaker and Whitaker, 1978:27) and screening (Papousek, 1974:1020-3). Some pottery making communities like Ticul (Yucatan), Chinautla (Guatemala) and Quinua (Peru) also sift their temper to remove larger pieces and assure a smooth fine textured paste (Arnold, 1971; 1972a; Arnold, 1978b). When the temper also contains some clay minerals as it does in these communities (Arnold, 1972b; Arnold, 1975b), moisture and high humidity can inhibit sifting. Without sifting of temper and clay, small rocks may be incorporated into the paste. These rocks weaken the vessel walls and cause uneven rates of expansion and contraction which produce stresses in the vessel walls and result in cracking and breakage during drying and firing.

Third, moisture also weakens vessel walls after partial drying, causing malformation, cracking and breakage. After vessels have dried partially, they are particularly susceptible to damage from moisture (e.g.,

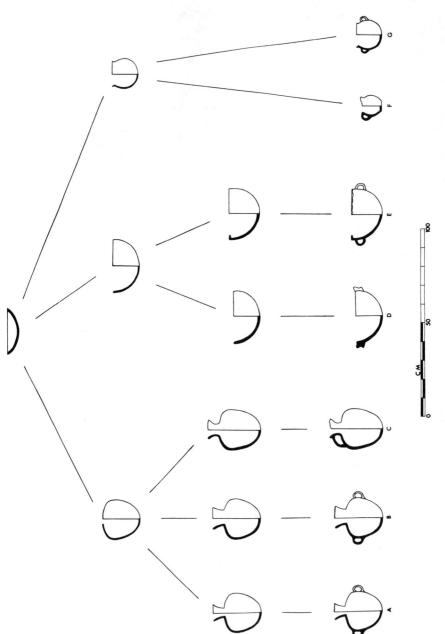

Figure 3.2 Stages of fabrication of several utilitarian shapes in Chinautla, Sacojito and Durazno, Guatemala. Stage 1 needs at least a day to complete and one day of drying time is necessary between stages 1, 2 and 3. Stages 3 and 4 are accomplished on the same day (reprinted from Arnold, 1978: Figure 10, p. 350).

Conklin, 1953:7). Partial hydration of any part of a vessel causes the moistened clay to expand, creating stresses with the adjoining clay and resulting in cracking. Furthermore, moisture may cause deformation of partially dried vessels when they are stacked. In Quinua (Peru), Ticul (Mexico) and Sacojito (Guatemala) dried vessels are often stacked prior to firing because of the lack of space in the potter's house (Arnold, 1972a; Arnold, 1978b). While the green strength of the dried clay is sufficient to withstand stacking without damage, contact with moisture causes the clay to lose its strength to withstand pressures of the stacked vessels, and the pottery becomes deformed.

Fourth, cold or damp weather often increases the time necessary to complete a pottery vessel. Ceramic vessels are often made in several stages which require sun drying between each stage in order to increase the strength of the formed portion to support a new section of fresh clay. Cold or damp weather can increase the drying time necessary between stages and delay the completion of the vessel. In Chinautla, Sacojito and Durazno, Guatemala, for example, narrow-necked water carrying jars require drying periods of one half to one day between each of the three stages (Figure 3.2; Arnold, 1978b:350) and rainy weather may retard the completion of the vessels by as much as three to six days. A similar drying period between stages is needed for shapes like the narrow-necked water carrying jar and the water storage jar in Ticul, Yucatan (Thompson, 1958:121). In Chitapampa near Cuzco, Peru, large earthenware jars are formed in three stages which require three successive days so that the clay is dry enough to support additional weight (Litto, 1976:21). Similarly, on Buka Island in Melanesia, vessels must be set aside to dry for hours to days between stages of construction. Large vessels may require three weeks to complete while medium sized vessels require as much as two weeks to complete (Specht, 1972:128). In Wagholi, India, production of one particular vessel shape requires five days to complete because of the drying periods necessary between stages (Gupta, 1966:70). Motu pottery (Melanesia) also requires partial drying between stages of manufacture (Groves, 1960:12). Yabob pottery (Melanesia) requires one week's drying time between forming the rim and forming the rest of the body and then one day of drying time between each of seven successive stages used in fabricating the body of the vessel (Smith, 1967:12).

Wheel thrown vessels may also require drying between stages. In Dera Ismail Khan in Pakistan, potters use a combination of the wheel and paddle and anvil techniques which requires at least a day of drying between each of the three major steps (Rye and Evans, 1976:53). Wheel thrown jars made by itinerant potters in Thrapsano, Crete, are made in six stages which require drying between each successive section (Voyatzoglou, 1974:20). In the northwest provinces of India, a large vessel requires a total of seven days for completion because of the drying periods that are necessary between stages of wheel forming, finishing by paddle and anvil and each of two types of slipping (Dobbs, 1897:4). Thus, cold or damp weather can prolong the drying period between stages of fabrication and increases the susceptibility of the pottery to malformation and breakage before the vessel is completed.

Fifth, cold damp weather also increases the drying time necessary between fabrication and firing and also increases the susceptibility to breakage. Drying time between these stages varies, but in some areas clay vessels may take as long as several weeks to dry properly (Table 3.1). In inclement weather, the drying time is often lengthened to such a degree that pottery making is impractical and unproductive. Rye and Evans (1976) noted that in the communities of Bannu, Musazi, Kharmathu, Zakhel Bala and Hala (Pakistan), vessels could not be dried sufficiently in the rainy season to make pottery during that time (Rye and Evans, 1976:31, 36, 38-9, 44, 78, 107). Furthermore, the snow and cold temperatures in winter in the Bomboret Valley, the Chitral Valley, Dir and Swat in northwest Pakistan also slowed drying time, preventing pottery production during that season. Increased drying time also increases the risk of breakage since pottery has to be moved in and out of the sunshine more than usual.

Table 3.1 *Length of drying time in various locations*

Community/ Group	Location	Length of total drying time (days)	Place	Source
Somali	East Africa	2–3	- -	Lewis, 1955:82
Siwah	East Africa	7	shade	Lewis, 1955:36
Toledo Disrict/Maya	British Honduras	4–5	shade of the hut	Thompson, 1930: 95
Chowra Island	Indian Ocean	9–12	- -	Man, 1894:24–5
Gisu	East Africa	8	- -	Fontaine, 1959: 22
Aragua	Venezuela	8–15	- -	Litto, 1976:201
Papua New Guinea	Melanesia	many months	inside	Tuckson & May, 1975:169
Fiji	Polynesia	several	partial shade	Roth, 1935:225, 232
Navaho	Southwest (U.S.)	1–2	- -	Hill, 1937:16

Table 3.1 (*Contd.*)

Community/ Group	Location	Length of total drying time (days)	Place	Source
Chitapampa	Peru	large jars require 2 days	sun	Litto, 1976:21
Papago	Arizona	2–3	shade	Fontana et al., 1962:68
Claros	Columbia	7	- -	Litto, 1976:160
San Sebastián, Teotihuacan	Mexico	2	inside	Charlton, 1976a: 141
Mito Alto	Peru	7–8	- -	O'Neale, 1977: 56
Musazi, Northwest Frontier Province	Pakistan	2–3	outside	Rye and Evans, 1976:34
Prang, Northwest Frontier Province	Pakistan	6	- -	Rye and Evans, 1976:38
Dera Ismail Khan, Northwest Frontier Province	Pakistan	3	- -	Rye and Evans, 1976:51
Barrio of Kinagabyan, Isabela (Ibanag)	Philippines	1.5–2.5	shade 1–2; sun 0.5	Solheim, 1954:305
Ifugao female potters	Philippines	3	racks above fireplace: 2; not specified:1	Solheim and Shuler, 1959:7
male potters		2–3	- -	Solheim and Shuler, 1959:6
Kalinga	Philippines	2–3	sun	Solheim and Shuler, 1959:9
Batanes Islands	Philippines	2	sun	Solheim, 1952a: 53

Table 3.1 (*Contd.*)

Community/ Group	Location	Length of total drying time (days)	Place	Source
Chinautla	Guatemala	1 or more; many more for large pots	indoors; 1 in sun	Reina and Hill, 1978:39
Quetta, Baluchistan	Pakistan	11–16	Before slipping: 2–7; inside:7; sun:2	Rye and Evans, 1976:7
Chalky Mount	Barbados	4–11	inside except for 1 hour in sun	Handler, 1963a:321
San Luis Jilotepeque	Guatemala	4–8	- -	Reina and Hill, 1978:1
Chinautla, Durazno and Sacojito	Guatemala	3	in sun	Arnold, 1978b: 351
Mixco	Guatemala	1	sun	Arnold, 1978b:342
Chalkis	Greece	1.5	sun	Matson, 1973:135
Moro/Yoruba	Nigeria	20	- -	Wahlman, 1972:324
Ilorin	Nigeria	3	- -	Wahlman, 1972:338
Buka Island	Melanesia	several	inside	Specht, 1972:129
Huehuetenango	Guatemala	8	sun	McBryde, 1947:56
Buhid	Philippines	4–6 (longer time for a larger pot)	warm, dry shaded spot (may be hung above the hearth)	Conklin, 1953:7
Ingalik Eskimo	Alaska	2	near the fire	Osgood, 1940:146
Mukalla	Southern Arabia	10	outside	Tufnell, 1961:30

Table 3.1 (*Contd.*)

Community/ Group	Location	Length of total drying time (days)	Place	Source
Catawba	North America	one to several; large vessels may require a week	shack outside, or airy place inside	Fewkes, 1944:88–9
Utekou/Edo	Nigeria	6	- -	Thomas, 1910:97
Sabongida/Edo	Nigeria	3	- -	Thomas, 1910:98
Sarayacu Quichua (cooking pot)	Ecuador	14	- -	Kelley and Orr, 1976:10
Talamanca (Boruca)	Costa Rica	15–1 month	house	Stone, 1949:19a
Tiv	Nigeria	several	- -	Bohannan & Bohannan, 1958:304
Beit Shebab	Lebanon	several weeks	indoors or undercover	Hankey, 1968:29
Bailén	Spain	24 hours	sun	Curtis, 1962:493
Ibibio	Nigeria	1 week	- -	Nicklin, 1973a:55
Nasioi	Bougainville	about 1 week	sun	Ogan, 1970:88
Wagholi	India	8–15 days depending on the vessel	shade	Gupta, 1966:70–1
Ghorepuripet, Poona City	India	4	shade	Gupta, 1966:73
Gwembe Valley	Africa	a few hours if hot and dry, but usually 1–2 nights	inside	Reynolds, 1968:146
Ajamoentenu, Eastern Highlands	New Guinea	1–2 weeks	in sun	Watson, 1955:123
Dangtalan/ Kalinga	Philippines	2.5–4	sun	Longacre, 1981:57

Table 3.1 (*Contd.*)

Community/ Group	Location	Length of total drying time (days)	Place	Source
Madang	New Guinea	6 weeks	shade and in house	Kakubayashi,1978: 138
Miadeba	Normanby Island, Papua, New Guinea	2–3 weeks	in house	Lauer, 1973:72
Yabob	New Guinea	several weeks	under the house	Smith, 1967:12
Central Moluccas	Indonesia	0.5 hour	sun	Ellen and Glover, 1974:357
Panaeati Island	New Guinea	a few days to a week	depends on weather	Tindale and Bartlett, 1937: 161
Wusi	New Hebrides, Melanesia	2–3 weeks	house	Shutler, 1968:17
Palau Islands	Micronesia	2 weeks	- -	Hobson, 1970:16
Nasama	Fiji	up to 7 (constricted neck jars)	often inside	Palmer and Shaw, 1968:67
		1 (bowls)	- -	Palmer and Shaw, 1968:57
Amphlett Islands	Melanesia	3–5	- -	Lauer, 1974: 146, 151

These problems associated with the time necessary for drying are characteristic of all pottery, but more acute with larger pottery. Large vessels with thick walls may take a long time to dry (Linné, 1925:121) and are more difficult to move without breakage than smaller ones. The longer they dry, the more frequently they must be moved and the greater the chance of cracking, breakage and becoming deformed because of contact with moisture. In Kharmathu, Pakistan, for example, potters make only small vessels in the winter months because of the difficulty of drying larger vessels (Rye and Evans, 1976:38-9).

Sixth, firing success may be be reduced significantly during rainy weather in three ways: (1) rainfall prevents fuel from drying prior to firing and thus increases the probability of firing failure; (2) rainfall reduces firing temperature during firing by dampening fuel, flame, pottery and kilns and; (3) during firing, rainfall or other moisture may cause breakage, blackening and uneven heating resulting in a defective and low quality product. In their survey of pottery techniques in Pakistan, for example, Rye and Evans (1976: 38-9, 44, 78, 106, 108) noted that wet weather adversely affects firing in Kharmathu, Bannu, Zakhel Bala and Hala. In Zakhel Bala, rain or a high degree of cloudiness during firing of unglazed pottery may cause up to a fifty per cent loss (Rye and Evans, 1976:36; 166). Similarly, in Quinua (Peru), Ticul (Yucatan, Mexico) and the Chinautla area of Guatemala, rainfall during the firing process may cause damage to the vessels and thus increases risk of loss. Potters here delay firing when rain threatens (Reina, 1966:192), but if it should rain during the firing process, potters exercise great care in increasing fuel consumption to compensate for the detrimental effects of rain (Arnold, 1972a; Arnold, 1978b). Thus, in rainy weather, firing costs increase because more fuel must be added to the firing and the pottery has to be fired for a longer period of time.

In order to further reduce risks produced by rainfall in these communities, care is always taken to protect the kiln and firing area from rainfall or moisture. In Ticul (Yucatan) and Quinua (Peru) the open parts of the kiln are covered when not in use. In the Chinautla area (including Sacojito and Durazno) of Guatemala, where pottery is fired without using a kiln, potsherds and ashes are spread on the ground in the firing area during the rainy season to prevent ground moisture from adversely affecting the pots during firing (Arnold, 1978b:353). Similar practices of spreading ashes on the firing area to mitigate dampness occur in Fiji (Roth, 1935:225) and among the Ibo of Nigeria (Murray, 1972:168).

Because of these problems, weather and climate can have a profound effect on pottery production. Pottery making is ideally a dry weather craft; cold and damp weather and climate provide a significant limiting factor for pottery production (Table 3.2). The most favorable weather and climatic conditions for pottery production thus occur during a time of sustained sunshine, warm temperatures, little or no rainfall and low relative humidity.

Table 3.2 *The regulatory effect of weather and climate on ceramic production*

Community/ Group	Location	Production time	Reason[1]	Source
Fulani	Cameroun	dry season	between harvest planting, availibility of dry fuel; drying of dung necessary for temper	David & Hennig, 1972:4, 5

Table 3.2 (*Contd.*)

Community/ Group	Location	Production time	Reason[1]	Source
Papago	Arizona	hot season	comfort and drying of pottery	Fontana et al., 1962:20
Vounaria	Greece	warm, dry season	dry weather; agricultural demands	Matson, 1972:220
Chalkis	Greece	more in hot, dry season	longer drying time in rainy season	Matson, 1973:135
Moro/Yoruba	Nigeria	when it is sunny (during the dry season)	less time needed to dry pottery and dig clay	Wahlman, 1972:3 317, 326; personal communication
Cocucho, Michoacán	Mexico	dry season	- -	Margret Hardin, personal communi
Yuma	U.S. Southwest	dry season	ground and fuel are driest, pottery will dry without delay	Rogers, 1936:4–5
Mixco	Guatemala	dry season	- -	Arrot, 1967
Chinautla, Durazno Sacojito	Guatemala	much more in the dry season (Dec. –April)	rains, dampness and wind may ruin pottery during firing	Arnold, 1978b; vis to community; Re 1966:60; Reina an Hill, 1978:32
Chowra Island	Indian Ocean	only small pottery made during rainy season	difficulty of drying unbaked pottery during the rains	Man, 1894:24
Kathmandu Valley/Newari	Nepal	dry season	potter's year ends with the monsoon (July–Sept) and no firing during the heavy rains	Birmingham, 197: 381
Barrio of Kinagabyan, Santa Maria, Isabela (Ibanag)	Philippines	when it is dry	- -	Solheim, 1954:30(
Amotag, Masbate Island	Philippines	when sunny and dry	- -	Solheim, 1952a:5

Table 3.2 (*Contd.*)

Community/ Group	Location	Production time	Reason[1]	Source
Mito Alto	near Huancayo, Peru	when and where it is sunny	(1) clay molded on a cloudy day does not hold its shape (2) eliminates waiting period for clay to dry out slightly	O'Neale, 1954:306
Catawba	North America	warm season (early spring to late fall)	- -	Fewkes, 1944:72
San Juan Metepec, State of Mexico	Mexico	dry season	- -	Whitaker and Whitaker, 1978:88
Guazacapán	Guatemala	not in the rainy season	- -	Reina and Hill, 1978:185
Yokuts/ western Mono	California	spring	ground was soft enough to dig clay (too dry in summer to dig clay) and sufficient sunlight and warmth to dry the pottery	Gayton, 1929:240
Ra Province/ Viti Levu Island	Fiji	- -	firing only when fine weather prevails with little or no wind	Roth, 1935:225
Temascalcingo	Mexico	dry season	adverse effects of rain	Papousek, 1974 1031
al–Hiba (sun dried pottery)	Southern Iraq	dry season	too cold to work comfortably in the rainy season and sun not strong enough to dry ware efficiently	Ochsenschlager, 1974a:164
Bomboret Valley, Kafiristan, Northwest Frontier Province	Pakistan	summer (May–July)	valley completely snowed-in in winter; people remain indoors	Rye and Evans, 1976:7
Chitral Valley Northwest Frontier Province	Pakistan	summer	heavy snows make firing impossible	Rye and Evans, 1976:13

Table 3.2 (*Contd.*)

Community/ Group	Location	Production time	Reason[1]	Source
Dir, Northwest Frontier Province	Pakistan	summer	during winter, snow makes access to clay deposits difficult and firing impossible	Rye and Evans 1976:17
Swat, Northwest Frontier Province	Pakistan	summer, especially at higher altitude	snow as in Dir above	Rye and Evans 1976:31
Musazi, Northwest Frontier Province	Pakistan	year around but production decreases Feb–April	difficulty of drying pottery on rainy days	Rye and Evans 1976:31
Kharmathu, Northwest Frontier Province	Pakistan	All year but 60% less time involved in winter	difficulty of drying large vessels and risk of rain during firing	Rye and Evans 1976:38–9
Bannu, Northwest Frontier Province (village of Shahbaz Ahmed Khel)	Pakistan	All year with slight seasonal variations	work is interrupted when there is rain because vessels can not be dried and the kiln cannot be fired	Rye and Evans 1976:44
Zakhel Bala, Northwest Frontier Province	Pakistan	unglazed ware not made in winter	pottery easily damaged or cracked in firing during rainy season	Rye and Evans 1976:36,78
		glazed ware produced year around but potters work less in winter especially during periods of inclement weather	during inclement weather, drying vessels is difficult and costs increase	Rye and Evans 1976:78
Dera Ismail Khan, Northwest Frontier Province	Pakistan	results best in summer	lowers firing losses	Rye and Evans 1976:54

Table 3.2 (*Contd.*)

Community/ Group	Location	Production time	Reason[1]	Source
Hala, Sind	Pakistan	full-time although production slows in rainy season during July –August	difficulties of dry-ing ware and firing in wet weather	Rye and Evans, 1976:107
Buka Island	Melanesia	production ceases in the wet season (Dec.–April)	difficulty of dry-ing and firing ves-sels	Specht, 1972:135
Chalkis	Greece	all year	longer drying time (usually inside) in winter and during rainy months; unfired vessels must be remov-ed from outside dur-ing rainy weather	Matson, 1973:125, 235
Vounaria	Greece	warm, dry season (April –Oct.)	pottery difficult to dry if rained upon before firing, and rain adversely affects firing during first stages and agricul-tural responsibilities	Matson, 1972:219–20
Ingalik Eskimo	Alaska	warm season (July– August)	clay will not bake in winter (cold season)	Osgood, 1940:147–8
Bailén	Spain	little made in rainy season (Sept.–Mar.)	fuel (prunings from olive trees) will dry without rotting	Curtis, 1962:488, 496
Andros	Greece	May–early July	too cold in winter	Birmingham,1967:36
Akama	East Africa	dry season	best time for pots to dry	Lindblom,1969:536–7
Ghorepuripet, Poona City	India	dry season mainly; generally only small vessels made in rainy season	demand for pitchers and water storing vessels is greatest in dry season	Gupta, 1966:73

Table 3.2 (*Contd.*)

Community/ Group	Location	Production time	Reason[1]	Source
Wagholi	India	dry season (mid-Feb.- mid-June)	weather assists seasoning the vessels	Gupta, 1966:767
Tonalá	Mexico	dry season	- -	Diaz, 1966:18
Wusi	New Hebrides, Melanesia	June –August	cool, dry months	Shutler, 1968:18
Ajamoentenu	Eastern Highlands, New Guinea	dry season	- -	Watson, 1955:123
Jipalom/Diola	Senegal	at end of dry season	- -	Linares de Sapir, 1969:2
Luo	East Africa	year round, but dry season preferred	potter can obtain dry materials and can protect vessels from rain	Ocholla-Ayayo, 1980:116
Orissa	India	not during the monsoon season (mid-July to mid-October)	intermittent rains and decrease in sun's heat prevents pots from drying	Behura, 1978:205
Tarahumara	Mexico	mid-April to late June early October to mid-November	little or no rain	Pastron, 1974:104

Notes

[1] When no reason is given and pottery is made during the warm and or dry season, clin[...] is assumed to be at least partly responsible.

Viewed from the perspective of cybernetics, weather and climate can provide either deviation counteracting feedback or deviation amplifying feedback for pottery production depending on the character of the climate. Since pottery making is best accomplished during a period of sunshine and dry weather to avoid damage to the pottery, these conditions provide deviation amplifying feedback permitting ceramic production to develop originally and eventually emerge into a full-time craft. For example, in areas of the world where warm-dry conditions (with little or no rainfall and a great deal of sunshine) predominate for the entire year with no significant change, weather and climate would provide deviation amplifying feedback; there would be no climatic restraints on ceramic production, and once pottery making began, it could evolve into a craft practiced on a year-round basis.

Since pottery making is adversely affected by cool temperatures, rain and high relative humidity, weather and climate can also be a regulatory mechanism preventing ceramic production and counteracting deviation from non-pottery making activities. Kilns and drying facilities (see Chapter 8) can mitigate the regulatory effects of weather and climate, but even in areas with these facilities, weather and climate still have a regulatory effect.

The process of regulatory feedback can limit ceramic production in the climates of the world primarily in two ways: (1) the feedback can be partial, permitting ceramic production for part of the year while limiting production for the remainder of the year, or (2) the feedback can be total, preventing the development of any ceramic production. Secondarily, weather and climate can also provide some regulatory feedback in hot dry climates causing pottery to dry too quickly and unevenly and producing cracking and breakage (Matson, 1965:211; Lackey, 1982:110; Kelley and Palerm, 1952:214). This situation does not provide the degree of negative feedback of damp climates and can easily be avoided by drying pottery in the shade (Pastron, 1974:106; Van de Velde and Van de Velde, 1939:32), indoors (Shepard, 1956:74; Matson, 1965:211; e. g. Diaz, 1966:144; Lackey, 1982:110), in a cave (*American Ceramic Society Bulletin*, 1961:543); by turning the pottery once or twice daily (Lackey, 1982:110); or by covering it with a moist cloth (Lauer, 1974:146) or damp clothes (Diaz, 1966:144), leaves (Lauer, 1974:146; Ocholla-Ayayo, 1980:16) or animal skins (Ocholla-Ayayo, 1980:16). Similarly, hot dry weather and climate can also be a regulatory mechanism for ceramic production because of a shortage of water in the dry season, as it does in Ocomicho, Michoacán, Mexico (Margaret Hardin, personal communication).

Weather and climate as a regulatory mechanism

The process of negative feedback affects the seasonality of ceramic production in different ways depending on the climate. First of all, dry climates interrupted by a substantial rainy season with heavy rains, fog, cloud cover, high relative humidity and cool temperatures result in partial negative feedback regulating pottery making to a seasonal pattern and limiting it to the relatively dry part of the year. Many areas in the tropical latitudes of the world fit into this category.

A. *Partial regulatory feedback: the Central Andes*

The Central Andes provide an illustration of the partial regulatory effect of weather and climate on ceramic production. The climatic pattern of the Central Andes consists of a marked wet season and dry season. The wet season extends from November until April with the greatest amount of rainfall occurring between December and March (Table 3.3). Generally, the heavy rains of this period are accompanied by high humidity,

Table 3.3 *The wet season in highland Peru*
Months that received 12.5% or more of the yearly precipitation according to number of reporting stations (compiled from Instituto Nacional de Planificacion, 1969:131-5). Total mean amount of rainfall = 724.26 mm (Median = 759 mm)

Month	November	December	January	February	March	April
Number of reporting stations[1]						
10			X	X	X	
19		X	X	X	X	
1	X		X	X	X	
2			X	X	X	X
Totals: 32	1[2]	19	32	32	32	2[2]
Absolute wettest month; no. of stations	-	2	6	19	5	-

Notes
[1] Data were summarized from the following weather stations in highland Peru: (1) in the Department of Ancash: Paron (Huaron), Ticapampa; (2) in the Department of Arequipa: Andahua, Cabanconde, Imata, Orcopampa, Pane, Sibayo, Yanque; (3) in the Department of Cajamarca: Cajamarca, Huacraruco, Sunchubamba; (4) in the Department of Cerro de Pasco: Cerro de Pasco, Laguna Huaron; (5) in the Department of Cuzco: Cuzco; (6) in the Department of Huancavelica: Accnacocha; (7) in the Department of Junín: Huancayo, Jauja, Pachachuca; (8) in the Department of Lima: Yauricocha; (9) in the Department of Puno: Azángaro, Capachica, Cojata, Crucero, Desaguadero, Isla Solo, Juli, Mazo Cruz, Puno, Putina; (10) in the Department of Tacna: Paucarany, Tacalaya.

[2] Some stations in northern Peru had a longer wet season.

persistent heavy cloud cover and hence little sunshine. The dry season occurs between May and October with June, July and August generally being the driest months (Table 3.4). This season is characterized by little or no rainfall, lower relative humidity than the wet season, and little, if any, cloud cover. Sunshine is persistent during this period; the hours of sunshine are greater during the dry season than the wet season even though the number of daylight hours is the shortest for the entire year. The dry season also constitutes the coldest months of the year (Instituto

Table 3.4 *The dry season in highland Peru*
Months that received 1.9% or less of the total yearly precipatation according to number of reporting stations (compiled from Instituto Nacional de Planificación, 1969:131-5).

Month	May	June	July	August	September	October
Number of reporting stations[1]						
20		X	X	X		
2	X	X	X	X		X
2	X	X	X	X	X	X
1	X	X	X	X	X	
1		X	X	X	X	
1			X	X		
2		X	X			
2	X	X	X	X		
1			X			
totals: 32	7[2]	30	32	29	4[3]	2[3]
Absolute driest month (no. of stations)	–	1	30	1	–	–

Notes

[1] Same as Table 3.3

[2] Some reporting stations around Lake Titicaca in southern Peru had a longer dry season.

[3] Some reporting stations nearer to coast (in the Departments of Arequipa and Tacna) had a longer dry season.

Nacional de Planificacíon, 1969:131, 135; Olivera, 1971; Rivera, 1967) with night frosts possible during June and July.

These seasonal climatic patterns are greatly affected by altitude and to a lesser extent by distance from the tropical forest to the east of the Andes. Generally, the intensity of the rainfall and cloud cover decreases as one moves down slope and westward away from the tropical forest. Temperature, of course, varies inversely with altitude. Furthermore, evapotranspiration increases as one moves down slope so that lower zones are warmer, drier and sunnier than the higher ones (Holdridge, 1947; Tosi, 1960).

The rainy season of the Central Andes provides regulatory feedback for ceramic production. Since pottery making requires dry weather and climate, the wet months of December to March limit production to a part-time activity during the dry season (Table 3.5).

Table 3.5 *Time of the year when pottery is made in some Central Andean communities in Peru*

Department (Province)	Community	Source	Pottery made during[1]
Huancavelica (Huancavelica)	Huaylacucho (Totorapampa)	Ravines, 1963-4:92	July–Aug.
Huancavelica (Huancavelica)	Acoria (Ccaccasiri)	Ravines, 1966:210	May-Oct.
Puno (Lampa)	Pucará	potter in Calca Market; Jorge Flores, personal communication; potters in Cuzco RR station	not in rainy season mostly in dry season when pottery will dr▪
Cuzco (Canchis)	Raqchi	visit to community; Dec. 1972; Orlove, 1974:199	dry season
Junín (Concepción)	Aco	La Vallee, 1967:104; David Browman, personal communication	June–Oct.
Ayacucho (Huamanga)	Ayacucho (Barrio of Santa Ana)	visit to barrio, Feb. 1967	after rainy season passes
Ayacucho (Huanta)	Luricocha (Pampay)	visit to area May, 1967	dry season, after harvest
Ayacucho (Huamanga)	Ticllas	informant in Ayacucho (marketing pattern)	dry season, after harvest

Table 3.5 (*Contd.*)

Department (Province)	Community	Source	Pottery made during[1]
Ayacucho (Huamanga)	Quinua	Arnold, 1972a, 1975a	mostly in dry season
Ayacucho (Huanta)	Huayhuas	marketing pattern, Feb.–June 1967	dry season
Ancash (Huarás)	Taricá	Donnan, 1971	harvest season, beginning Mar.–May
Cochabamba, Boliva (Quillacollo)	Calcapirhua	Litto, 1976:57, 61	dry season May–Oct.
Cuzco (Cuzco)	Chitapampa	Litto, 1976:21	August
Chuquisaca, Bolivia (Yamparaez)	Villamalecita	Grace Sherman, personal communication	dry season
	Tarabuco	Grace Sherman, personal communication	dry season

Notes

[1] Litto's (1976:218) data (except for Chitapampa near Cuzco) contradict these data, and can be attributed only to her brief visit in the communities, her reliance on secondary sources rather than direct observation and perhaps her lack of fluency in Spanish.

The degree to which the wet climatic pattern affects ceramic production, however, is dependent on altitude. Colder, higher, cloudier and wetter ecological zones limit ceramic production more than warmer, lower, sunnier and drier zones. In fact, these lower tropical and subtropical dry zones may affect pottery production negligibly. Thus, the degree to which regulatory feedback affects ceramic production depends upon the ecological zone in which potters live. Since the montane prairie, the lower montane savannah, and the montane steppe are the most important ecological zones for agriculture in the Andes and contain most of the highland population (Tosi, 1960:101,109), one would expect most of the potters to live in these zones. Furthermore, climatic data from one station (Cuzco) in the montane prairie or moist forest (Olivera, 1971) and one (Ayacucho) in the lower montane savannah or dry forest (Rivera, 1967) indicate that pottery production in these zones would experience total regulatory feedback during the wet season. Conversely, the dry season would provide deviation amplifying feedback permitting ceramic production.

Central Andean ethnographic data reveal that potters tend to live in the highly populated zones in which the rainy weather and climate needed for agriculture prevent ceramic production during the rainy season. There are twenty-seven communities of potters for which the location was sufficiently precise to pinpoint the ecological zone in which they lived using Tosi's (1960) map (Table 3.6). Of these twenty-seven communities, 59 per cent (16) occurred in the montane prairie or moist forest, 26 per cent (7) in the lower montane savannah or dry forest, 11 per cent (3) in the sub-alpine and alpine zones of higher elevation and 4 per cent (1) in a lower and drier zone—the lower montane thorn steppe. Thus, Central Andean weather and climate provide significant regulatory feedback during the rainy season in the ecological zones that contemporary pottery making communities occupy.

Table 3.6 *The ecological zones of some Andean pottery making communities*

Community (District)	Department	Province	Source	Zone[1]
Pucará	Puno	Lampa	Spahni, 1966:53–67	Mp
Checca (Pucará)	”	”	Spahni, 1966:36–50	”
Santiago de Pupuja	”	Azángaro	Spahni, 1966:53	”
Quota Ayllu (Chucuito)	”	Puno	Tschopik, 1950:205	”
Palala Ayllu (Chucuito)	”	”	”	”
Q'arukaya (Chucuito)	”	”	”	Mp or SAwp
Qolokachi (Chucuito)	”	”	”	Mp
Tinta	Cuzco	Canchis	notes	”
Raqchi	”	”	notes on visit	”
Machacmarca	”	”	”	”
Qea	”	”	notes	”
Colquemarca	”	Chumbivilcas	notes	”
Huayllay estancias	Pasco	Pasco	Tschopik, 1947:52–3	SAwp or Art
Huaychao estancias	”	”	Tschopik, 1947:54	SAwp or Art
Aco	Junín	Concepción	LaVallee, 1967:103–4	LMs
Mito	”	”	Tschopik, 1947:36	LMs

Table 3.6 (*Contd.*)

Community (District)	Department	Province	Source	Zone[1]
Orcotuna	,,	,,	,,	,,
Muqui	,,	Jauja	Tschopik, 1947:48	Mp
Totorapampa (Huaylacucho)	Huancavelica	Huancavelica	Ravines, 1963–64:92	Mp
Ccaccasiri (Acoria)	,,	,,	Ravines, 1966:210	Mp
Huayhuas	Ayacucho	Huanta	notes	LMs
Pampay (Luricocha)	,,	,,	notes on visit	LMs
Ayacucho, Barrio of Santa Ana	,,	Huamanga	,,	LMs
Ticllas (San Jose de Ticllas)	,,	,,	notes	,,
Quinua	,,	,,	Arnold, 1972a, 1975a	,,
Hualcan (Carhuás)	Ancash	Carhuás	Stein, 1961:91–2	Mp
Taricá	,,	Huarás	Donnan, 1971	Mp

Notes

[1] Key for zones: Mp–Montane prairie or moist forest; LMs–Lower Montane savannah or dry forest; SAwp–Sub-Alpine wet paramo; Art–Alpine rain tundra; LMts–Lower Montane thorn steppe.

B. Total regulatory feedback: the Northwest Coast

A second way in which weather and climate affect ceramic production is by total regulatory feedback. In areas where a wet, cold and foggy climate persists for the entire year, the negative feedback is totally effective in preventing the development of pottery making, even if the craft is introduced by innovation or diffusion.

In the Northwest Coast culture area of North America, a combination of climatic factors exists which provides total negative feedback for the development of pottery making. With rainfall averaging 100-300 cm a

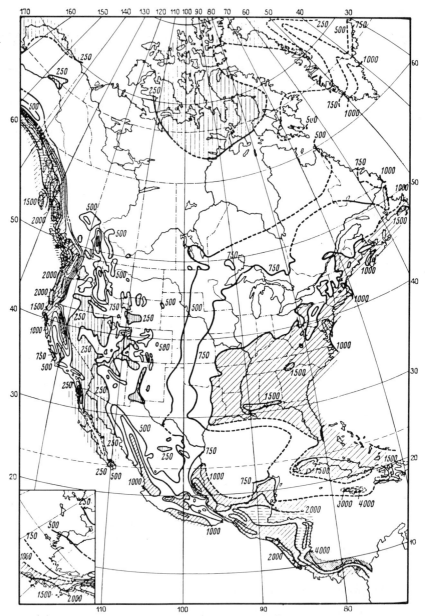

Figure 3.3 Mean annual rainfall (in mm) for North America (from
Ward et al., 1972: Figure 32; reprinted with the permission of Kraus
Reprint, a division of Kraus-Thomson Organization Limited).

year (Ward et al., 1972:Figure 32; Ginsberg, 1970:31; Blair, 1942:Figure
27), and most places receiving 150-200 cm of rainfall per year (Ward et
al., 1972:Figure 32), it is the wettest area of North America north of the
tropics (Figure 3.3). Although the extreme southern portion of the

Northwest Coast area has 90-120 days annually of precipitation over .025 cm (.01 inch), most of the region has 150-200 such rainy days (Koeppe, 1931:61; Environmental Data Service, 1968:56). The Northwest Coast has a mean annual cloudiness of 60 per cent or more of the sky covered (Koeppe, 1931:Figure 38; Ward et al., 1972:168). Finally, with an average of 40 days per year with dense fog, the Northwest Coast and the eastern tip of the coast of Maine share the highest total of foggy days in North America (Ward et al., 1972:169).

Even though most of the rainfall and cloudiness (60-80 per cent of the daytime sky covered in January) occurs during the winter months (Koeppe, 1931:Figure 34; Ward et al., 1972:Figures 34-9, 44), when pottery would not be made anyway (because it is too cold, wet and cloudy), the warmer summer months (May – August) are only slightly more favorable for making pottery. Even though these months have a combination of the warmest temperatures, the least rainfall and less cloudiness, there are several reasons why they still do not provide favorable conditions for pottery production. First of all, the mean temperature in the region for July is a chilly 12-18 degrees C. (Paullin, 1932:Plate 5b; Koeppe, 1931:Figure 29; Blair, 1942:Figure 26; Ginsberg, 1970; Ward et al., 1972:Figures 15, 19). Secondly, rain still occurs during this period. The July rainfall, for example, averages from less than 25 mm in the extreme southern part of this region to 100 mm or more in the northern portion (Ward et al., 1972:Figure 37; see Figure 3.4). Thirdly, the relative humidity at this time is very high with the average at noon during July at 65-90 per cent in the southern three-fourths of the region (Paullin, 1932:Plate 4d; Ward et al., 1972:Figure 43). Finally, even in the summer, there is little sunshine, with an average daily cloud cover of 50-70 per cent in most places (Ward et al., 1972:Figure 45; see Figure 3.5). Thus, even in the warmer summer months, the weather and climate provide significant regulatory feedback for pottery production in the Northwest Coast.

Ethnographic surveys reveal that no pottery is made on the Northwest Coast. Murdock's *Ethnographic Atlas* indicates that there are no potters in any of the 32 Northwest Coast societies in his sample (Murdock, 1967:104, 108) and these data are confirmed by Driver and Massey (1957:Map 127; Driver, 1969:Map 27; see Figure 3.6). In summary, then, the combination of heavy rainfall, fogs, mists, cool temperatures and lack of clear days provides total regulatory feedback for the development of pottery making in this region, and these ecological factors are important reasons why there are no potters there. Other factors (like the factors influencing demand which will be discussed later) are probably also responsible for the lack of pottery making in the Northwest Coast, but in the greater part of the area, the weather and climate provide total regulatory feedback for the craft.

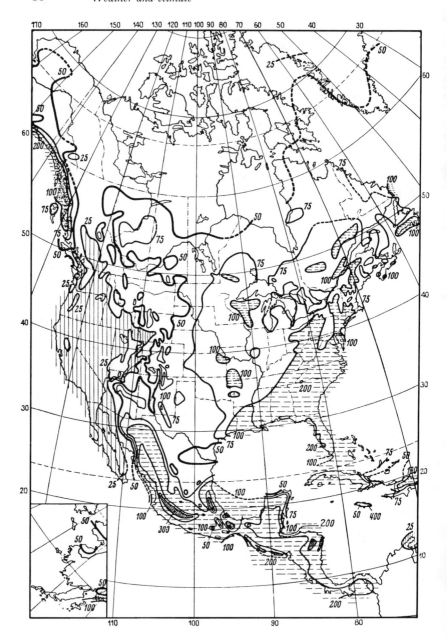

Figure 3.4 Mean July rainfall in mm for North America (from Ward et al., 1972:Figure 37; reprinted with the permission of Kraus Reprint, a division of Kraus-Thomson Organization Limited).

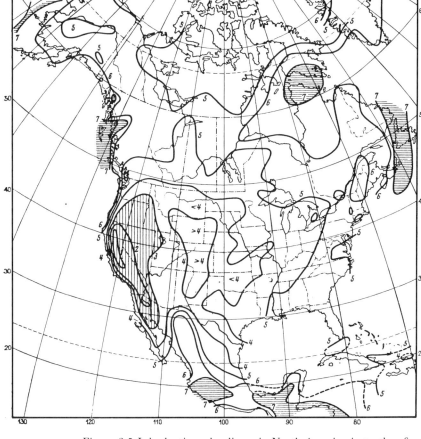

Figure 3.5 July daytime cloudiness in North America in tenths of the sky covered (from Ward et al., 1972:Figure 45; reprinted with the permission of Kraus Reprint, a division of Kraus-Thomson Organization Limited).

C. Regulatory feedback elsewhere in North America

The total regulatory effect of weather and climate also helps explain why most of the California Indians do not make pottery. Pottery is not made in California except in the drier, sunnier and warmer areas such as the Colorado river region (among such groups as the Yuma and Mohave), extreme southern California (among the Digueño, Luiseño, Cupeño, Serrano and Cahuilla) and the southern San Juaquin Valley and south central California among the Central Yokuts, Tubatulabal and Western Mono (Heizer and Whipple, 1951:20-1). In these areas, the climate provides more of a deviation amplifying feedback–at least seasonally. The regulatory effect of weather and climate on pottery making in

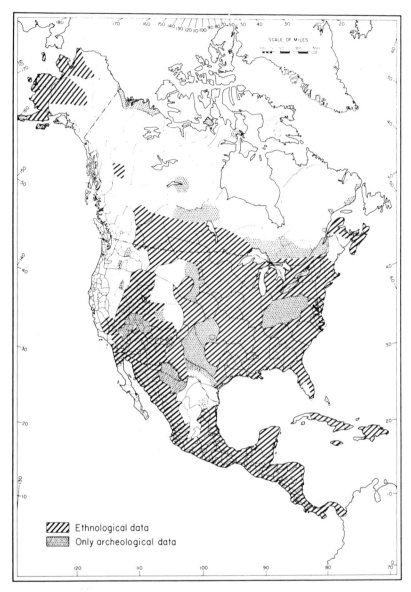

Figure 3.6 Distribution of the cultures of North America which make pottery vessels (reprinted from Driver and Massey, 1957: Map 127; used by permission; see also Driver, 1969: Map 27).

California, however, thus appears to be less significant than in the Northwest Coast, and in both areas other feedback mechanisms (like factors influencing demand: see Chapter 6) are operating as well.

Another factor which may provide total regulatory feedback for pottery making is cold weather. Cold temperatures retard drying time. This factor is probably an important reason why pottery occurs far less frequently in the Arctic and Sub-arctic than in other culture areas (except the Northwest Coast and Calfornia culture areas discussed

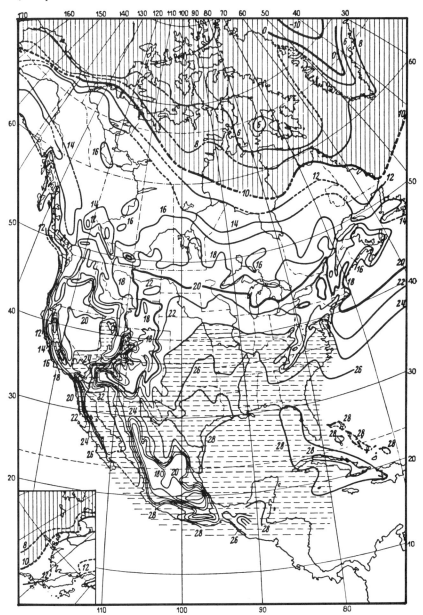

Figure 3.7 Actual temperature for North America for July (from Ward et al., 1972:Figure 19; reprinted with the permission of Kraus Reprint, a division of Kraus-Thomson Organization Limited).

earlier) of North America (Driver and Massey, 1957:Map 127; Driver, 1969:Map 27; see Figure 3.6). Aside from a few exceptions, the northern limit of archaeological and ethnographic pottery in North America (Figure 3.6; Driver and Massey, 1957: Map 127; Driver, 1969:Map 27) corresponds fairly well to the 16 degree C. mean isotherm for July (Figure 3.7), the most favorable time of the year climatically when pottery would be made. The exceptions are: (1) groups in cold areas that make pottery (such as certain Eskimo groups), and (2) warm, dry areas where pottery is not made (most of the Plateau and Great Basin culture areas). These exceptions suggest the complex interplay of other feedback mechanisms which affect pottery production besides weather and climate. The Eskimo pottery is unique in that it is a product of low demand with high non-plastics content and certain firing innovations (see Osgood, 1940). The lack of pottery among the Great Basin and Plateau groups is probably more affected by lack of sedentariness (see Chapter 5) and availability of other kinds of containers (see Chapter 6).

Weather and climate as a deviation amplifying mechanism

Since damp weather and climate provide a regulatory feedback for seasonal ceramic production, a perpetually warm, dry climate with much sunshine and little or no rainfall provides deviation amplifying feedback for pottery production, favoring the original development of pottery making in a society with the potential for full-time specialization. Parts of the Peruvian coast, for example, would be an ecologically favorable area for the development of pottery making into a full-time craft. Most of the coast is extremely dry with no rainfall and little precipitation (Table 3.7). Although some of the coast (particularly the central coast) is covered with fog during the months of May – August (Table 3.8), the river valleys in the foothills of the Andes away from the coastal strip have no fog, constant sunshine and little rain. Many of these valleys are favorable for human occupation and provide ideal conditions for the development of the full-time, year-round ceramic specialization that was responsible for such complex ceramic traditions as Nazca, Paracas, Moche and Chimu.

In order to remove the climatic constraints on ceramic production, minimize the regulatory feedback of weather and climate and thus create deviation amplifying feedback for the craft, one or more of the following 'kicks' would have to be set into operation: (1) a climatic change towards dessication; (2) movement of potters into a drier area where climate did not limit the craft; or (3) the development of kilns, ovens or drying facilities. The initiation of these changes alone, however, would not bring the development of full-time ceramic specialization. For part-time potters, subsistence needs are partially met by other means (such as agriculture) besides pottery making, so full-time potters must depend

Table 3.7 *The driest months (0-1.9% of the precipitation) in coastal Peru*
(From data in Instituto Nacional de Planificación, 1969:131,135)

Region (number of reporting stations)	Month	J	F	M	A	M	J	J	A	S	O	N	D
North coast (13)													
0-1.9% prec.						7	10	11	11	10	7	6	4
Driest month						1	1	2	7	2			
Inland cities on south coast (5)													
0-1.9% Prec.						5	5	5	5	4	5	4	2
Driest month							1	2		1	1		
Central south coast (8)													
0-1.9% prec.		3	3	4	4	2						1	1
Driest month		1		3	1	1						1	1

Table 3.8 *The wettest months (12.5+% or more of monthly precipitation) in coastal Peru*[1]
(From data in Instituto Nacional de Planificación. 1969:131,135

Region (no. of reporting stations)	J	F	M	A	M	J	J	A	S	O	N	D	Mean amount in mm (median)
North coast (13)													
12.5%+	7	11	11	9	1								46.4
wettest month		3	9		1								(18.5)
South coast inland cities (5)													
12.5%+	5	5	5										45
wettest month		5											(22)
Central/south coast (8)													
12.5%+				1	6	3	6	7		1			41.8
wettest month				1	1	1	1	4					(25)

Note
[1] Almost all the precipitation in the coastal areas comes in the form of fog.

upon sufficient demand on the one hand and adequate methods of distribution and exchange on the other in order to meet all of their basic subsistence needs. These factors involve other feedback mechanisms for pottery production and will be discussed later in this book.

Application for archaeology: the Central Andes

Given the adverse effect of rainy weather and climate on ceramic production, it is possible to make several predictions about patterns of ceramic production in ancient Andean society. Firstly, if potters lived in the same ecological zones as they do today, then pottery production would be restricted to the dry season and potters would also have to be part-time agriculturalists in order to subsist during the wet season when the weather and climate precluded pottery production. Secondly, if ancient potters were year-round, full-time specialists (and it is assumed that they were in some areas), then it would be impossible for them to practice their craft in the same zones as their modern counterparts because of the inclement weather during the wet season. This limitation is particularly important when one considers the labor-intensive ritual wares made in the ancient Andes. Breakage would be a great risk for potters because of the trememdous investment of labor in this kind of pottery. Thus, full-time potters would have had to work in dry areas where agriculture, if it was practiced at all, was not dependent on rainfall, but depended on irrigation for moisture. It is thus possible to predict the location of full-time ceramic specialists in the Andes on the basis of climate.

Where could full-time ceramic specialization take place in the Central Andes, given the ecological limits on the potter's craft? By examining Tosi's ecological map, it is possible to suggest those areas which were ecologically favorable for full-time ceramic specialization. Generally speaking, the most favorable zones are the lower montane thorn steppe and the subtropical thorn forest—the two driest zones of the Central Andean highlands. Both of these zones receive 250-500 mm of rainfall per year, but have a mean annual temperature between 12 and 24 degrees C. (Tosi, 1960:Figure 1). Probably the most important factor in these zones, however, is the evapotranspiration potential between 2 and 4, indicating that theoretically 2 to 4 times the rainfall in these zones is lost through a combination of evaporation and transpiration.

Assuming that the climate of the Central Andes has not changed significantly since the first appearance of ceramics at the beginning of the Initial Period (c. 1800 B. C.), these same areas represent regions where full-time ceramic specialization could have taken place in the past as well. If climatic change has occurred since the Initial Period, it would probably have affected the intensity and duration of the rainy season and modified the boundaries of the ecological zones. In any case, these proposed dry areas represent general areas favorable for full-time ceramic specialization with boundaries subject to fluctuation due to climatic change. Thus, they are only *general* areas which are climatically favorable, but do not represent areas which corresond exactly to the boundaries of such zones in the past.

These dry zones occur in highland valleys along the following rivers (Figure 3.8): (1) the Santa river in the northern half of the Callejón de Huaylas; (2) the Huallaga River in the vicinity of the city of Huánuco; (3) the Huarpa River in the Ayacucho Basin; (4) the Mantaro River from 12 degrees 45′ to 12 degrees 17′ S; (5) the Apurimac River from 13 degrees 35′ S to 13 degrees 22′ S, including the following tributaries: (a) the lower Pachacaca from 13 degrees 50′ S (south of Abancay) and two of

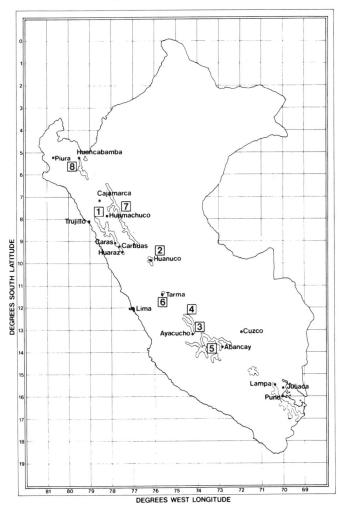

Figure 3.8 Distribution of dry ecological zones in the Andes (the lower montane and subtropical zones) which have the most favorable weather and climate for full-time ceramic specialization (data from Tosi, 1960).

its tributaries, the Antabamba and the Chalhuanca, and (b) the Pampas River from 74 degrees 40' W including its tributaries: the Pampamarca, the Chicha, and the lower San Miquel; (6) the area around the city of Tarma; (7) the Marañon from 9 degrees 10' S to 8 degrees 10' S and from 7 degrees 0' S to 6 degrees 40' S including the following tributaries: (a) the lower Chasgon from 7 degrees 40' S, (b) the Puccha from 9 degrees 22' S, (c) the lower Chontano from 6 degrees 15' S, and (d) between Cajamarca and Huamachucho along the Condebamba from 7 degrees 40' S downward along the Criquegas to the Marañon. (8) Other tributaries of the Marañon where one finds these zones are: (a) the Huancabamba River south of the city of Huancabamba and along its lower tributaries to the Chamaya, and (b) the upper Anaolla in a small area in the vicinity of 5 degrees 20' S and 79 degrees 10' W east of Huancabamba.

The only other region outside of thse zones where full-time ceramic specialization might have been possible is the montane steppe in the high plains in the upper Pampas and Pachachaca drainage and west of Lake Titicaca. Like the lower montane thorn steppe and the subtropical forest, this zone receives 250-500 mm of rainfall annually, but its mean annual temperature (6 to 12 degrees C.) and evapotranspiration potential (1 to 2) are lower than in the former zones. This region, therefore might have been too cold for much ceramic production.

The high probability that full-time ceramic specialization was limited to these dry areas has great implications for the study of culture history as it is currently understood in the Andes. Most interpretations of Central Andean archaeology rest upon distributions of various ceramic styles which are assumed to reflect the culture history of the region. If it was indeed true that large quantities of complex ceramics were produced by full-time potters in relatively few climatically favorable locations in the Central Andes, then it is possible that reliance on ceramics for reconstructions of culture history may give a distorted picture of Central Andean prehistory. Ecological factors may condition the location of pottery production centers and thus affect the distribution of ceramic styles. There are several reasons for this.

First, favorable climate for year-round full-time ceramic specialization exists in relatively few areas of the highlands. Complex highland ceramic styles such as Huari, Cajamarca, Recuay, and Marañon occur in or near areas climatically favorable for full-time ceramic production. All of these areas – the Ayacucho Basin (the Huari Styles), the Cajamarca Basin (the Cajamarca Style), the Callejón de Huaylas (the Recuay Style), and the middle Marañon drainage (the Marañon Style) – include the lower montane thorn steppe zone, an ecological zone favorable for full-time ceramic specialization (see Tosi, 1960). It is reasonable to assume that dry sections favorable for full-time ceramic production also existed within these areas in the past and that full-time potters could have worked there.

Although climatically favorable, the driest zones in the Andes (i. e. the lower montane thorn steppe and the subtropical thorn forest) would not necessarily be suitable for the development of full-time ceramic specialization for other reasons. Firstly, some of these regions may be excessively steep with non-existent valley floors and would be unsuitable for human habitation. Secondly, suitable ceramic resources may not be present. Good quality ceramic resources exist in the Ayacucho Basin (Arnold, 1972a, 1972b; 1975a) and near Huamachuco in the northern highlands where kaolin is readily available (John Thatcher, personal communication): it was probably used to manufacture the white Cajamarca Wares during the Middle Horizon. Finally, full-time specialization would need a sizeable demand and market for pottery to support full-time potters (see Chapter 6).

A second reason supporting the belief that ecological factors may affect the distribution of ceramic styles is the existence of long distance pottery trade and exchange. Long distance trade was probably responsible for the widespread distribution of ceramics in the Precolumbian Andes so that full-time pottery production did not need to occur in every climatically favorable location. There were probably two major pottery distribution mechanisms: (1) vertical control, and (2) long distance trade via llama caravans. Vertical control provided distribution on a relatively local scale across vertically arranged ecological zones except in the vertical archipelago model in which distribution occurred at some distance (Murra, 1972; Brush, 1977:1-16). Llama caravans (Browman, 1974; 1976) were also widely used, often as a product of state control, to transport great amounts of goods (including pottery) over long distances.

Since trade was very important in the Precolumbian Andes, pottery produced in areas ecologically favorable for full-time specialization could have a wide distribution without significant culture-historical contact. Huari, the capital of a Middle Horizon Empire, is a case in point. Huari is located in an area of favorable climate for full-time ceramic production and is near excellent ceramic resources in the Ayacucho Basin (Arnold, 1972b; 1975a). These factors played an important role in accounting for the wide distribution of Huari pottery throughout the Central Andes during the Middle Horizon. In fact, the existence of this distribution also suggests the existence of long distance trade. Huari also had a large population which along with a long distance trading network could have supported full-time potters. Except for some sparse architectural information from Pikillaqta in the southern highlands (Sanders, 1973), Huari (Isbell and Schreiber, 1978) and Jargampampa (Isbell, 1977) in the central highlands, the inferences and interpretations of the Middle Horizon are based almost exclusively on ceramic evidence and stylistic data (e.g., see Menzel, 1964; 1968). Is the wide distribution of Huari pottery in Peru due to the imperialistic conquest of the Huari state or to its ecologically superior location for ceramic production? More importantly, were there other Andean states which have escaped our notice because they did not lie in such ecologically favorable areas for pottery production? The highland cultures which inhabit the comparatively few climatically favorable areas for full-time ceramic production and have access to ceramic resources probably have more archaeological visibility than those which did not occur in such favorable areas. The abundance of these ceramics in the Andes may not necessarily reveal an accurate picture of the culture's importance.

The limitations of most other highland regions for full-time production and the probable importance of ancient trade thus suggest that ecological factors rather than culture-historical ones were involved in the distribution of ancient Andean ceramic styles. The study of ancient ceramics has provided important chronological controls in many areas, but do ceramics reflect culture history?

In summary, there are relatively few areas of the Central Andes where climatic conditions favor the development of full-time ceramic specialization. If other environmental and cultural factors are taken into consideration and critically examined, the list of suitable locations would probably be shorter. Nevertheless, the ecological and ethnographic data suggest that full-time ceramic specialization is not possible everywhere in the Andes and those complex ceramic styles of highland origin which are assumed to be products of full-time specialists were probably made in few locations and widely traded. From the archaeologically best known areas in the Central Andes (Lanning, 1967:31) and the list of climatically favorable areas for full-time ceramic specialization, it is reasonable to suggest that full-time potters could have worked in the Ayacucho Basin, in the region around Huánuco, in the Cajamarca – Huamachuco area, in the northern half of the Callejón de Huaylas and in parts of the Titicaca Basin. The Ayacucho region is already recognized as the source area of some Middle Horizon styles (Menzel, 1964) and this region also has the ceramic resource potential, favorable climate and presumably large population during the Middle Horizon to support full-time potters (Arnold, 1975a). The existence of full-time potters in other dry areas mentioned here, however, will have to await further archaeological research.

Summary

Since the weather and climate are so important for pottery production, different climates in the world will affect the initial development of pottery making and its evolution into a full-time craft. First of all, areas of warm and sunny climate which persists for the entire year with little or no rainfall provide deviation amplifying feedback with no regulatory feedback from climate both in the initial development of pottery making and its evolution into a full-time craft. Secondly, dry areas interrupted by a substantial rainy season with heavy fog and cloud cover provide favorable weather and climate for ceramic production, but only for a part of the year. Similarly, warm, sunny climates with cold snowy winters would also permit pottery making for only a part of the year. Thus, if optimum conditions for pottery making exist for at least part of the year, these conditions provide deviation amplifying feedback and ceramics can emerge as part of the technological system. Full-time ceramic specialization probably could only develop in such areas with a series of technological innovations like elaborate drying facilities or kilns which could mitigate the effect of the negative feedback of weather (see Chapter 8). Thirdly, perpetually cold, wet and rainy climate provides total regulatory feedback for pottery production, preventing the origin of the craft and its development into a full-time specialization. Although certain Eskimo societies have apparently overcome the severe limiting effect of weather and climate on a very small scale (e.g., Osgood, 1940), the regulatory feedback of weather and climate can be successfully overcome in such areas only by the elaborate kilns and drying facilities of the industrial world (See Chapter 8).

Interactions with other feedback mechanisms: resources

The amount of non-plastics in a paste, whether naturally present or added by the potter, can affect the negative feedback of weather and climate. One of the factors affecting the rate of drying of clay products is the amount of non-plastics present. Non-plastics open up the clay to speed and facilitate drying and control shrinkage (Shepard, 1956:25). Yuma pottery, for example, dries in just a few hours, because it contains 80-86 per cent non-plastics (Rogers, 1936). If no non-plastics were present, the amount of drying time would be increased and would thus increase the chances of damage or breakage.

   Increased non-plastics in pottery permit ceramic production in a wider range of environments than would otherwise be possible. Just as increased temperatures and reduced relative humidity speed drying time, cold temperatures delay it. Because of this problem, increased non-plastics in the pottery reduce drying time that would ordinarily be lengthened because of cold temperatures. A clay body with abundant non-plastics (whether naturally present or added by the potter), for example, permits pottery to be made in a colder climate. It is probably the use of large amounts of non-plastics that permitted pottery manufacture to be carried out among certain Eskimo groups (see Figure 3.6) and in the high cold regions of the Andes (like the Altiplano). Prehistoric

Alaskan pottery (Oswalt, 1953; Dumond, 1969), for example, contains abundant and highly variable non-plastic materials. Thus, paste with a large amount of non-plastics helps protect the potter's investment of labor in his pottery and is particularly important in cold areas that produce labor-intensive pottery where breakage would mean great loss. Since non-plastics tend to weaken vessel walls, however, there is a limit to how much potters can add as an adaptation to a cold climate. Some wares from prehistoric Alaska, for example, are friable and crumble easily (Oswalt, 1953; Dumond, 1969). Thus, the adaptive value of non-plastics for making pottery in the Arctic were counterbalanced by resulting problems of paste hardness and friability.

Conclusion

Besides the importance of weather and climate in a general theory or model of cultural process, there are some important conclusions that can be derived from a general discussion of weather and climate and their effect on ceramic production. Firstly, because of the nature of ceramic materials, climate can limit ceramic production, and the cultural process involved in the adaptation of ceramic production to the environment can be established independently of any direct historical relationships between the present and the past by inferring the nature of the ancient climate. Secondly, ceramics do not occur universally, and because of the negative feedback of weather and climate, centers of ceramic production have at least some climatic base and would not necessarily reflect culture-historical forces in the ancient society. Thus, ceramic history, while revealing important aspects of technological history, would not necessarily reveal a culture history.

4
Scheduling Conflicts

The transition of a population to making pottery also depends on the successful solution of two inter-related problems: (1) scheduling pottery making so that it does not interfere with subsistence activities, and (2) if it does, solving this problem by allocating the craft to one sex or the other (or both) without conflicts with other responsibilities.

The necessity of warm, dry weather for pottery production can create potential scheduling conflicts with various subsistence activities. If there are substantial subsistence activities (like agriculture) during the period of optimum weather for pottery making, the resulting scheduling conflict provides regulatory feedback for the origin of pottery making and its development into a year-round, full-time craft. Thus, scheduling conflicts are a feedback mechanism produced by the interaction of the climatic restraints on pottery making on the one hand and subsistence requirements on the other.

There is ample ethnographic evidence that conflict with subsistence activities has a regulatory effect on pottery making. Litto, for example, made this observation in her survey of pottery making in South America:

In many places we discovered that potting is a seasonal occupation for people who make their main livelihood through farming. If we arrived at planting or harvesting time, no one was potting, no clay was prepared and all the work had long since been sold. (Litto, 1976:9)

We had picked a poor time to see work in process in Quinchamalí. It was April and the harvest season was in full swing. There was grain to reap and fruit to pick. No one had the time to work with clay. (Litto, 1976:82)

In Tenango in Chiapas, Mexico, potters produce their wares in the dry season because of the agricultural responsibilities in the wet season (Blom and La Farge, 1927:382). In Wusi, New Hebrides, potters work only during the slack agricultural season when people are free for extra work (Shutler, 1968:18). Similarly, in the Gwembe Valley in Africa, potters work in the slacker times of the year when the gardens make fewer demands on their time (Reynolds, 1968:144). Among the Diola in Senegal in West Africa, potters work only after they have completed the rice and peanut harvest (Linares de Sapir, 1969:2). On the Greek island of Andros, potters work only when they are not involved in agriculture (Birmingham, 1967:36). This same pattern also occurs in some parts of Mexico (Whitaker and Whitaker, 1978:27,30) and Quinua, Peru (Arnold, 1975a). Similarly, scheduling conflicts exist between pottery making and agriculture in Tonalá, Mexico, but farming responsibilities take precedence (Diaz, 1966:158). In Moveros and Pereruela, Spain, female potters must interupt pottery making to help their husbands in the fields (Cortes, 1958:97; 1954:154).

Some anthropologists argue that the seasonality of pottery making is explained solely by scheduling conflicts with subsistence activities. Hammond (1966:59), for example, explains the seasonal production of pottery among the Mossi by arguing that the primacy of agricultural tasks precludes pottery making in the rainy season. While there are times when all of the members of the family are required to help in the fields, another important reason that pottery is not made in the rainy season is because the inclement weather would adversely affect pottery production. Conflict with subsistence activities occurs only at the end of the rainy season when the favorable dry weather for pottery making coincides with the millet harvest. Similarly, Longacre (1974:64) points out that the conflict with agricultural activites among the Kalinga accounts for the seasonal pattern of pottery making. While conflict with subsistence certainly does preclude pottery making at this time, the rainy season undoubtedly has a limiting effect on the craft as well (see Chapter 3). Thus, scheduling does not explain entirely the seasonality of pottery making, but rather explains only why pottery is not produced in a climatically favorable season when there are conflicting subsistence activities.

Scheduling conflicts of subsistence activities with good weather and climate for pottery production do not always occur. When they do occur, however, a successful resolution of this conflict must be made in order to make pottery. Such a solution then creates deviation amplifying feedback for the development of the craft, and commonly occurs through the sexual division of labor. When the scheduling of subsistence activities conflicts with the time of optimum weather and climate for ceramic production, a society may assign each of the discordant activities to different sexes to eliminate conflict. In a case where no such conflict exists, other factors affect the sex of the potters. In any case, allocating pottery making to one sex or the other is affected by three main factors: (1) the compatibility of pottery production with household tasks, (2) the subsequent female advantage in making pottery, and (3) the male involvement in subsistence activities which may require time away from his residence.

For part-time, seasonal potters, pottery making is primarily a household craft. Because the potter probably seldom has the capital (cash or goods) to construct structures to use only for pottery making (see Lackey, 1982:70), the potter's house serves a number of important uses. Firstly, it serves as a relatively dry storage facility to store ceramic raw materials like clay, temper and fuel. Secondly, it provides an easily accessible place to produce pottery. Thirdly, it provides a relatively dry, safe and secure place to dry pottery prior to firing and to store it after firing before it is sold. Since females tend to be closely attached to the household by the requirements of pregnancy, infant care and other household tasks, they have an advantage in performing tasks (like making pottery) that can be accomplished within the household. This advantage is supported by several factors. First, pottery making is easily compatible with child care responsibilities. Indeed, Burton, Brudner and White (1977:249-50) found that childbirth and the nursing of infants were the main constraints on the sexual division of labor in an entailment analysis of fifty tasks in a sample of 185 societies (the Murdock and Provost sample, see Murdock and Provost, 1973). Second, pottery making is easily accomplished in the home and does not require periods of absence from the home. Females are at a disadvantage in undertaking tasks which must be performed away from the household (Murdock and Provost, 1973:211) because of household and childcare responsibilities. Third, it is not dangerous and does not thus provide a hazard for children. Fourth, it is relatively monotonous and does not require great concentration, can be carried out in spite of interruptions and can be easily resumed. Fifth, it is easily compatible with household chores like cooking and women can easily make pots in the house in their spare moments. Sixth, once the process has begun, it requires almost daily attention and thus it is an ideal craft for females tied to the household (Murdock and Provost, 1973; see also Brown, 1970). (These explanations from Brown (1970) and Murdock and Provost (1973) were not offered for the group of activities that included pottery making. Rather, these authors regarded pottery making as a swing activity sometimes associated with males, sometimes with females. This claim is probably related to their failure to control for social complexity in this portion of their analysis (see the latter part of this chapter). Nevertheless, the explanations presented here fit the advantages of pottery making even though Murdock and Provost provide a different explanation.) Seventh, pottery making can be economically important in some societies (such as peasant societies) in which women do not contribute significantly to subsistence activities (such as agriculture). For this reason, in some societies like Panajachel (Tax, 1941:25) and Chinautla (Reina, 1966:57), Guatemala, women can make a substantial economic contribution to the household through pottery making. Finally, having women potters also reduces the risks inherent in the craft and the risks involved in doing anything besides direct subsistence activities. Pottery making involves more risks of loss than subsistence activities. Rainy and cold weather can create problems with drying and firing (Chapter 3).

Moreover, the fragile unfired pottery must be dried and stored in the home for periods of time and this practice increases the likelihood of breakage. In contrast to agricultural pursuits, the potter's family can not eat the fruits of her labors. Pots must be sold or exchanged for food or cash. Thus, making pottery involves more economic risks to a family than subsistence activities and diverting male labor from subsistence to making pottery (unless that labor is unused or unnecessary because of limited or unavailable land) increases the risks of loss of income or food from subsistence activities. Women, then, have a distinct advantage making pottery because it can be easily accomplished in the home between doing other tasks and is compatible with pregnancy, childbirth and nursing responsibilities (Figure 4.1). The female advantage in pottery making is further confirmed by a relatively low position (43/50) in the ranking of male participation of 50 technological activities in a world-wide sample of 185 societies (Murdock and Provost, 1973:207). Pottery making in this sample has an index of male participation of 21.1/100 (where total male participation has an index of 100 and total female participation has an index of 0). The only activities that had more female participation are gathering of wild vegetal foods (19.7), dairy production (14.3), spinning (13.6), laundering (13.0), water fetching (8.6), cooking (8.3) and preparation of vegetal foods (5.7).

Figure 4.1 A Kanjobal woman potter in Coyá, San Miguel Acatán, Guatemala, interrupts the forming of a water carrying vessel to nurse her child. Pottery making in a household context is an activity which is compatible with pregnancy, nursing and child care responsibilities and can easily be interrupted if necessary.

This female advantage in pottery making is reinforced by male dominated patterns of subsistence that take them away from the home. Because childbirth and the nursing of infants are the main constraints on the sexual division of labor (Burton, Brudner and White, 1977:249-50), there is universally a strong tendency for men to be allocated tasks within production sequences beginning with the more distant and dangerous while women are allocated production sequences beginning with low risk tasks closer to home. Thus, men are frequently involved in activities like hunting and agriculture or related tasks that take them away from the home. Often these activities occur during the optimum time for making pottery and females are therefore in the best position for producing ceramics. If females are potters, then there is no scheduling conflict with major subsistence activities that are male dominated and take males away from the home for any length of time. Women, then, can still participate in gathering tasks for subsistence and participate in harvest, but only when these activities are relatively near the household. If, however, females are involved in extensive gathering activities (a female dominated activity with a male participation index of 19.7/100; see Murdock and Provost, 1973:207) which are crucial to subsistence during the optimum time for making pottery, the resulting scheduling conflict serves as a regulatory mechanism preventing the origin of the craft in a society and may also help explain why there are so few fully nomadic, semi-nomadic and semi-sedentary societies which make pottery (see Chapter 5).

Females, however, are not always the potters in a society. Given the female advantage in pottery making, it is possible to suggest a model which explains (and to a certain extent predicts) male involvement in part-time pottery making. This model focuses on ecological criteria rather than the role of market demand or pottery making techniques (as suggested by Foster, 1965). In societies where men are responsible for most subsistence activities and where rainfall limits pottery production to the dry season, male involvement in the craft depends on the relative lack of substantial subsistence responsibilities during the optimum weather for making pottery. Three examples illustrate this principle.

In areas such as highland Peru where winter frosts and lack of rainfall preclude agricultural activity, where there are no significant or prolonged subsistence responsibilities in the dry season and no activity takes men away from the household during this time, potters tend to be predominately male (Kolb, 1976; Tschopik, 1950:205; Ravines, 1966; 1963-64:92). In Quinua (Peru), for example, there is little conflict in scheduling because the optimum time for pottery production corresponds to a relative lull in agricultural activities. Production during the rainy season is prevented anyway because of rainfall and fog. Thus, men are potters in Quinua (see Arnold, 1972a), with some female participation, and no major scheduling conflicts exist between potting and agriculture.

In tropical areas where groups utilize slash and burn agriculture, there are significant agricultural responsibilities in the dry season and potters tend to be women. In the tropical forest east of the Andes, for example, the optimum time for ceramic production occurs during the dry season when new fields must be cleared and burned before the heavy rains return. In this area as well as other tropical areas of the world, some agricultural tasks, like land clearance and burning, tend to be a masculine activity (Murdock and Provost, 1973:209) and must be accomplished in the dry season. Murdock and Provost (1973:209) put land clearance as a quasi-masculine activity, ranking it 90.5/100 in male dominance in a world-wide sample of 185 societies. In Central and South America, however, land clearance has an even higher index of male involvement (95.2/100) which indicates that this activity is almost exclusively male dominated in this area. Since the dry season is an optimum time for making pottery, the male cannot carry out this activity because he is preoccupied with agricultural responsibilities. Thus, potters tend to be women, freeing the men to pursue the necessary agricultural activities in the dry season and thus avoiding a scheduling conflict. In 37 societies from southern Mexico and Central and South America that practice extensive agriculture and for which data were available on the sex of the potters, 84 per cent (31) had female potters, 8 per cent (3) had potters of both sexes with females predominating and 8 per cent (3) had male potters (Murdock, 1967). If the sample is restricted to the tropical forest of South America, where extensive agriculture predominates, then 9 out of the 10 societies in Murdock's sample had female potters, with the remaining society having potters of either sex with females predominating.

The Plains and eastern Woodlands of North America provide another example. The optimum time for making pottery in these areas is summer and early fall when there is sunshine and warm temperatures. Pottery making was probably difficult if not impossible in the winter because of cold and wet inclement weather preventing the drying and firing of the pottery. Agriculture, too, was impossible in the winter but did conflict with the optimum season for pottery production. Thus, in the societies which made pottery, women were the potters, freeing the men to pursue the necessary agricultural activities in the summer and thus avoiding a scheduling conflict (Murdock, 1967:116). In non-agricultural societies of the Plains culture area, summer and early fall were probably times of important hunting and gathering activities which took place only to a limited extent in the winter. A male dominated activity like hunting (cross-cultural male participation index = 99.3 (large land fauna) from Murdock and Provost, 1973:207) might require absences from the camp, whereas a woman could gather food nearby. Thus, women were potters in the non-agricultural societies in the Plains, freeing the men for subsistence activities like hunting (Murdock, 1967:112). This generalization is supported by Driver (1969:170) who noted that when hunting predominates as a subsistence type, women tend to perform tasks other than hunting.

The adaptation of the sexual division of labor to reduce scheduling conflicts between pottery making and both subsistence and non-subsistence tasks is illustrated in the community of Chinautla, Guatemala. The exploitation of ceramic resources for pottery making and the exploitation of the forests for making charcoal are integrated into the economy so as not to interfere with subsistence agriculture. First of all, males are agriculturalists and carry out many of these activities during the wet season, leaving females to make pottery for much, if not most of the year. Secondly, men make charcoal during the dry season when many fields must be cleared and burned. Charcoal production is thus not only compatible with agricultural responsiblities during the dry season and supplements pottery making and agriculture in a family, but occurs during the optimum time for making pottery (see Reina, 1966:46-57) when the waste from charcoal production (cones, needles and bark) can be used for pottery firing and there is the greatest demand for pottery (Reina, 1966:55). Furthermore, agricultural and charcoal activites may take men away from the household. Thus, since pottery making is compatible with household activities, women are potters in the Chinautla region.

In some complex societies, other strategies besides the sexual division of labor must be used to resolve scheduling conflicts between pottery making and agriculture. For example, the optimum time for making pots in Japan is during the summer agricultural season. In order to accomplish both agriculture and pottery making, potters may have to hire assistance to make pottery during this time (Rhodes, 1970:126).

The problem of scheduling ceramic production around subsistence activities is primarily a problem for part-time potters. This mechanism operates when potters are working part-time, when weather and climate limit ceramic production for part of the year and when potters practice subsistence or other activities during the part of the year in which they do not make pottery. With seasonal limits on ceramic production, there must be other means during the inclement weather to provide support for the potter; he must practice agriculture or some other subsistence activity during this time (e. g. Orissa potters, see Behura, 1978:225). He cannot intensify his craft into a full-time, year-round speciality because although rainfall provides moisture for agriculture, it provides regulatory feedback for pottery making.

In order to neutralize the regulatory effect of scheduling conflicts for full-time ceramic specialization, there must be several kicks that put deviation amplifying feedback into operation. First, in a society where a part-time craft conflicts with subsistence activities, full-time ceramic specialization could not evolve without population pressure (discussed more in chapter 7). If weather conditions do not permit a potter to practice his craft for the entire year, he must also practice agriculture to survive during the wet season when pottery cannot be made. Without decreasing subsistence activities there would be no incentive to intensify the craft. Intensifying the craft in an area limited by weather and climate would not be possible without either of two factors occurring: (1) technological innovations which mitigate the negative affect of climate or increase the efficiency of craft activities (Chapter 8), or (2) movement out of the area into a drier, more favorable area. In warm dry areas that utilize irrigation rather than rainfall for agriculture, however, technological innovations or migration would not be necessary and intensification of pottery making could occur without any new technology that could mitigate the effects of weather and climate. As traditional subsistence strategies (like agriculture and hunting) were reduced and ultimately eliminated by population pressure (see Chapter 7), pottery making would become the primary activity for a livelihood. Since there would be no scheduling conflicts with subsistence activities, male potters would become more involved in the pottery making process and eventually would replace female potters, since the use of females for making pottery on a part-time basis is related to the female advantage in making pottery in a household and a solution to scheduling conflicts. Furthermore, any cultural change that produced dependency on pottery making as a livelihood, required sustained long term production and removed it from the household would also reduce female participation in the process. Thus, when potters become itinerant craftsmen (like those in Thrapsano on Crete (Voyatzoglou, 1974) and in the Callejón de Huaylas in Peru (Donnan, 1971)) and must travel away from their household, potters are male.

One example of the change of pottery making from a female to a male activity has occurred in Ticul, Yucatan. In several communities of the Yucatan (Mama, Maxcanu, Akil and Peto), potters tended to be women. (Akil and Peto were not mentioned by Thompson (1958). In October 1968, there were only two potters in Akil and these worked seasonally making bowls for use during the All Saints' Day festivities. In Peto, only one family of potters were located and they had stopped making pottery several years earlier.) In Ticul, however, pottery making was a full-time household craft and both males and females were potters. Females did not work as consistently as males. Between 1965 and 1970, several workshops existed where one potter hired the services of others on a wage basis. A workshop existed within the houselots of each of two potters. The two hotels at the ruins of Uxmal also had workshops near their hotels and hired Ticul potters to make specific items for sale to tourists and, in some cases, decorative items for the hotel itself. (The

Hotel Uxmal began hiring Ticul potters before 1964. In November 1979, Ticul potters were still working there. The other tourist hotel at Uxmal only hired potters immediately before and for an unknown period after it opened (probably around 1971). In 1979, no potters worked there.) In all of these pottery workshops that existed outside the potter's home, only male potters were involved. A wife or female relative of the workshop owner may also make pottery in a workshop, however, if the workshop is in her household. Thus, the increased dependency on pottery making as a livelihood and its removal from the household creates a change to male potters because women potters can no longer fulfill nursing, childcare and household responsibilities in the home.

With the intensification of the craft, women potters provide deviation counteracting feedback for the craft because of the scheduling conflicts between the increased time necessary to make pottery and their childcare and household duties. Women with young children may be too busy to work very much and any woman must interrupt pottery making to perform childcare and household tasks, as they do in Tonalá (Diaz, 1966:158-9) and Veracruz (Krotser, 1974:133), Mexico, and in the Gwembe Valley (Reynolds, 1968:144). Among the Shipibo-Conibo (De-Boer and Lathrap, 1979:124), households with suckling infants produce less pottery than households free of children or with less demanding children. The regulatory feedback that the scheduling conflict of women potters with young children has on pottery production is most dramatically illustrated by Nash (1961:189). In comparing the pottery production of three households in Chiapas, Mexico, the household with no children had a far greater production of pots than two households with children under the age of three (Figure 4.2). Thus, widows or elderly women may be the only females who can make pottery regularly (Nicholson, 1931; David and Hennig, 1972:4) and have much output. When pottery making becomes the sole means of livelihood, however, potters must work constantly. As potters come to depend more and more on their craft for a livelihood, men must participate more and more in the pottery making process and females must limit their participation to avoid scheduling conflicts with household responsibilities and childcare. Again, widows would have more of an advantage in being able to work regularly if they had to be economically dependent on the craft. Finally, with the removal of the pottery making from the household, females can no longer participate at all unless they have no household or childcare responsibilities.

Two kinds of data support the generalization that the cultural evolution into complex societies and thus full-time ceramic specialization corresponds to the change from female to male potters. First, male involvement in pottery making is associated statistically with certain characteristics of complex societies. Factor and cluster analyses by Smith and Crano (1977) revealed a consistent association (with a high

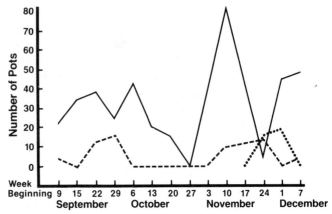

Figure 4.2 Pottery production of all types of ware in three households in Amatenango, Chiapas. The solid line indicates household
thirteen which has four women producers and no children. The
dashed line refers to household six which has two women producers
and three children under the age of three. The dotted line is household fourteen which has two women producers and one child under
three years of age. Female potters in households with young children produce less than potters in households with no children
(redrawn from Nash, 1961: Figure 2; used with permission of the
Royal Anthropological Institute of Great Britian and Ireland).

load factor of above .60) of supra-jurisdiction, class stratification and
political integration. Male involvement in pottery making is also associated with this cluster, but it was weaker and not central in both kinds of
analyses. These data suggest a tendency towards male involvement in
pottery with increasing internal stability between the sectors of the
society, political integration and class stratification, and thus indicate
that male potters tend to be associated with more complex societies.
Second, factor analyses of cross-cultural comparison of sexual division of
labor by Murdock and Provost (1973:215) also suggest that pottery
making by males is associated with intense and complex agriculture such
that as the intensity and complexity of agriculture increases, pottery
making tends to be assigned increasingly to males. These agricultural
patterns are often associated with complex societies.

5
Degree of Sedentariness

The degree of sedentariness is a feedback mechanism relating the pottery production of a population to the relative mobility of that population. At the outset, it would seem that mobile societies provide total negative feedback for the origin of the craft and its evolution into a full-time specialization. Conversely, sedentariness would provide deviation amplifying feedback for both the origin of pottery making and its evolution into a full-time craft. As this chapter will demonstrate, these generalizations are basically correct, but are oversimplified.

Pottery making has traditionally been associated with sedentary societies. This idea goes back at least to 1876 when Lewis Henry Morgan used the presence of pottery making as a criterion for one of his stages of cultural evolution (Lower Barbarism) and claimed, 'the manufacture of pottery presupposes village life...' (Morgan, 1963:13). While the relationship of pottery production to sedentary life is implied in this quotation, Morgan makes no other statement relating pottery making to sedentariness more precisely. Otis Mason's *The Origins of Invention*, originally published in 1895, expresses this same relationship, but more explicitly.

But, just as soon as people had fire, became sedentary, ate farinaceous food, the pot came to be born. (Mason, 1966:154)

The converse of this assertion is that mobile groups which are not fully sedentary do not make or use pottery. This aspect of the relationship of ceramics and the degree of sedentariness was noted by Nordenskiöld in 1919 and Linné in 1925 in their studies of South American ceramics:

The absence of pottery among the Tehuelche is due to their life being so bound up with that of the horse; fragile earthenware is unsuitable for an equestrian people. (Nordenskiöld, 1919:211)

The rest of the potteryless tribes likewise being nomadic it may be supposed that they had not been driven by any very urgent necessity to learn this art... (Linné, 1925:6)

It is possible that clay vessels would have been a hindrance in their wanderings. (Linné, 1925:4)

In fact, Linné views lack of sedentariness as even more important than weather and climate as a limiting factor for the development of pottery making.

> The raw and rainy climate of Tierra de Fuego, and the humid atmosphere of the primeval forests of Brasil, perhaps make difficult the drying of clay vessels, and, subsequently, is a hindrance to firing. But that is no reason for their not being able to make pottery. Rather, it has to be taken into consideration that clay vessels would prove impractical to these nomadic peoples on their perpetual wanderings. (Linné, 1925:3)

Finally, in his summary of the section on pottery making and sedentariness, Linné argues that in becoming settled there was a transition from making water-tight baskets to producing clay vessels (Linné, 1925:13).

The alleged reason given for the relationship between sedentariness and pottery making is the fragility of pottery and its susceptibility to breakage. If pottery was fired at a low temperature or contains large amounts of non-plastics, it is particularly fragile. Thus, mobile societies presumably have a greater probability for breaking pottery than sedentary ones because of movement.

> It is only the sedentary peoples that can make full use of pottery because pottery is difficult to transport without breakage. (Driver and Massey, 1957:231)
> It seems likely that the semi-nomadic way of early Plains and Basin life, with its frequent moving in search of food, tended to limit the amount of pottery because pottery was both heavier and more breakable than basketry. (Driver and Massey, 1957:229)

The use of other kinds of containers presumably reduces the risk of breakage and the need for continual replacement.

The argument that mobile peoples do not make pottery because of its fragility has been overemphasized. Pots are important enough to some groups that they may be safely transported without breakage using adaptations such as carrying slings, net bags (Gupta, 1966:71), or special shapes that are easily carried, or by cushioning pottery by careful packing (Nicklin, 1979:453-4). Water carrying vessels in Nurar, Pakistan, for example, have lugs for attachment to a camel saddle (Rye and Evans, 1976:49) for easy transport. Among the Ingalik of Alaska, pots carried from one village to another are tightly packed with grass in a birch bark basket (Osgood, 1940:148). The Yanomamo of Venezuela transport their pottery in a basket with a cushion of bark around the pot (Lizot, 1974:17). Furthermore, peasant potters, traders and middlemen consistently transport great quantities of pottery over long distances without much breakage using relatively simple technology such as net bags (e. g. Gupta, 1966:71; Reina and Hill, 1978:207; Nash, 1961:187; Van de Velde and Van de Velde, 1939:34), carrying frames (e. g. Reina and Hill, 1978:208; Willett and Connah, 1969:134) or by packing pine needles (Bock, 1970:14), grass (Nash, 1961:187), henequen waste, corn husks, cloth, or paper between pots tied in bundles (Thompson, 1958:101-3; Figure 5.1a-e). Potters in Luricocha (Department of Ayacucho), Peru, for example, transport cooking pots by stacking them four or five vessels high and tying the handles together tightly. Two bundles are then laid horizontally on the side of a burro, covered with a blanket and then fastened securely to the animal.

Using this simple technology of careful packing and carrying frames or slings, pottery can be transported great distances without significant breakage. In a brief survey of the literature, Foster (1965:56) indicated that pottery may be transported up to 250 km by the original sellers. Pottery from Ticul, Yucatan, is consistently transported to many parts of the northern Yucatan peninsula as far as 250 km by road (to towns such as Peto, Sotuta, Tizimín, and Valladolid). Chinautla pottery is transported throughout southwestern Guatemala up to an airline distance of 125 km (Reina, 1960:72 compared with McBryde, 1947:Map 1). In brief, then, the fragility of pottery is not the main reason that mobility produces negative feedback for pottery making, since both non-sedentary societies and sedentary societies transport their pottery. The

Figure 5.1a-e Several ways in which potters transport pottery without breakage:

a. Grass used as a packing material for pottery placed in a rope net. (The pottery is probably from Pucará, Peru, 240 km away, being unloaded at the railroad station in Cuzco, Peru.)

main difference is that potters in non-sedentary societies transport it during use while potters in sedentary societies transport it for distribution prior to use. In terms of the possibility of damage to fragile pots, there is little qualitative difference between mobile and many non-mobile societies.

Although the fragility of pottery is a rather dubious factor in limiting pottery use among non-sedentary societies, do the above data mean that there is no relationship between sedentariness and the presence or absence of pottery making? In order to test the relationship of sedentariness and the presence of pottery making cross-culturally, a sample of world-wide societies was drawn and compared statistically. The sample consisted of the 60 societies in the HRAF (Human Relations Area Files) Probability Sample, a randomly selected sample of societies drawn from the larger HRAF that can be used for cross-cultural comparisons. These

b. Paper or cardboard used as packing material between pottery placed in a net bag for carrying. (Man using a tumpline to carry pottery from the market in Chichicastenango, Guatemala.)

c. Carrying frames (right) or a simple cloth sling (left) used for carrying pottery on the back (Chichicastenango, Guatemala).

societies were matched against the societies in the *Ethnographic Atlas* (Murdock, 1967) using the sample unit concordance developed by the HRAF (Lagacé, 1977:496-7). Data were selected from column 48 (pottery) and column 30 (settlement pattern). Column 48 gives sex of the potter, but the data from each society in this column were recoded as either presence or absence of pottery making. Column 30 lists the settlement pattern by type (Table 5.1). For societies not listed in the Atlas, data were obtained directly from the HRAF (Table 5.2). Data on pottery making were not available for one society (the Shluh). All the sedentary codes in the Atlas were recoded as fully sedentary (see Table 5.1). The settlement pattern codes were then arranged into progressive degrees of sedentariness (from nomadic to fully sedentary) and cross-classified with the presence or absence of pottery making. For statistical comparison, the significance level was set at .05. Chi-square and Cramer's V were computed from the resulting table (Table 5.3) and revealed a strong association between the presence of pottery making and a greater degree of sedentariness (Chi-square = 18.537 with 4 degrees of freedom, significance = 0.001, Cramer's V = 0.56052).

(There has been some question in the past whether Chi-square can be utilized for cells that have an expected value of less than five. Plog (1980:123), citing Dixon and Massey (1969:241), criticizes the Chi-squares used by Clemen (1976) as being invalid because more than 20 per cent of the cells fall below an expected value of five. Citing the work of Hopkins and Glass (1978), however, Minium and Clark (1982:382)

d and e. Net bag and cardboard used as packing material for pots tied together for transport. (Pottery being loaded at potter's house in Ticul, Yucatan, for transport to other parts of the northern Yucatan peninsula.)

Table 5.1 *List of societies in the Probability Sample Files showing breakdown by presence/absence of pottery making and degree of sedentariness*

Degree of sedentariness	Non-sedentary	Partly sedentary			Fully sedentary
Ethnographic Atlas category	Nomadic	Semi-nomadic	Semi-sedentary (Transhumance)	Impermanent settlements moved every few years	
Ethnographic Atlas code	B	S	T	W	H,N,V,X
Societies which do not make pottery	Aranda Blackfoot Lapps Ona Pigmies Somali	Copper Eskimo Klamath Sanusi	Tlingit		Kapauku Tikopia Truk

116

Table 5.1 (*Contd.*)

Degree of sedentariness	Non-sedentary	Partly sedentary			Fully sedentary
Ethnographic Atlas category	Nomadic	Semi-nomadic	Semi-sedentary (Transhumance)	Impermanent settlements moved every few years	Fully sedentary
Ethnographic Atlas code	B	S	T	W	H,N,V,X
Societies which make pottery	Chukchee Masai	Andamans Bororo Mataco Yakut Yanoama	Cagaba Kurd Lozi Ojibwa Pawnee	Bemba Tucano	Amhara Lau Ashanti Santal Aymara Serbs Azande Sinhalese Bahia Brazilians Taiwan Bush Negro Tarahumara Cuna Thailand Dogon Tiv Ganda Toradja Garo Trobriands Guarani Tzeltal Hausa Wolof Highland Scots Hopi Iban Ifugao Iroquois Kanuri Khasi Korea

Table 5.2 *Data on pottery making and sedentariness in societies*
in the HRAF present in the Probability Sample Files
but not in the Ethnographic Atlas

HRAF code	Society	Source	Pottery making	Sedentariness (Ethnographic Atlas code)
FA16	Dogon	Palau Marti, 1957:8, 25, 26	Present (women)	Sedentary (V)
MS14	Kanuri	Rosman, 1966:129	Present	Sedentary (V)
		Cohen, 1960:268	Present (women)	
		Cohen, 1967:5-6		Sedentary (X)
NG6	Ojibwa (southern Ojibwa focus)	Densmore, 1929:162	Present in former times	
		Landes, 1937:2, 4, 76		Semi-sedentary (T)
		Ritzenthaler, 1953		
NV 9	Tzeltal	Villa Rojas, 1969:207	Present (women)	Sedentary (X)
SR8	Bush Negro	Kahn, 1931:203	Present	
		Hurault, 1959:19		Sedentary (V)
		Geijskes, 1954:141		
MT9	Libyan Bedoin (Sanusi focus)	Evans-Pritchard, 1949:49	Absent	Non-sedentary, semi-nomadic (S)
ES10	Highland Scots	Thompson, 1973:112	Glass industry present	
		Parman, 1972:22ff.		Sedentary (X)
		Geddes, 1955:229		
		Moisley et al., 1962: 15		
		Ducey, 1956:41–2		

point out that Chi-square will give reasonable results for contingency tables even when the expected values in them are less than five. Nevertheless, for the 2 × 2 contingency tables used in this chapter, the Fisher Exact probabilities (the Fisher Exact Test is only appropriate for 2 × 2 tables) were also calculated. These exact probabilities are smaller than

Table 5.3 *Comparison of sedentariness and pottery making among societies in the HRAF Probability Sample Files* (Total sample = 59/60 societies in the files)

Degree of sedentariness	Non-sedentary		Partly sedentary		Fully sedentary	Row totals
Ethnographic Atlas category	Nomadic	Semi-nomadic	Semi-sedentary (transhumance)	Impermanent settlements moved every few years		
Number of societies which do not make pottery	6	3	1	0	3	13
Number of societies which make pottery	2	5	5	2	32	46
Column totals	8	8	6	2	35	59

Note

χ^2 (df = 4) = 18.536; p = 0.001; Cramer's V = 0.56052

those based on corrected Chi-square, but the differences do not affect the interpretations presented here.)

The degree of sedentariness acts as a regulatory feedback mechanism for pottery production in two ways: first, the lack of sedentariness limits the amount of time that is available to make pottery in any given location. Pottery makes fragile containers, but is even more fragile during the process of fabricating, drying and firing, and can be easily broken during this time. Movement from one location to another during the pottery making process greatly increases the risk of breakage of the unfired pottery. Thus, pottery is best made in a single location until after firing to lessen the risk of breakage. In a non-sedentary population which depends upon movement for subsistence, the amount of time in one location may be insufficient to fabricate, dry and fire pottery. Secondly, if a society is sedentary long enough to make pottery, the temporary sedentariness may not occur in a location with ceramic resources or a favorable climate. Conversely, the most favorable time of year to make pottery may occur when a population is not in that ecological niche nor located near ceramic resources. Thus, pottery making by a non-sedentary population may be complicated by the negative feedback of the lack of either resources or a favorable climate, or both, which prevents the original development of the craft. Materials more closely related to subsistence (like hides) would be easier to obtain, and fabricating these types of containers would not be limited by weather or climate or the lack of ceramic resources.

In general, then, the lack of sedentariness provides negative feedback for pottery making. In non-sedentary societies (i.e., nomadic, semi-nomadic, transhumant or semi-sedentary societies and impermanent settlements moved every few years), a lack of sedentariness would be a regulatory device because the following factors need to co-occur: (1) the availability of water and suitable clay nearby; (2) a favorable climate for making pottery; and (3) enough time in one location to fabricate, dry and fire the pottery. This perspective was anticipated by Schofield in 1948:

...people whose main livelihood is derived from hunting must follow the game in its migrations. They seldom stay long enough in one place for the complicated business of making, drying and burning of pottery... (Schofield, 1948:8)

Thus, the lack of sedentariness provides negative feedback for pottery production not primarily because of its fragility, but because settlement impermanence limits the amount of time in one place needed to make pottery, can complicate obtaining suitable resources and may reduce opportunities for making pottery in a favorable climate.

In spite of the problems with non-sedentary populations making pottery, however, the negative feedback of mobility is not total, and there are many non-sedentary societies of the world that make pottery. In the sample of the 862 societies listed in the *Ethnographic Atlas* (Murdock,

1967), 33 per cent (282) were non-sedentary societies (Column 30). Of these, 37 per cent (103) made pottery (Column 48). (There may be more, but data on pottery making were lacking for many societies.) Of these 103 societies that made pots, 15 were nomadic bands (Murdock's code 'B'), 45 were semi-nomadic societies (Murdock's code 'S'), 36 were transhumant or semi-sedentary societies (Murdock's code 'T') and 7 were impermanent settlements moved every few years (Murdock's code 'W').

The probable reason for pottery making in non-sedentary and partially sedentary societies is that they are not as limited by climate or by the distance to resources as sedentary groups are; migratory groups could move into ecological niches which have ceramic resources and favorable climate. The primary problems for such populations, however, consist of the availability of a favorable resource niche in the general area through which they move, and the scheduling of their movements so that the population will be in this niche during favorable weather and remain there long enough to make pottery. Presumably, the cultures in the *Ethnographic Atlas* (as well as others in the world) which make pottery, but which are not fully sedentary, have successfully adapted to these problems.

This adaptation is particularly evident in the Plateau/Great Basin area (Murdock's 'Nd' group) of North America. Because this region has excellent climate for making pottery seasonally from approximately May to September, pottery making would not be limited by climate during this period but only by presence of resources and length of residence. Presumably, these were not significant regulatory mechanisms since 42.1 per cent (16/38) of the societies that were not fully sedentary (including 1 nomadic society, 34 semi-nomadic societies and 3 semi-sedentary or transhumant societies) in this culture area also made pottery (Murdock, 1967). Thus, a society does not have to be fully sedentary to make pottery, and even temporary sedentariness in a favorable resource and climate niche provides deviation amplifying feedback for pottery production.

In order to test the role of partial sedentariness on the presence or absence of pottery making, the earlier 5×2 table from the HRAF Probability Sample was collapsed into a 3×2 table (compare Table 5.3 with Table 5.4) with all non-nomadic and non-fully sedentary populations in one category of partial sedentariness (i.e. semi-nomadic, semi-sedentary or transhumant societies and impermanent settlements moved every few years). Chi-square and Cramer's V were computed from the table and revealed a strong association of pottery making and degree of sedentariness (Chi-square $= 16.839$, significance $= 0.0002$ and Cramer's V $= 0.53423$).

The impact of partial sedentariness on making pottery can be tested by comparing the presence or absence of pottery making among totally

Table 5.4 *Contingency table of presence of pottery making and degree of sedentariness among nomadic, partly sedentary and fully sedentary societies*

	Nomadic societies	Partly sedentary societies	Fully sedentary societies	Row totals
Societies which do not make pottery	6	4	3	13
Societies which make pottery	2	12	32	46
Column totals	8	16	35	59

Note

χ^2 (df=2) = 16.839, p = 0.0002;
Cramer's V = 0.53423

non-sedentary (nomadic) and partially sedentary populations using the HRAF probability sample. The resulting 2 × 2 table includes two non-sedentary and 12 partially sedentary societies which make pottery and 6 non-sedentary and 4 partially sedentary societies which do not make pottery (compare Table 5.4 with Table 5.5). The Chi-square and Phi (a measure of correlation similar to Cramer's V but for 2 × 2 classification tables) were computed and indicated a moderately strong

Table 5.5 *Contingency table of presence/absence of pottery making among non-sedentary and partly sedentary societies*

	Non-sedentary	Partly sedentary	Row totals
Societies which make pottery	2	12	14
Societies which do not make pottery	6	4	10
Column total	8	16	24

Note

Corrected (for continuity) χ^2 (df = 1) = 3.621; p = 0.057; Phi = 0.47809

Table 5.6 *Contingency table of presence and absence of pottery making among partly and fully sedentary societies*

	Partly sedentary societies	Fully sedentary societies	Row totals
Societies which make pottery	12	32	44
Societies which do not make pottery	4	3	7
Column total	16	35	51

Note

Corrected (for continuity) χ^2 (df = 1) = 1.3076; p = 0.2528; Phi = 0.22152

association between partial sedentariness and pottery making (corrected Chi-square = 3.621 with one degree of freedom, significance = 0.057 (p=0.0259833 with the Fisher Exact Test), Phi = 0.47809). This measure of association suggests that even temporary sedentariness nullifies the regulatory aspect of movement and acts as a deviation amplifying mechanism. Conversely, the effect of full sedentariness over partial sedentariness appears to have less effect on pottery making than the effect of partial sedentariness over no sedentariness. In order to test this relationship, the presence and absence of pottery making among partly and fully sedentary societies was compared. This sample consisted of 4 partially sedentary and 3 fully sedentary societies which do not make pottery and 12 partially sedentary and 32 fully sedentary societies which make it (compare Table 5.4 with Table 5.6). Chi-square and Phi were computed from the values in this table and indicated a weak relationship between the presence of pottery making and fully sedentary societies (corrected Chi-square= 1.3076 with one degree of freedom, significance = 0.2528 (p=0.10289 with the Fisher Exact Test), Phi = 0.22152). These measures of association suggest that the transition from nomadism to partial sedentariness provided more deviation amplifying feedback for the development of pottery making than the transition from partial sedentariness to full sedentariness. Thus, partial sedentariness was more crucial for the original development of the craft than full sedentariness.

The negative feedback of poor weather and climate takes precedence over the deviation amplifying effect of sedentariness. This relationship can be illustrated by comparing the percentages of sedentary societies in the Northwest Coast culture area with several North American culture

Table 5.7 *Comparison of percentage of fully sedentary pottery making societies in cultural areas of North America that have favorable climate for making pottery*

Culture area	Ethnographic Atlas code (Murdock, 1967)	Percent fully se-dentary (raw ratio)	Percent that make pottery (raw ratio)	Climate for pottery making (see text)
Southwest	Nh	70.8 (17/24)	95.8 (23/24)[1]	seasonal, excellent
Plateau/Great Basin	Nd	0 (0/38)	42.1 (16/38)	seasonal, excellent
California	Nc	3.3 (1/30)	33.3 (10/30)	parts are excellent (central and south)
N. Mexico	Ni	57.2 (4/7)	85.7 (6/7)	excellent
Plains	Ne	5 (1/20)	30 (6/20)	very seasonal, good
S. Plains	Nf	5.8 (2/35)	57.1 (20/35)	seasonal, good
Eastern Woodlands Southeast	Ng	66.7 (6/9)	100 (9/9)	seasonal, good
Northwest Coast	Nb	43.8 (14/32)	0 (0/32)	poor

Note

[1] Data for one society are missing

areas (Table 5.7). The percentage of fully sedentary societies in each culture area ranges from 0 per cent to 70.8 per cent, yet the per cent of societies which make pots in each culture area ranges from 30 per cent to 95.8 per cent. The Northwest Coast, on the other hand, has 43.8 per cent sedentary societies and no society with potters (Murdock, 1967). A sedentary community in the Northwest Coast area is always prevented from producing pottery because of the inclement weather regardless of the availability of resources. By way of contrast, pottery production among sedentary societies in a dry area like the Southwest is only partly regulated by the climate, but mostly by the presence of resources. Furthermore, production in the Southeast/Woodlands culture area is only partly limited by the climate (in the colder winter months from November to March), but also by resource availability. Thus, the degree of sedentariness only operates as a deviation amplifying feedback mechanism in an area where climate provides deviation amplifying feedback for at least part of the year.

Although partial sedentariness was more important for the original development of ceramic production than full sedentariness, full sedentariness also has a deviation amplifying affect on pottery production such that there is a greater frequency of pottery making among fully sedentary societies than partially sedentary ones, given equal climatic restraints. One can demonstrate the deviation amplifying effect of full sedentariness when one compares the degree of sedentariness and percentage of pottery making societies of several adjacent culture areas in the western United States where excellent climate exists for pottery production. First, the Southwest has the most winter sunshine in North America with 40 per cent or less of the sky covered with clouds (Ward et al., 1972:Figure 44). The amount of sunshine in the summer (the best time to make pottery) is not any different, however, than much of the western half of the United States, with 40 per cent or less of the sky covered during July (Ward et al., 1972:Figure 45; see Figure 3.4). Areas further west and north in the Great Basin, the Plateau area and in parts of California have even more sunshine, with 30 per cent or less of the sky covered in July. Second, the Southwest shares the warmest temperatures in North America with many parts of the southern United States throughout the year (Ward et al., 1972:Figures 12-17). Third, the amount of rainfall is no less than the western half of the country in mean amount per year (Blair, 1942:Figure 27; Ward et al., 1972:Figure 32; see Figure 3.3) and in amount per month (Ward et al., 1972:Figures 34-9). In fact, there are areas farther west and north in the Great Basin and the Plateau area that receive less rainfall per year (Ward et al., 1972:Figure 32; Blair, 1942:Figure 27) than the Southwest and less during July and September, the best season for making pottery. Fourth, low relative humidity during July is shared by many areas in the Southwest, Great Basin and Plains culture areas (Ward et al., 1972:Figure 43). Although low relative humidity is generally restricted to the Southwest in January (Ward et al., 1972:Figure 42), pottery would probably not be made during that time anyway (see Fontana et al., 1962:20; Rogers, 1936:4-5).

As for pottery making societies, the Southwest has the greatest percentage (95.8 per cent) that make pottery in comparison to nearby culture areas which also have favorable climate for pottery production (Table 5.7). By way of contrast, 42.1 per cent of the societies in the Plateau/Great Basin make pottery. In California, 33.3 per cent make pottery while in the Plains and the southern Plains area, 30.0 per cent and 57.1 per cent of the societies make pottery respectively.

The climatically favorable areas alone do not explain the presence of a high percentage of pottery making societies in the Southwest (Table 5.7). Rather, the degree of sedentariness is a major factor in widespread pottery production. From the *Ethnographic Atlas*, the Southwest has the highest percentage of sedentary cultures in North America, with 70.8 per cent of the cultures being fully sedentary. By way of contrast, the Plateau/Great Basin has no fully sedentary societies, the Plains 5 per cent, and the southern Plains area has 5.8 per cent fully sedentary societies. Thus, the high percentage of fully sedentary societies in the Southwest and the favorable climate there are important factors for the existence of a large number of pottery making societies since a very high percentage of fully sedentary societies distinguishes the Southwest from nearby climatically favorable areas that have fewer societies that make pottery. The only other areas with a relatively favorable climate for ceramic production for at least part of the year and a large percentage of fully sedentary societies are the eastern Woodlands (66.7 per cent) and northern Mexico (57.2 per cent). These two areas also have high percentages of societies that make pottery, with 100 per cent of the societies making pottery in the Woodlands and 85.7 per cent in northern Mexico.

The advantage of sedentary societies, then, is that if they are located near good quality ceramic resources and live in a favorable climate for at least part of the year, pottery making could emerge as part of the cultural pattern. In sedentary societies, of course, the negative feedback of mobility no longer operates. Furthermore, the lack of movement makes the use of breakable ceramic containers more feasible, and the relative permanence of pottery makes it easily adapted to sedentary populations (discussed in Chapter 6). Thus, while pottery can be produced by non-sedentary and partially sedentary societies, the dominance of pottery as a container is most closely related to sedentary modes of life (Driver, 1969:156) and in contrast to other areas of North America, pottery is the predominant non-cooking and cooking container among the more sedentary peoples of the Southwest and Meso-America (Driver, 1969: Map 23; Figure 5.2) where it is used for dishes, water jars, food storage, incense burners, and burial urns (Driver, 1969:155).

The regulatory effects of any lack of sedentariness are too great to permit the evolution of ceramic specialization into a full-time craft. Total sedentariness provides deviation amplifying feedback for the development of the full-time specialization for several reasons. First, any mobility, as has already been demonstrated, provides regulatory feedback for ceramic production – full-time as well as part-time, because of the amount of time in one place necessary to make pottery and the need of a favorable climate and an ecological niche that has adequate resources. Second, populations of most mobile societies are too small to provide enough demand for full-time potters. Only total sedentariness provides deviation amplifying mechanism for the evolution of full-time production, releasing the society from the regulatory effects of mobility and low demand.

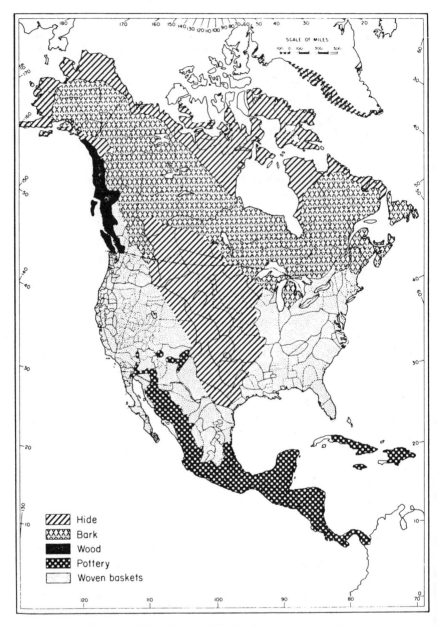

Figure 5.2 Materials used for the dominant non-cooking containers in the cultures of North America (reprinted from Driver and Massey, 1957: Map 120; used by permission).

6
Demand

Because culture consists of a dynamic system made up of interacting parts, ceramics have a systemic relationship with the rest of culture. Since ceramics are also the result of an adaptation of a particular population to the environment, they are a product of the systemic interaction of culture with the environment, and are also a channel for the flow of information between parts of the ecosystem. In this case, the information consists of water, calories, vitamins and minerals which move from the environment to human beings to meet their nutritional needs. Ceramics, in fact, make it possible to increase this nutrient flow. It is the importance of ceramics as a channel for this type of information flow which is partially responsible for the demand for ceramic vessels in an area. Besides nutrients, ceramics can also provide a channel for ideological and/or social structural information between members of the society when vessels (in shape and/or decoration) reflect mythical themes and/or are used in ritual. This new use of ceramics broadens the channel of information flow and represents a more evolved state of ceramics from their use as a strictly utilitarian channel.

Demand can provide both regulatory and deviation amplifying feedback for ceramic production. If there is no demand for ceramic containers, there is no advantage in making pottery and demand acts as a deviation counteracting mechanism preventing the development of the craft. If demand for ceramics is limited, demand acts as a deviation counteracting mechanism, permitting some production, but limiting its development into a full-time craft. If, however, demand for ceramic vessels is great or growing, demand acts as a deviation amplifying mechanism which results in the intensification of pottery making and its evolution into a full-time craft.

Demand for ceramic vessels is a function of several factors which relate to the use of ceramics as a channel of information flow in a culture. Firstly, demand is closely related to the container needs of a population. These needs result, in part, from the technological advantage and subsequent desirability of ceramics over other types of vessels as a channel of nutrient flow. Secondly, demand is related to the utilitarian and technological advantages of particular vessel shapes. This factor relates to the specific characteristics of the channel for effective nutrient flow in a particular environment. Thirdly, demand is related to the rate at which a population breaks ceramic containers and thus the amount of ceramics necessary to replenish and maintain the channel. Fourthly, demand is affected by the size, density and growth of the population. Here the channel must be provided to all of a population. Fifthly, demand is affected by the degree to which ceramic objects are tied to the ideological and social structural subsystems of culture. In this case, the channel is expanded from just nutrient flow from the environment to human beings to include information which flows *between* human beings. Finally, demand is closely related to the existence of distributive systems which place ceramic channels of information flow and its benefit into the hands of consumers.

The technological advantage of clay vessels

As a channel for energy and nutrient flow, ceramic vessels provide a number of advantages over containers of other materials like basketry, hide, wood, stone or more regional materials like bamboo, coconut shells, gourds or calabashes. First, the refractory properties of pottery permit the direct and sustained heating of water and food. Cooking using ceramic vessels makes it easier to process food by boiling or steaming. These procedures render food more digestible or palatable by limiting the cooking temperature to 100 degrees C. and by preventing carbonization of food surfaces and the excessive loss of water content. Moreover, cooking directly on the fire without using a container of some kind exposes the cook to accidental burning (Ikawa-Smith, 1976:513).

The use of ceramic vessels also requires less effort and attention than indirect methods of cooking like stone boiling in vessels of basketry, wood or hide (Driver, 1969:90; Ikawa-Smith, 1976:514; Van Camp, 1979:74). Stone boiling requires constant attention necessitating the heating of stones, placing them in a container and then removing and reheating them if food needs to be cooked longer (Driver, 1969:89-90; Van Camp, 1979:74).

The hot stones were removed from the fire with two sticks, paddles, or a pair of tongs made for the purpose and were frequently dipped for an instant or two into a vessel of clear water for cleaning before being placed in the container with the food. The stones had to be renewed at frequent intervals, at least until the mess reached the boiling point. All in all the process was more laborious than direct fire boiling, but was faster if sufficient stones were used. (Driver and Massey, 1957:231)

In contrast, ceramic vessels can be left on the fire unattended for long periods of time, permitting the cook to carry out other activities simultaneously (Van Camp, 1979:74). Furthermore, in contrast to roasting

Table 6.1 *Toxic constituents of plant foodstuffs that can be reduced or destroyed by processes involving ceramics*[1] (Scientific names of plants listed only the first time they appear if available)

Plant	Toxic constituent	Effect of toxicity	Treatment necessary to significantly reduce or eliminate toxicity	Source
Soybeans (*Glycin max*)	protease inhibitor	inhibits activities of enzymes that break down proteins	heat	Liener & Kakade, 1969
Oats (*Avena sativa*)	"	"	"	"
Jack bean (*Canavalia ensiformis*)	"	"	"	"
Lima bean (*Phaseolus lunattus*)	"	"	"	"
Barley (*Hordeum vulgare*)	"	"	"	"
Rye (*Secale cerale*)	"	"	"	"
Corn (*Zea maize*)	"	"	"	"
Potato (*Solanum tuberosum*)	"	"	cooking	Browman, 1981:112
Peanut (*Arachis hypogaea*)	"	"	heat	Liener & Kakade, 1980:34-7
Broad bean (*Vicia fava*)	"	"	"	"
Navy bean	"	"	"	"

Table 6.1 (*Contd.*)

Plant	Toxic constituent	Effect of toxicity	Treatment necessary to significantly reduce or eliminate toxicity	Source
Most frequently found in *leguminosae* and *euhorbiaceae* including:	hemagluttinins	agglutinates red blood cells[2]	heating; heating of soaked beans most effective (household cooking)	Jaffé, 1969; 1980
Jack bean	,,	,,	,,	Jaffé, 1980
Red, kidney and black bean (*Phaseolus vulgaris*)	,,	,,		Jaffé, 1969
Lentil (*Lens esculenta*)	,,	,,		,, ,,
Sweet pea	,,	,,		,, ,,
Runner bean (*Phaseolus mutifloris*)	,,	,,		,, ,,
Lima bean	,,	,,		,, ,,
Soybean	,,	,,		Jaffé, 1980
Broad bean	,,	,,		Jaffé, 1980
Garden pea (*Pisum sativum*)	,,	,,		
Field pea (*Doloichos lablab*)	,,	,,		Jaffé, 1980
Cassava (manioc) Sugar cane	cyanogenic glucoside	cyanide has a strong affinity for cytochrome	hydrolysis occurs when plant is chop-	Montgomery 1969;1980

Table 6.1 (*Contd.*)

Plant	Toxic constituent	Effect of toxicity	Treatment necessary to significantly reduce or eliminate toxicity	Source
Sweet potato beans (especially Lima bean) Yams Millet (especially *Sorghum vulgare*) Bamboo Maize Blackeyed pea (*Vigna sinensis*) Garden pea		oxidase which inhibits cellular respiration. Death results from cytotoxic anemia with the brain being the most susceptible organ (Montgomery, 1969:14).	ped, soaked in water and thoroughly cooked (HCN volatizes on boiling with lid removed). Discard cooking water.	
Common bean (*Phaseolus vulgaris*)	same as above	same as above	soaking and cooking	Browman, 1981:106
Soybean	anti-Vitamin D	interferes with effectiveness of Vitamin D	heating (autoclaving) for 60 min.	Liener, 1969
Kidney bean	anti-Vitamin E	interferes with effectiveness of Vitamin E	heating (autoclaving) for 60 min.	Liener, 1969
Soybean	metal binding constitutents	increases physiological requirements of zinc, manganese, copper and perhaps iron	heating (autoclaving)	Liener, 1969

Table 6.1 (*Contd.*)

Plant	Toxic constituent	Effect of toxicity	Treatment necessary to significantly reduce or eliminate toxicity	Source
Peas	same as above	increased requirement for zinc	heating (autoclaving)	Liener, 1969
Chick pea (*Lathyrus sativa*) Flat podded vetch (*Lathyrus cisera*) Spanish vetchling (*Lathyrus clymenum*)	lathrogen neurotoxin " " " "	spastic paralysis of legs as a result of neurological lesions of spinal cord degeneration; death may result in extreme cases	steeping seeds in hot water; steeping and boiling dehusked seeds; roasting seeds at 150° for 20 min. reduces toxin by 85%	Sarma & Padmanaban 1969:267
Soybean	goitrogen	hypothyroidism with enlargement of thyroid	heating	Van Etten, 1969:131
Tarwi (*Lupinus mutabilis*)	alkaloid lupinine	respiratory problems and ultimately respiratory failure and death	combined drying, soaking and cooking	Browman, 1981:114
Quinoa (*Chenopodium quinoa*)	nitrate accumulator; hydrocyanic acid; alkaloid saponin[3]	irritates mucus membranes of gastrointestinal tract; if absorbed into blood can cause destruction of red blood cells	grinding and repeated washing	Browman, 1981:106–13
Cycads	cycasin	not available	either: soaking for 7–10 days, sun drying, fermentation or cooking	Yang & Michelson, 1969

Plant	Toxic constituent	Effect of toxicity	Treatment necessary to significantly reduce or eliminate toxicity	Source
Common bean	micro toxins	interferes with calcium metabolism	cooking	Browman, 1981:106
Fava bean	unknown	hemolytic anemia (destruction of red blood cells)	drying or cooking reduces effect of toxicity	Mager, Chevion & Glaser, 1980
Green pea	allergens	allergic reactions	heat above 100°C	Perlman, 1980
Wheat	"	" "	heat above 120°C	" "
Rice	"	" "	heating reduces effect	" "
Barley	"	" "	heat above 100°C	" "
Potato	"	" "	reduced or destroyed with heat " " "	" "
Carrot	"	" "	" " " "	" "
Squash	"	" "	" " " "	" "
Celery	"	" "	" " " "	" "
Banana	"	" "	heat reduces effect	" "
Pineapple	"	" "	" " " "	" "
Mustard	"	" "	" " " "	" "
Chocolate	"	" "	" " " "	" "
Coffee	"	" "	" " " "	" "
Yeasts and molds	"	" "	" " " "	" "
Rye	"	" "	" " " "	" "

Table 6.1 (*Contd.*)

Notes

[1] This list includes only plants for which the method of destroying the effects of toxicity is known and for which the processes can be accomplished easily with ceramic vessels. There are more toxins and many more examples of the plants which contain them.

[2] This toxin causes a variety of problems including intense destruction of epithelial cells, edema, hyperemia, hemorrhages in lymphatic tissues and degeneration of fatty tissues in the liver. Capillaries of all organs may be extended and filled with blood clots (Jaffé, 1969:86).

[3] Birk (1969:201) says that although saponins are toxic when injected into the blood of warm blooded animals, they are not absorbed through the intestinal walls and thus are not toxic to these animals.

directly on the fire and stone boiling, cooking using ceramic vessels can maintain heat for long periods of time (Ikawa-Smith, 1976:514; Van Camp, 1979:74). Cooking thus can be more efficient with ceramic vessels because of direct and sustained heating of the food.

These advantages of cooking with ceramic vessels would have expanded the range of potential food resources. First, prolonged heat under a ceramic vessel can render certain resources more digestible and palatable (Ikawa-Smith, 1976:515). Leafy plants, for example, can be heat treated without loss of flavor or texture through carbonization or dehydration (Ikawa-Smith, 1976:515). Some plant or animal resources may be more acceptable when cooked in various combinations (Ikawa-Smith, 1976:515). Shellfish, especially bivalves such as clams, open automatically when heat is applied causing the muscle binding the two valves to lose its elasticity. Grains that are staples of the diet like wheat, maize and rice require cooking before consumption in order to be made more palatable. Second, cooking in ceramic vessels prevents loss of meat or juice into the open fire (Ikawa-Smith, 1976:514). Bivalves can be heated on the open fire, but not without loss of juices and danger from accidental burning. Third, cooking in ceramic containers through steaming and boiling detoxifies some plant and animal products making them safe and palatable for human populations (Ikawa-Smith, 1976:515). The most obvious way this occurs is through sterilizing food contaminated by bacteria or fungus (Ikawa-Smith, 1976:515). Although some toxins of mold origin (such as the fungus *Fusarium* sp. which grows on cereals) are detoxified by cooking, other such toxins are not so easily broken down (Friedman and Shibko, 1969:392-4). A less obvious way that cooking in ceramic containers detoxifies plant products is that ceramic vessels permit sustained cooking and other food preparation processes that break down and render harmless natural toxins that are innate in some plant products. In most cases, it is the prolonged heating at cooking temperatures which detoxifies many such toxins (Table 6.1). Bitter manioc, for example, contains the toxic chemical hydrocyanic acid (HCN). A minimum lethal dose of this toxin for humans is between 0.5 and 3.5 mg per kg of body weight (Montgomery, 1969:150). Both baking the resulting pulp and cooking the extracted juice effectively detoxifies them for human consumption (Lathrap, 1970:48-53; Driver and Massey, 1957:233). There are a wide variety of other plant foods that are detoxified by heating, roasting, soaking or other processes (Table 6.1) for which ceramic vessels are indispensible. Since many domesticated plants have such toxins, the use of ceramics for detoxifying domestic plant foods is crucial in many agricultural economies to maintain the integrity of the channel for energy and nutrient flow and alleviate the deleterious effects of certain plants on the populations. The use of ceramic vessels for processes of food preparation such as heat treating would thus provide a population with improved chances of survival

(Ikawa-Smith, 1976:515) by expanding the range of usable plant resources.

The difference between the wide spread distribution of pottery vessels and the limited use of pottery for non-cooking containers in the North America (compare Figures 3.6 and 5.2) indicates the importance of pottery as a cooking container. This importance is further confirmed by the widespread use of pottery as the major direct fire boiling vessel (Figure 6.1). This distribution, in turn, suggests the genuine technological advantage of pottery for cooking as opposed to stone boiling.

Second, the refractory properties of the clay expand the range of food preparation and preserving techniques not possible with other non-metal containers. Without ceramics, food preparation techniques are more limited. Besides stone boiling and direct roasting of food, stems of bamboo may be used for cooking as they are among the Perak Semang of the Malay peninsula (Skeat and Blagden, 1966:3), in the Philippines (Kroeber, 1928:45), or for cooking sago flour in the central Moluccas (Ellen and Glover, 1974:361-2). Some tribes filled a paunch of wood, hide, or part of the intestine of an animal with blood and meat and baked it in the ashes of the fire, but the container lasted only from one day to a month (Driver and Massey, 1957:229, 331). Food may also be cooked by: (1) wrapping it in green leaves and roasting it over the fire; (2) placing it between hot flat stones; (3) using a vessel made from the stalk of the sago palm (Ellen and Glover 1974:361-2), or (4) using an earth oven. An earth oven consisted of a hole in the ground in which hot stones and food were placed to cook. Food was wrapped in leaves or bark to keep it clean and the hole was covered with earth and the food allowed to cook overnight (Driver and Massey, 1957:233).

The use of ceramic vessels, however, permits a wider range of food preparation techniques than is otherwise possible. The use of pottery vessels permits toasting of grains or seeds such as the making of toasted and popped maize in Meso-America (Driver and Massey, 1957:247) and the Andes. Similarly, brewing, distilling (see Ocholla-Ayayo, 1980:Figure 60) and associated activities are possible only with pottery because of the necessity of direct sustained heating of the mash and the need for containers which will not break during fermentation and storage. Similarly, the use of ceramic griddles for thin maize cakes (*tortillas*) in Meso-america (Arnold, 1978b:338; Reina and Hill, 1978; Driver and Massey, 1957:246) and for cakes of manioc flour in the tropical forest of South America (Lathrap, 1970) permit a food preparation technique not possible without pottery. Thus, the refractory properties of clay vessels expanded food preparation techniques and hence the range of potential food resources available for human populations, and increased the carrying capacity of the habitat by broadening the resource base (Ikawa-Smith, 1976:515).

Third, food preparation processes involving pottery also enhance the

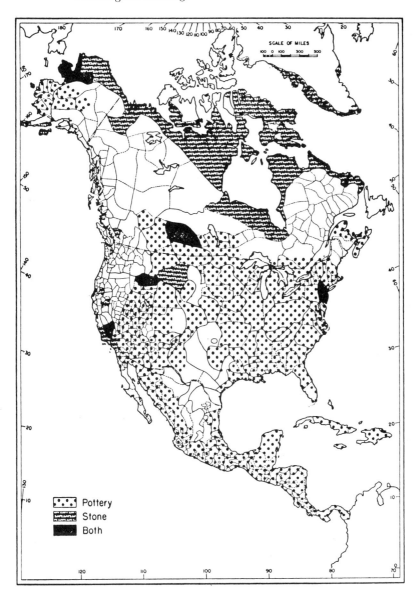

Figure 6.1 Materials used for the major direct fire boiling vessels in the cultures of North America (reprinted from Driver and Massey, 1957: 230, used by permission).

nutritive value of plant foods. The process of alkaline soaking of maize (Katz, Hediger and Valleroy, 1974) in much of tropical America enhances the amount of physiologically usable protein in the maize and increases the amount of niacin. The relatively caustic nature of these alkaline solutions (like lime, lye, soda or wood ashes–see Katz et al.,

1974) would damage containers of organic origin. Cooking enhances the nutritive value of legumes like beans (Jaffé, 1969) and many plant foods with protease inhibitors (see Table 6.1; Liener and Kakade, 1980:51). Ceramic vessels would greatly facilitate this process.

Fourth, the plastic properties of clay permit its fabrication into a wide range of shapes and sizes usable for a variety of purposes. Baskets are more limited in form and usage because of the kinds of material used and the tightness of the weave. For example, certain kinds of baskets with a coarse weave would not be suitable for liquids but adequate for carrying fish, nuts or berries, while a ceramic vessel could be used for virtually any purpose including many types of heating and preserving mentioned earlier. Only baskets with a tight weave could be used for carrying or storing water (see Driver and Massey, 1957:231) while virtually any fired pot could be used for this purpose. Wood, hide, bark and stone also have a more limited range of shapes possible due to the nature of the material. Wood could be used for an open bowl, but a bulbous vessel with a tall neck narrower than the greatest circumference of the vessel would be difficult if not impossible to carve from wood. The use of internal organs of animals such as stomachs and bladders would extend the range of possible shapes made from hides somewhat, but there are only a few organs that are suitable for this purpose and each has a similar shape. The shape range possible with bark vessels is similarly limited by the flat nature of the material and the necessity to sew the edges of the bark together to form a container. The resulting shape thus limits the use of these vessels. Finally, stone containers are practical for certain shapes and uses and share the refractory characteristics of pottery (e.g., Mason, 1966:154). Stone, like wood, however, has a more limited range of shapes than clay vessels. Coconut shells, bamboo and gourds are also used for containers, but their shape greatly restricts their use. Ceramic containers, then, are more versatile than these materials because clay can be molded into almost any shape. Thus, the versatility of the form and use of pottery vessels is much greater than that of wood, basketry, hide, stone or other materials. Pottery can thus provide convenient containers of variable shape for packaging and transportation of agricultural produce like oil, wine (Matson, 1972:212), grains or root crops.

Fifth, because of the porous walls and free soluble salts in the fired clay body, pottery can often impart a desirable taste to food and liquids during cooking or storage through the process of leaching. Rye (1976:13) explains this advantage in terms of the food residues which collect in the porous walls. In Guatemala, beans are said to have better taste when cooked in ceramic vessels than in metal vessels (Arnold, 1978b:350). Among the Newari of Nepal, clay containers provide the best flavored pickles of lemon, cucumber and mangoes (Birmingham, 1975:378, 383) and impart a benficial taste to milk products. In South America, Litto (1976:9) noted that *chicha* (a fermented maize beer) will be made only in traditional ceramic vessels because of the distinctive flavor clay vessels give the beverage. Clay vessels can impart a good taste to water and to local dishes such as *arepas* (Venezuelan corn-flour cakes), fried bananas rice, *chicharon* (fried pork) and toasted corn (Litto, 1976:9). Among the Yoruba of Nigeria, food is said to taste better when cooked in earthenware pots (Wahlman, 1972:335). In Spain, cooks and potters alike claim that ceramic vessels season and impart a distinct flavor to food (Reese, 1974:28). In India, ceramic cooking pots are preferred by an overwhelming number of families in the state of Orissa because of the taste they impart to rice (Behura, 1978:229). Even cooks in industrial societies recognize that cooking in clay pots imparts a desirable flavor to food (Hay, 1973:3).

The taste of food is sometimes an important and tenaciously held value in cultures and has been known to inhibit cultural change (e.g., Foster, 1962:76). This value not only sustains demand for cooking vessels, but is is one factor that mitigates the replacement of cooking pottery with metal pots in societies in the modern world.

Sixth, the porosity and subsequent permeability of fired pottery allows seepage through the vessel walls, permitting evaporation on the external surface of the pot, removing the heat and thus cooling the liquid in the container (Linné, 1925:63-6; Shepard, 1956:126-7). This characteristic of pottery makes it an ideal storage container for water in hot climates like the eastern Mediterranean (e.g., Matson, 1974:347; Matson, 1972:212; Birmingham, 1967:35), India (Gupta, 1966:73; Behura, 1967:37), Mexico (Charlton and Katz, 1979:47; Whitaker and Whitaker, 1978:64; Van de Velde and Van de Velde, 1939:36, 40), South America (Linné, 1925:63-6), Burma (Henderson et al., 1971:118) and the hotter regions of Guatemala (Reina and Hill, 1978:199) where the water cooling properties of ceramic vessels are recognized and greatly appreciated. Dry climates with low relative humidity enhance evaporation from the surface and cool the water more than in wet humid areas.

This advantage also provides the basis for resistance to massive technological change such as metal pots and centralized municipal water systems. In Ticul (Yucatan), Mexico, for example, the installation (between 1965 and 1970) of a central piped water supply did not eliminate the need for water storage pots. Since water pipes were laid near the ground surface, the hot tropical climate consistently produced warm tap water. In order to obtain cool drinking water, local inhabitants removed water from the tap and placed it in large ceramic storage vessels. Similarly, inhabitants on the Greek island of Andros retained limited use of water storage jars even with the cheapness and availability of plastic and aluminium vessels and the expansion of piped water systems (Birmingham, 1967:35).

Sometimes porosity may be excessive and the vessel walls will have enough permeability to allow liquids to move through them. Glazing, slipping and the use of organic liquids, however, give the potter more control over the porosity and permeability of the pottery. Glazing (Birmingham, 1967:35) seals the pores of pottery inhibiting its permeability to fluids (e. g., Hodges, 1964:42-53; Litto, 1976:152; Casson, 1938:469), making pottery an ideal vessel for liquids. Slipping of the pottery with clay or other inorganic material like lime (Tufnell, 1961:31) also accomplishes this to a lesser extent (Linné, 1925:125) but may still permit some permeability. Sometimes the addition of organic liquids on the interior or exterior of the pot after firing (e.g., Solheim and Shuler, 1959:4) can help decrease porosity when it is not desired (Shepard, 1956:191; Rye, 1976:119).

There is a great diversity in controlling porosity in this manner. At Amotag, on the island of Masbate in the Philippines, pots are coated with the sap of a local tree to decrease porosity (Solheim, 1952a:51). Linné (1925:148), Shepard (1956:93), Thompson (1958:99-100) and Ellen and Glover (1974:357) note similar practices for South America, the Southwest, Yucatan (Mexico) and the Central Moluccas respectively. The placement of salt and coconut milk inside the newly fired vessels at Makabog on the island of Masbate, Philippines, also decreases porosity (Solheim, 1952a:52). Coconut milk alone is used for this purpose on Panaeati Island, east of Papua New Guinea (Tindale and Bartlett, 1937:161). Farabee (1924) noted the use of cassava (manioc) juice for a similar purpose among the central Caribs of Brazil. Willett and Connah (1969:138) report a similar practice near Benin City in Nigeria using a liquid prepared by boiling a large bean and a particular type of wood in water. Among the Motu speaking people of New Guinea, Groves (1960:11) reports that the porosity of water pots is decreased after firing by rubbing them with the leaves of the pawpaw or passiflora vine. Porosity is also decreased by dabbing newly fired pots with a solution of mangrove bark in water in New Guinea (Groves, 1960:17). Among the Sarayacu Quichua of eastern Ecuador, potters place organic liquids like resins, melted beeswax and juices from leaves (alone or in combination) on storage, cooking and service vessels to decrease porosity (Kelley and Orr, 1976).

All of these techniques give ceramic containers more flexibility when permeability is not a desirable characteristic for pottery. Glazing (and to a lesser degree slipping) has the added benefit of providing an increased repertoire of colors and thus increased aesthetic potential (see Hodges, 1964:42-53). This potential provides the basis for greater functional and decorative variability. Glazing, however, requires the use of a kiln and is dependent on that innovation.

Seventh, pottery has a greater permanence and durability in comparison to basketry, skin and wood in tropical climates. In these areas, containers of wood, skin and basketry are easily destroyed or rendered unusable by rodents, fungus, algae and insects (like termites). Even in more temperate climates, baskets that are subjected to long periods of heating and water soaking deteriorate quickly (Van Camp, 1979:74). The value of the permanence of pottery is reflected in the distribution of various kinds of non-cooking containers in North America (Driver, 1969:Map 23). Pottery predominates in the warmer areas like Meso-America, Central America, northwestern Mexico and parts of the South-west (Figure 5.2). In other more temperate areas further north where insects and fungus are far less of a threat to perishable materials, hides or wood are used for containers, and thus pottery does not have the advantage of greater permanence over other materials.

This durability and permanence of ceramic vessels for storage may have enabled populations (particularly in the tropics) to be more sedentary because of increased and more permanent storage capacity. Baskets could also have an important use in storing dried foods like fish because of the ventilation provided by the weave. Furthermore, some crops like manioc and tobacco that have some resistance to insects and disease (because of their natural toxins) may be profitably stored in baskets. The use of ceramic vessels, however, provided deviation amplifying feedback for agricultural production by providing permanent vessels for storage, permitting heavier dependence on stored plant foods. Water, too, could be stored for longer periods of time in pottery than in baskets.

Eighth, except for basketry materials, clay is probably more universally available than either hide, wood or stone. Obviously there must be forests to obtain wood and game animals must be available for the use of hides. Stone (such as soapstone (steatite) or serpentine) that is suitable for making containers like cooking pots is less common and is not found universally. In areas like the Chumash region of California where serpentine and Catalina steatite were readily available, stone was used for bowls and cooking pots and no comparable ceramic vessels were made (see King, 1976). Clays, then, are a far more universal resource for use as a container than other kinds of materials.

Finally, pottery has the advantage of being inexpensive (David and Hennig, 1972:24) and therefore disposable (Rye and Evans, 1976:13). Clay vessels are easily replaced relative to other kinds of vessels. Some baskets (like plaited or open twined baskets) can be made quickly and are therefore disposable whereas other baskets (like fine coiled and fine twined and coiled baskets) require a long time to make (Ronald Weber, personal communication). It is these latter baskets that would be more comparable to pottery in terms of use, but they would take a longer time to make than a pot of the same size. Thus, baskets with similar uses to pots would probably be less disposable than pottery because of the great amount of time invested in these pieces. Pottery is inexpensive in Tzintzuntzan where Foster (1960a:608) found that there was never dismay over a broken pot. Replacement was never a problem and was not a significant item of yearly expense. Disposability is also an important attribute of ceramic vessels among the Newari of Nepal. Birmingham (1975:386) found that entire groups of vessels were disposable; pots made in payment to Brahmins for priestly duties, festival pots, daily offering pots, tea pots and dishes for distilled rice beer (*rakski*) were all thrown away after use.

The technological advantages of ceramics can best be illustrated in modern communities that have access to a variety of metal and non-metal containers. The advantages of ceramic vessels are recognized in these communities and pottery is preferred for some uses complementing the advantages of baskets, wood and metal vessels.

Among the Newari of Nepal, baskets are used widely as carrying containers because of their lightness and strength, but also for the storage of dry goods, *chilis*, grains, lentils, and flour, presumably because of the aeration permitted by the weave (Birmingham, 1975:385). Metal vessels also have unique advantages, particularly in light of the disadvantages of ceramics which include fragility and lack of cleanliness for storing cooked foods. The Newari prefer metal containers for a wide range of storage, serving and cooking uses because of their long life, versatility, shape, strength, cleanliness and attractive appearance (Birmingham, 1975:385). Metal is particularly preferred for the storage of cooked food (Birmingham, 1975:385).

Ceramics, on the other hand, provide a different set of advantages. Clay vessels are preferred because of their cheapness, availability, refractory properties, strength and versatility in forming, and the flavor they impart to their contents (Birmingham, 1975:383). First, the Newari will buy cheaper ceramic copies of brass, aluminium and silver vessels when they cannot afford an unbreakable metal vessel which is thirty to forty times the cost of a ceramic pot. Second, ceramic vessels are used to provide extra pots in households that already have some brass vessels. Because of their cheapness and availability, ceramic vessels are disposable in a domestic or religious context (Birmingham, 1975:383). Third, the Newari exploit the refractory properties of clay for ceramic vessels like braziers and ovens. Finally, clay pots give a beneficial taste to their contents and thus the Newari use ceramic vessels for collecting the spirit in making rice beer, for milk products and for certain types of pickles (Birmingham, 1975:386).

In Guatemala, cast iron, plastic, porcelain and galvanized steel vessels are readily available, but the rural population of indians and *ladinos* prefer pottery vessels (even though they can afford vessels made out of more modern materials) because of their low cost, utility and availability and because of the 'taste' they impart to substances cooked or stored in them (Reina and Hill 1978:219). Even middle class urban *ladinos* will purchase ceramic vessels for preparation of native dishes (Reina and Hill, 1978:219). In New Guinea, some people prefer clay pottery in spite of the availability of aluminium vessels because of the flavor it imparts to the food (Groves, 1960:10; Tuckson, 1966:9). In the urban centers of Nigeria, there is an increasing number of plastic and aluminium vessels, but people prefer ceramic vessels because they are cheaper (Wahlman, 1972:335).

Metal vessels sometimes replace clay vessels because of their superior durability and permanence relative to ceramics. For example, in Yucatan and some areas of Guatemala, pieces of metal have largely replaced *tortilla* griddles because the refractory properties of metal were similar to ceramic griddles but the metal ones were more durable (Figure 6.2). Yet in Veracruz, Mexico, Krotser (1974:132) reports that metal griddles tend to overheat and produce *tortillas* that lack the toasted corn flavor. Similarly, metal cooking pots have largely replaced ceramic ones in Yucatan and among Plains groups of North America for the same reason (Driver, 1969:513). Rye and Evans (1976:13) also noted the decline in demand for pottery in the Chitral Valley in the Northwest Frontier Province of Pakistan because of the availability, competitive price and greater durability of aluminium pots in comparison to pottery. Among the Fulani in the northern Cameroon, metal vessels and salvaged tin cans and bottles are more efficient, durable and easier to transport than pottery (David and Hennig, 1972:25). On the other hand, uses which exploit the unique advantages of ceramic vessels that are not matched in

Figure 6.2 Making *tortillas* in San Pedro La Laguna, Guatemala. Metal *tortilla* griddles (like this cover of a 55 gallon drum) have replaced ceramic griddles in many areas of Guatemala because ceramic vessels offer few, if any, advantages over metal for this purpose and are less durable.

other materials, such as cooling and storing water, cost and imparting a desirable taste, sustain a demand for ceramics in many areas.

Although plastic vessels offer an advantage of durability, ceramic vessels are superior in other ways. In recent years, for example, plastic water carrying vessels have been manufactured in Guatemala, but were not received well by indians in spite of their superior durability because of lack of porosity and because they heated rather than cooled the water placed in them. In Greece, Matson (1973:133-4) also noted that plastic vessels did not keep water cool, but even so were slowly being accepted when a piped water supply became more accessible to householders. When ceramic vessels offer no particular advantage, however, plastic vessels may replace pottery vessels. Matson (1973:133) also noted that plastic yogurt bowls had completely replaced ceramic ones in Greece.

In summary, these practical advantages of ceramic containers make pottery vessels desirable to human populations. As a result, they provide a demand for ceramics in a population, producing deviation amplifying feedback for the origin and maintenance of the craft.

Utilitarian factors that affect demand for pottery

Besides the technological advantages of ceramic vessels as opposed to other vessels, there are several utilitarian factors which go one step beyond the technological advantages of ceramics to the advantages of particular vessel shapes. These factors affect the demand for ceramics and also provide deviation amplifying feedback for the origin of pottery production.

First of all, the shape of a vessel may be related to its utility as a cooking vessel. Because cooking pots are subjected to heat, they must avoid thermal shock if they are to prove useful for cooking. Fabricating a vessel to withstand thermal shock involves the use of certain resources discussed in Chapter 2, but it also involves the shape of the vessel. Cooking vessels are best adapted to withstand thermal shock if they are formed in a spherical shape with a rounded bottom and no sharp changes in direction. This shape minimizes the different thermal gradients from one part of the vessel to the other when the vessel is heated (Rye, 1976:114, 207).

Second, micro-environmental considerations can affect the demand for different vessel shapes in different areas. In the northern Yucatan Peninsula, Mexico, for example, the demand for water storage and carrying vessels is related to the different characteristics of water sources on the peninsula. With a karst limestone topography, the northern Yucatan has only subsurface drainage and is thus without surface lakes or streams. The only significant natural sources of water exist where the surface limestone has collapsed down to the level of the subsurface water table which varies from a meter or less in the north to 25 meters or more below ground level in the south. Until the recent advent of a piped water supply in several cities of the peninsula, communities supplemented their water from natural sinkholes by digging wells. In communities without sinkholes (like Ticul and other communities in the south), the water supply of the entire community depended on these wells.

The potters of Ticul who sell their pottery in all parts of the peninsula know that the demand for water storage vessels is greater in the northern Yucatan than in the south near the Puuc (hills) where the demand is greatest for water carrying vessels. Potters, for example, will transport large water storage vessels (like *tinajas* and *barriles*) to sell in cities of the north such as Tizimín, Valladolid, Dzitas and Sotuta whereas they will sell primarily water carrying vessels in Peto, Tzucacab and Tekax in the south near the Puuc hills. Conversely, few if any water carrying vessels are sold in the north while comparatively few water storage vessels are sold in the south.

The primary reason for this pattern is a combination of height of the water table, the availability of water sources and the cost of digging a well. With the high water table in the north, virtually any natural sinkhole would have water in it. Furthermore, wells are shallow and both easy and relatively inexpensive to dig. Probably most people can afford them. Thus, water needs to be carried only a short distance from the well to the house for storage and no special vessel is needed to transport the water. If one is used, it is used relatively briefly. Since water storage vessels are used all over the peninsula to cool the water, the people of the northern Yucatan peninsula prefer to purchase these rather than water carrying jars. In contrast, the water table in the south near the Puuc (hills) lies 25 meters below the surface at Ticul and much deeper near Peto to the southeast. Natural sinkholes with an exposed water table are infrequent and wells serve as the primary water sources. Wells are about a meter in diameter and difficult and expensive to dig, requiring a great amount of labor, time and the use of dynamite. Few people can afford this expense and thus many people must use a single well. Water then must be transported into the house from outside the house lot, using a bulbous narrow-necked ceramic jar (called a *cantaro*; see Thompson, 1958) to minimize spills. More frequent use of these vessels provides a greater opportunity for breakage and as a result, there is a continued demand for water carrying vessels in areas of deep wells where water must be carried long distances.

Topography and distance to water sources can also affect the demand for water carrying vessels. The more often water must be transported to the house, the greater the risk of breakage and thus the greater the demand for water carrying vessels. Settlement around the village of Quinua in the Peruvian Andes, for example, is spread out over a highly variegated topography stretching over a slope with a vertical distance of approximately 1000 meters. Most of the population lives in the rural area in a highly dispersed settlement pattern. Water sources consist primarily of streams and irrigation canals that flow down from the mountains and dissect much of the topography. During the rainy season (lasting about 3-4 months) discarded pottery placed under the eaves provides water for domestic use. Houses in the dispersed settlement outside of the town have cisterns which are filled by rain or irrigation water (Mitchell, 1976:32). During much of the year, however, people must walk to either a stream or an irrigation ditch. Irrigation ditches with a constant supply of water can provide water for only three to six months a year in some areas (see Mitchell, 1976), but irrigation ditches with a constant and reliable source of water during this time are still some distance from houses. The most reliable sources of domestic water, however, lie at the bottom of deep, highly eroded gorges and stream cuts. Descending into these gorges to obtain water and ascending again involves a great risk of breaking ceramic vessels. The risk and breakage resulting from it provides a demand for water carrying vessels, and Quinua potters respond to this need by producing four shapes which can be used to carry water. Much of the utilitarian pottery produced in the community and sold in local markets consists of one or more of these shapes. In recent years, people have also obtained water from the municipal water supply in the village of Quinua, but the same kind of risks are present—particularly for people who live in the dispersed settlement outside the village.

Similarly, in the valley of Guatemala, potters in Chinautla, Sacojito and Durazno produce a narrow-necked water carrying jar which is marketed all over the southwestern Guatemala highlands. The demand for the shape is partly related to the fact that the households are often located far away from permanent water sources. Some communities, like Chinautla, have a piped community water supply, but not everyone can afford the cost of a hook-up or the monthly fee. Thus, water must still be carried some distance and vessel shapes such as the narrow-necked jar must be used that minimize spills.

The great distance to water sources in this area is well illustrated in Sacojito, a small pottery making hamlet northwest of Chinautla. This area is a highly eroded region with flat table lands interspersed with steep sided gorges as much as 300 meters deep. Sacojito lies on the table land between two of these gorges, so that water must either be carried from a hacienda approximately 1 km away or from the streams in the bottom of the gorges. There is no piped water supply. Across the valley in Durazno, the situation is similar. Houses in the Durazno area are more dispersed than in Chinautla or Sacojito. Water sources are located well away from the houses. In the rainy season, mended and discarded pots catch water from the roof of the house, but during the dry season people must utilize other water sources located some distance away. Water carrying jars with their narrow neck to avoid spills are extremely important vessels for this purpose and this use helps sustain demand locally and elsewhere in Guatemala where water sources are distant from the households.

A similar effect of the micro-environment on demand occurs in the village of Bé in the Fulani area of the northern Cameroon. Although a narrow-necked water carrying vessel is part of the potters' shape repertoire, it is not used in the community. The village lies close to the river and women have to walk only a few meters to obtain water. Since calabashes are lighter and more convenient to carry, any loss of water from them is inconsequential because of the nearness of the river. The inhabitants thus prefer calabashes for carrying water instead of ceramic vessels (David and Hennig, 1972:8).

Motor habit patterns also can affect the demand for pottery, influencing the kinds of vessel shapes desired. Motor habit patterns are unconcious but customary muscular patterns which result from habitual use of certain muscles which are ultimately strengthened relative to other muscles. Any body posture that does not use those muscles is difficult to maintain and any task that requires muscles other than the habitually strengthened ones is difficult to accomplish. Similarly, tools require certain patterns of muscular use and if these patterns are not developed, the tool can not be used properly, efficiently or with ease. Tools that require one set of motor habit patterns can be used by persons who do not have those motor patterns only with difficulty. Of the almost unlimited variation of muscular movements, few are restricted by anatomical considerations. Relatively few are customarily used and these are systematically applied to a variety of situations. These habitual patterns are culturally linked, are characteristic of a given culture and vary from culture to culture. The constellation of patterns of a particular culture is learned by members of that culture, tends to be rigid and is thus altered only with difficulty (Spier, 1967:97-8). Motor habit patterns may be sex-linked due to a variety of factors (see Jenni and Jenni, 1976) such as differences in role behavior between men and women (men may never carry water pots) and sexual differences in hip width and shelf (e. g. women carry water jars on the hip more easily than men).

Motor habits in a culture are often congruent with particular vessel shapes and can create a demand for these shapes. In the northern Yucatan peninsula of Mexico, for example, water carrying vessels are carried resting on the hip with the arm around the high neck of the vessel. This motor habit pattern is reflected in three requirements for the vessel shape: (1) a sharp angle between the base of the vessel and the vessel walls so that the pot will not slip off the hip; (2) a long extended neck for placing the arm around it and holding it in place; and (3) a particular height of the body of the vessel in order for it to fit comfortably between the hip and the bent arm. In addition, two horizontally placed strap handles occur on the body of the vessel for lifting it to the hip.

In India, one potter in the community of Chirag Dilli produced a different shape of water carrying vessel for each of two populations with different motor habit patterns (Gupta, 1969:19). Shapes produced for local consumption had shorter necks and could be stacked one on top of the other. A shape with a higher neck was sold to Punjabis who came from Pakistan after the partition. The higher neck permitted the Punjabi women to use four fingers to support the pitcher while they carried it from the well on their hips.

Reina and Hill found that the shape of the water carrying jar (the *tinaja*) made in various communities of Guatemala corresponded to motor habit patterns used for carrying the vessel in large areas of the country (see Reina and Hill, 1978:Map 10; Figure 6.3). The potters in the central part of the country (e. g. in Chinautla) produce a water carrying jar with two opposing vertical strap handles which are used for lifting the vessel to the top of the head where it may rest on a coil of cloth during transport. The two vertical strap handles also serve to secure the vessel with a rope for carrying the jar on the back using a tumpline. Most of the country carries the jar in this way. In the northeastern part of Guatemala, vessels are produced with three vertical strap handles equidistantly spaced on the upper body. This placement corresponds with the motor habit pattern of carrying the vessel on the hip so that one hand can easily grasp one of the handles. In the southeastern part of the country, potters produce a slightly different shape which consists of one handle from the rim to the upper body and two strap handles placed on the upper body. All three handles are equidistant from one another. This handle placement permits a woman to carry one vessel on her hip using the smaller handles and to place another on her head using the larger handle to steady it. The motor habit patterns for water carrying vessels in the northwestern part of the country represent a third variation. San Miquel Acatán and its surrounding hamlets, for example, make *tinajas* with a long neck and a pointed base. The pointed base prevents the vessel from being carried on the head or the hip, but instead is ideally suited to carrying the vessel on the back with a tumpline over the extremely variegated topography of the Cuchumatanes mountains where people must traverse a great distance to obtain water. Because this area is mostly limestone, mountain streams quickly percolate down into the porous limestone, and surface streams lie hundreds of meters below communities located on the slopes of the mountains. The long neck and pointed base increase the volume of the vessel and result in fewer trips to water sources, and the long neck prevents spills over difficult terrain. Motor habit patterns that involve carrying the water jar on the head (like that used in most of Guatemala) would probably result in more breakage than the tumpline pattern.

Motor habit patterns involved in carrying water vessels also affect the shape of pottery vessels elsewhere. Water carrying vessels in the

Figure 6.3 Shapes of water carrying jars and accompanying motor habit patterns used in Guatemala (reprinted from Reina and Hill, 1978: Map 10, p. 230; used by permission).

Gwembe valley in Africa have a rounded base so that they may balance easily on the carrying pad placed on the head (Reynolds, 1968:154). Water jars in the pueblo of Santo Domingo in the U. S. Southwest are also produced with a rounded base so that they will comfortably rest on a woman's head (Chapman, 1977:9).

The combinations of motor habit patterns, spatial arrangement of household furniture and micro-environmental considerations can also combine to effect the shape of utilitarian vessels. Among the Amahuaca of eastern Peru, for example, cooking pots have a pointed base, out-slanting sides and constricted neck. This shape is an adaption to the Amahuaca method of cooking which consists of placing firewood around a conical depression in the dirt floor in which the vessel is placed. Since stone or non-combustible material is scarce in the tropical forest, cook-ing pots can not be easily be raised above the fire. This shape thus eliminates the need for rocks or ceramic pot supports to raise the cooking vessels above the fire. By way of contrast, the Amahuaca community of Chumichinía lives in houses with platforms to permit use of mosquito nets and provide refuge from flooding. There, cooking pots have a flat rather than a conical base and are ideally suited for placing on the fire on the house platform (Dole, 1974:152). Cooking pottery in Madang, New Guinea also has a pointed base for stabilizing the pot between three stones during cooking (Kakubayashi, 1978:138).

The demand for certain shapes is often tied to economic values in a community. Among the Quechua in the Peruvian Andes, for example, most of the repertoire of utilitarian shapes is associated with maize agriculture. Ceramic vessels are used for general cooking and for car-rying water, but more utilitarian shapes are used for cooking and prepar-ing maize than for any other single crop. In contrast to a wide variety of other cultigens available, like a variety of root crops, maize is highly valued because it can be stored for longer periods of time than root crops (Murra, 1973). It is probably the most important single protein source (William Mitchell, personal communication) and is prepared in several ways. Fresh unshelled maize (*choclo*) or kernels of shelled maize (*mote*) can be boiled. Maize kernels can be toasted (*camcha*) and certain types can be popped. Finally, maize can be prepared as a fermented drink called *chicha*. There are two kinds of maize *chicha*, a fermented kind made of germinated corn and a nonfermented kind made of dark red or purple maize. A third type of *chicha* is not made from maize, but is made by fermenting the small fruits of the pepper tree (*molle*). Maize *chicha* is important for religious rituals and these rituals reinforce the high value placed on maize (Murra, 1973).

These uses of maize require preparation techniques which are associ-ated with particular ceramic vessels. Cooking pots are used for the preparation of *choclo* and *mote*. Several variations of ceramic toasters (*toqto*) are used for toasting and popping maize, while brewing *chicha* requires two large ceramic vessels (*maqma* and *urpu*) which can also be used for general storage. *Chicha* is stored and transported in tall, narrow-mouthed jars (*tumin*) to avoid spilling (Figure 6.4). Both wide- and narrow-mouthed pitchers can be used for serving *chicha* as well as water.

The same relationship between traditional ceramics and preparation techniques of highly valued food is evident in highland Guatemala. Maize is the most important crop in the traditional diet in Guatemala and it is elaborately classified (Butler and Arnold, 1977), reinforcing its

Figure 6.4 A *chicha* vendor at the Sunday Market in Urcos, Peru. *Chicha* is transported in the large narrow-necked vessel (pictured here) which is made in the Raqchi area (see Chapter 8) approximately 60 km south of Urcos. The pitchers are used for dispensing *chicha* from the larger vessel into the glasses on the table.

position as a highly valued crop. It is a staple of the diet, with some maize product eaten at every meal and regular between-meal snacks (Henne, 1977). As in the Andes, specific vessel shapes are associated with specific maize preparation techniques. Ceramic vessels are used to soak corn in lime water (the *apaste*) and this alkali processing enhances the nutritional quality of the maize by increasing the niacin and usable amino acids (Katz et al., 1974). Ceramic *comals* serve as griddles for making thin corn cakes (*tortillas*) and ceramic vessels are used for making *tamales* (a meat-filled corn cake). A similar relationship between maize and ceramic vessels also occurs among the Tajín Totonac (Kelley and Palerm, 1952:214-15) and this pattern is probably wide spread in Meso-America. Thus, a strong relationship exists between specific ceramic vessels and the economic values of growing and processing of food in domestic contexts (Reina and Hill, 1978:204).

Non-utilitarian factors that affect demand

The utilitarian advantages of ceramics created a demand which provided a deviation amplifying mechanism for the original development of pottery. Besides the technological and utilitarian advantages of ceramics, there were three other processes that created demand for ceramics.

The first factor that affects demand is the rate at which people break their pottery. Breakage rates vary a great deal from society to society and vary according to shape. There are, however, several principles (derived from Foster, 1960a) of ceramic longevity which provide a guide for the relative demand for vessels based on breakage rates.

Table 6.2 *Pottery life expectancies in Tzintzuntzan[1]*
(Data from Foster, 1960a; ages in years by household (number of vessels))

Household	Otilia Zevala	Micaela Gonzalez	Carmen Pena	Concepción Tzintzun	Mean Age	N=
Vessel						
Large casserole (not in daily use)	5.0(1)	8.0(1)			6.5	2.0
Smaller casserole (daily use)	0.5(2)	0.75(1)	2.0(1), 0.5(1), 0.25(1)	1.5(1), 3.0(1)	1.13	8.0
Plates				0.5(2)	0.5	2.0
Fiesta cups	10.0(3)				10	3.0
Water storage jars	12.0(2)	2.0(1)	0.5(1)	5.0(1)	6.3	5.0
Cooking vessels			0.5(5)		0.5	5.0
small	0.33-1.0(8)				-	-
large			40.0-50.0(1)		-	-
Milk boiling pot		1.0(1)			1.0	1.0
Pot for soaking maize		1.0(1)			1.0	1.0
Bean pot		1.0(1)			1.0	1.0
Water carrying pot		4.0(1)			4.0	4.0
Griddle for fiestas			0.5(1)		0.5	1.0
Cups for drinking chocolate				1.0(2)	1.0	2.0

Notes

[1] Only precise data are included – not statements like 'a variety of small cooking p‹ range from new to 2 1/2 years old' or 'other pottery pieces not in daily use w‹ estimated at from one month to 6 or 7 years old' (Foster, 1960a:607).

The first principle involves the strength of the vessel. Vessels without glaze and fired at a lower temperature without a kiln are weaker and break more often than glazed, kiln-fired vessels (Foster, 1960a). Furthermore, friable vessels with an excess or the wrong kind (see Chapter 2) of non-plastic materials also have lesser strength. The relative weakness of Tarahumara cooking pottery, for example, is probably the reason that some of Pastron's (1974:109) informants reported that it broke on the fire.

The second principle of ceramic longevity involves the frequency with which people use particular shapes. Generally, those vessels which are used more frequently have shorter lives than those which are not used as frequently. In Tzintzuntzan, Foster (1960a:608) noted that griddles, cooking vessels and bean pots in daily use have the shortest life of all while service ware such as plates, cups and casseroles last a little longer (Table 6.2). Pottery used only for fiestas will last a long time. Among the Shipibo-Conibo (DeBoer, 1974; DeBoer and Lathrap, 1979), vessels in daily use such as food bowls, beer mugs and medium cooking pots have the shortest life (Table 6.3). Among the Kalinga in the Philippines, cooking vessels used daily have the shortest life (Longacre, 1981:63-4). Similarly, among the Fulani in Africa, pots used in the preparation and serving of food are broken and replaced much more frequently than those used for other purposes (David and Hennig, 1972:19).

A third principle of ceramic longevity involves the mode of use. Vessels which are movable and handled a lot will break faster than vessels which are not as movable and more stationary. The greatest cause of breakage of cooking pottery among the Tarahumara is rough handling and mistreatment, since 55.5 per cent of the Tarahumara surveyed (N=27) said that cooking pottery broke by being dropped or having something dropped on it (Pastron, 1974:109). Longacre (1981:64) expresses this principle as 'the larger the pot is, the longer it lasts'. Since large pots cannot be moved easily and are relatively stationary, they have a longer use-life while more movable smaller pots have a shorter life. Movable vessels include utility ware and service ware whereas more stationary vessels are usually storage pottery. Large vessels used for storage or utilitarian purposes have the greatest longevity of most Shipibo-Conibo pottery (Figure 6.3). Within the class of movable pottery, there may be differences in breakage rates due to motor habit patterns. Foster (1960a) found that service and utility ware used exclusively at waist height lasted longer than utility ware that was used near the ground. Similarly, water carrying pots carried on the head would probably break more frequently than those carried on the back with a tumpline. Although storage vessels may be used daily, they have the longest life in Tzintzuntzan (Foster, 1960a) and among the Fulani (David and Hennig, 1972). In Tzintzuntzan, water storage vessels are placed in a frame and are located in a protected area of the kitchen.

Table 6.3 *Age in years of various kinds of vessels in Shipibo, Kalinga and Fulani societies*

	Shipibo/Conibo (DeBoer and Lathrap, 1979:128) Median age in years	Kalinga (Longacre, 1981:63–4)	Fulani (David & Hennig, 1972) Median age in years
Food bowl	.31[1]	-	2.7
Beer mug	.24[1]		
Small cooking pot (for preparing medicines)	1.13		2.7
Cooking pot	.88[1]	2–3[1]	2.5
Large cooking vessel (brewing beer)	1.38	9–10 (cooking)	10.2 (cooking/ storage)
Beer carrying jar	.75		
Ceramic Kiln	1.00		
Canteen	.71		
Water carrying jar	.78	10–15	
Beer/wine storage vessel	1.13	~30	12.5 (storage)

Note

[1] Daily use

Among the Fulani, storage vessels have a fixed position in the hut. Relatively stationary storage vessels exist in other societies and even though breakage rates are not known, these vessels would be expected to last a long time. In Ticul, Yucatan, for example, water storage vessels such as *tinajas* and *barriles* may be used several times daily, but their position in the cooking hut is relatively fixed. Similarly, in Quinua, Peru, large ceramic storage vessels may be buried in the ground inside the house. In both Ticul and Quinua, storage vessels would thus be expected to have low breakage rates and last a long time.

The fourth principle of ceramic longevity involves the presence of domestic animals. While breakage rates involving frequency and mode of use involve housewives' carelessness and children's fumblings (in that order in Tzintzuntzan according to Foster, 1960a), the presence of domestic animals in a household is also a significant factor in pottery breakage in Tzintzuntzan (Foster 1960a) and among the Kalinga (Longacre, 1981:64). Indeed, Longacre believes that domestic animals account for 10 per cent of the breakage among the Kalinga.

A fifth principle of longevity is the degree to which pots 'wear out' before they are broken. Among the Kalinga (Longacre, 1981:63), when the resin on the pot dissipates and the interior of the pot begins to turn white, the rice cooked in it begins to taste bad and the pot is used for another purpose. Among the Tarahumara, 18.8 per cent (4) of Pastron's sample (1974:109) of potters (N=27) said that cooking pots broke because they 'wore out' (Pastron, 1974:109). These principles of ceramic longevity provide a complex picture of pot breakage rates, but the overall replacement rate is at the lower end of the range of 2-12 (or about 3-6) domestic pots per household per year based on rather meagre cross-cultural data (see Table 6.4).

Second, population size, density and growth can act as either a regulatory or a deviation amplifying mechanism. Small, isolated societies of low population size, density and growth would have little demand for ceramics. The craft would be limited to making utilitarian pottery and the low density and isolation of these communities would mean great distances to nearby groups, little contact between groups and thus little or no demand for ceramic vessels outside the local community. Demand would be limited to replacing the broken vessels (see Table 6.4). Thus, in societies characterized by mechanical solidarity and hence no part-time or full-time specialists, demand would be a regulatory factor limiting the production of pottery to the few pots necessary to replace the vessels broken in one's own household.

Table 6.4 *Yearly replacement of pots per household*

Pots replaced per year	Group	Location	Reference
3.14	Fulani	North Cameroon	David & Hennig, 1972:20
6–12	Kalinga	Philippines	Longacre, 1981:63
4[1]	Ajamoentenu	East Highlands, New Guinea	Watson, 1955:126
3 (average house)[2]	Siuai	Solomon Islands	Oliver, 1967:297
2–5[3]	Tarahumara	Mexico	Pastron, 1974:108

Notes

[1] Based on the figure of three pots broken during an eight months' stay.

[2] 7–8 pots are used yearly if the household contains a feast-giving leader.

[3] New pots made each year to replace broken ones.

To act as a deviation amplifying mechanism, population size and density would have to increase, but the relationship is not direct or immediate. Population growth would not result in a significant increase in demand until the number of households (as opposed to the number of people) increased. Population growth through a rise in fertility would not be reflected in an increase in demand until a generation later when children grew up and formed their own households and needed pots for them. Even in a generation, however, the demand for pottery probably would not increase significantly enough to produce deviation amplifying feedback. With more mouths to feed, however, and increased vessel breakage because of the presence of children, there may be some increase in demand for service ware in a household.

Even with the establishment of new households, however, the increase in demand from population growth through natural fertility may not be significant. If newly married couples were absorbed into existing households (by means of virtually any residence pattern that required newly married couples to live in the same household as an older and more established family), the increase in demand would also be for service ware. Even so, family members may eat at different times (like males eating at a different time than females) using the same eating utensils and thus the family may not require any additional vessels. Demand, then, would be very limited even with population growth and even if it existed, it probably could be absorbed by the already existing potters. In many small societies, however, cultural factors existed (such as infanticide, restricted marriage rules or delayed marriages) that checked population growth so that growth in demand for ceramic vessels would not occur through population growth alone.

Increase in population size in itself may thus ultimately provide some increase in demand, but it is unlikely that it was sufficient to create deviation amplifying feedback that led to the evolution of full-time ceramic specialization until a specific threshold was reached. With a yearly replacement rate of three to six pots a year per household, increase in population size probably did not create significant deviation amplifying feedback for ceramic specialization until communities which used the pottery reached a threshold population of about 1000, when the number of new pots needed per year would probably be in the hundreds.

It is not so much the increase in the number of people that creates the deviation amplifying feedback for pottery making, but an increase in the number of households. The creation of another household independent of an already existing household would mean an increase in demand for the entire repertoire of household pots (Table 6.5) which would increase the demand for pottery from 2 to 15 times the rate for the yearly replacement of utilitarian pots alone. Thus, any process that resulted in an increased number of households (like settlement nucleation and

Table 6.5 *Number of pots per household*

Group	Number of pots per household	N=	Reference
Shipibo-Conibo	18.7	18	DeBoer and Lathrap, 1979:122–3
Tarahumara	7–19 (7–8 minimum number needed per household)	–	Pastron, 1974:108–9
Tzintzuntzan	60.8	3	Foster, 1960a:607
Fulani	20.9 (S.D.=8.6)	15	David and Hennig, 1972:17

urbanization) would create a demand for ceramic vessels that would create deviation amplifying feedback that would lead eventually to full-time specialization.

The third and probably most important factor that increased demand for ceramic specialization was the cultural changes brought about by the innovation of new uses for ceramics. In some cases the introduction of new shapes for utilitarian uses had a deviation amplifying effect on ceramic production. This new use for ceramics broadened the channel for information flow in a culture. For example, the use of ceramic vessels for sugar molds and for draining off molasses in the sugar plantations in Barbados provided deviation amplifying feedback for a plantation-based industry oriented primarily to sugar production after the craft was introduced in the seventeenth century (Handler, 1963a). This demand continued until a new method of drawing off molasses was discovered in the early nineteenth century when a cottage industry in ceramics developed based on the new utilitarian shapes and a new type of demand. At present, however, with the decline in use of ceramic vessels and the lack of development of new shapes (Handler, 1963b), demand is dropping and is creating a deviation counteracting effect that may soon be total.

It is possible that new cooking and food preparation techniques would also provide such positive feedback, but these new techniques are few and would not significantly increase the demand leading to full-time specialization. On the other hand, the development of cultural changes which provided new uses outside of utilitarian ones increased the desirability of ceramic products and provided new outlets for them. These uses developed outside the technological subsystem and involved the establishment of a new link between the technological subsystem of culture and the ideological and social structural subsystems through the ceramics. These changes broadened the use of ceramics as an information channel to include ideological and social structural content rather than just biological nutrients, and provided the kick which set into motion deviation amplifying feedback which had the potential of culminating in the evolution of a full-time craft.

There were two primary kinds of cultural changes which lifted the restriction of ceramics to utilitarian uses and provided a new kind of demand for these craft products. First, ceramics became vehicles of expression for ideological content. The most obvious way in which this occurred consisted of using painting, incising or plastic decoration to reflect mythical or ideological themes. This change in the ceramics created a new demand for pottery when the population wanted to use these ceramics as symbols of divine or mythical beings or religious activity. This use of ceramics to express mythical themes was important in the Central Andes, Meso-America and other parts of the world where civilization developed. On the coast of Peru, for example, pottery began to reflect ideological content during the Early Horizon (after 1000 B. C. at the latest) in the Cupisnique and Paracas styles, and reached its zenith in the Moche (Donnan, 1978, Sharon and Donnan, 1974) and Nazca (e.g., Roark, 1965; Proulx, 1968) styles during the Early Intermediate Period (200 B. C.–A. D. 600). This development began in the Ayacucho Basin in the southern highlands of Peru not later than the beginning of the Middle Horizon (about A. D. 600). The impetus for using elaborate ceramic decoration as a vehicle for ideological content in the Ayacucho Basin came from Nazca on the south coast of Peru where ceramics had been used in this manner since the first millennium B. C. (the Paracas style, see Menzel, Rowe and Dawson, 1964). The contact with Nazca then pre-adapted the Ayacucho population to use ceramics as a vehicle for the religious expression that came subsequently from the site of Tiahuanaco in the Titicaca Basin. This influence from Tiahuanaco co-existed with development of the Huari state.

The innovation of relating ceramics and ideology is found in the modern pottery making community of Quinua in the Ayacucho Valley, Peru, where potters still produce some traditional ceramics that reflect mythical themes. One such vessel is the *ukumari*, a legendary half human/half bear with exceptional strength who lives in caves in the jungle and captures men or women (depending on the sex of the *ukumari*) in order to have sexual relations with them. The use of pottery as vehicles for ideological content is also found in other contemporary pottery making communities. The expression of mythical themes is found in south India where potters make images of the gods (Dumont, 1952:Figure 3). Among the Yoruba of Nigeria, special pottery decorated with mythical symbols in high relief is made for local deities (Wahlman, 1972:342-4). Similarly, some pottery made for tourists in Acatlán, Mexico, reflects mythical symbols such as toads which bring good luck (Lackey, 1982:80).

The second kind of cultural change of an ideological nature that accelerated demand for ceramics consisted of using ceramics for certain practices of an ideological nature such as ritual and ceremony. There are a number of examples of using ceramics for ritual in contemporary cultures throughout the world. Among the Yako of the Cross River area of eastern Nigeria, pottery is used in ritual by the male lineage head (Forde, 1964:68). The Yoruba of Nigeria have special pottery which is used in ritual (Wahlman, 1972:342-4). Similarly, the Luo of the Sudan have special ritual pots for rain making ceremonies and the announcement of twins (Ocholla-Ayayo, 1980:117, Figure 48). The inhabitants of the Gwembe Valley have special small undecorated bowls for ritual use which are hung at hunting shrines and/or graves or at the rain shrine (Reynolds, 1968:159). In India, ritual pots are used for marriage, death and other ceremonial occasions (Behura, 1967:32, 35).

There are several classes of ritual vessels. First, there is the use of ceramics for ritual offerings. In Yucatan, for example, small ceramic serving dishes are used to make houshold offerings of food to the spirits of dead relatives during the All Saints' Day festivities. Similarly, ceramic censers are used in household *novenas* (nine nights of ritual prayers recited in memory of a saint or relative) in Yucatan and were also used by the ancient Maya of that region during the late prehistoric period (Smith, 1971). Reina and Hill (1978:240) also report the widespread use of ceramic censers for personal ritual performed by specialists in Guatemala. Household censers are also made and used among the Tajín Totonac (Kelley and Palerm, 1952:215). Among the Newari of Nepal, ceramic offering vessels include small lamps for oil, bowls for incense and small offering pots and saucers (Birmingham, 1975:386).

A second ritual use of ceramics is their use for musical instruments. The ancient Moche and Pucara cultures of Peru, for example, used ceramic trumpets. Drums made with hide stretched over a ceramic base are used among the Tuareg of the Sahara in north Africa (Hambly, 1937:450) and made with parchment stretched over the ceramic base in the northwest provinces of India (Dobbs, 1897:2). Ceramic pot drums are used among the Ibibio, Ibo and other groups in Nigeria (Nicklin, 1973a; Jeffreys, 1940:116-7; see Figure 6.5).

A third ritual use of ceramics consists of the use of special containers for ritual eating and drinking activities. In Quinua, near Ayacucho, Peru, ceramic bulls are used for the serving and drinking of *chicha* at fiestas. On occasion, specially made interconnected double pots are made in Quinua and in Sacsamarca (south of Ayacucho) for drinking *chicha* to ritually symbolize marriage (Litto, 1976:45) and fictive kinship (*compadrazgo*) bonds. Among the Ibibio in eastern Nigeria, special vessels are used for ceremonial drinking of palm-wine (Nicklin, 1973b).

The deviation amplifying effect that ritual use has on demand is illustrated by the importance of ceramics in the celebration of All Saints'

Figure 6.5 A women's choir from the town of Miago, Nigeria, playing pot drums in a church service in nearby Jos. The use of pottery for non-utilitarian purposes such as musical instruments helped establish a new link between the ideological and the technological subsystem of culture and stimulated the demand for pottery (photo courtesy of SIM Publications, used by permission).

Day in Yucatan, Mexico. During the festivities and rituals associated with All Saints' Day, the people of Yucatan offer food to the spirits of dead relatives on the altars in their houses. One of the traditions associated with these responsibilities is that the food must be prepared and served to the dead in newly made pottery. In preparation for these important ceremonies, families must procure newly made cooking pottery and serving bowls (*cajetes*). Recently, the market for new cooking pottery has lessened greatly; as late as 1970, few, if any, potters in Ticul still made this pottery. The demand for serving bowls, however, was still strong. Thus, the months before late October are periods of great demand for these bowls which are distributed and sold all over the northern Yucatan peninsula. Some potters in Ticul begin making them as early as late August and it is not unusual for individual potters to produce hundreds of these vessels before demand slackens in November. Some potters make over 1000 such vessels during this time. Other pottery making communities in Yucatan with few potters (like Akil) take advantage of this demand and also produce these bowls during this period. Thus, the ritual value of these bowls for food offerings during the All Saints' festivities sustains a demand for pottery during this time of year.

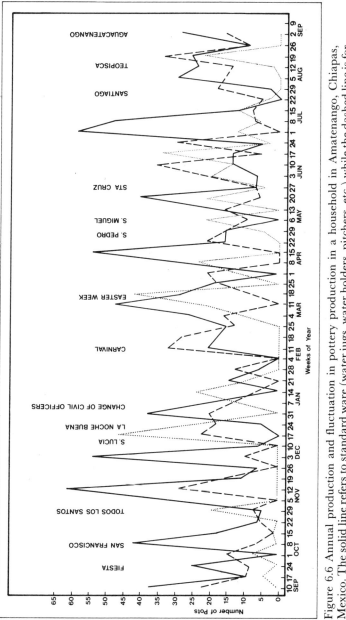

Figure 6.6 Annual production and fluctuation in pottery production in a household in Amatenango, Chiapas, Mexico. The solid line refers to standard ware (water jugs, water holders, pitchers, etc.) while the dashed line is for fiesta ware (vases, incense burners, etc.). The dotted line refers to ware that requires a special order (flower pots, braziers, etc.) (redrawn from Nash, 1961: Figure 1; used with permission of the Royal Anthropological Institute of Great Britian and Ireland).

A similar practice was noted in San Jose Peten in Guatemala. As in Yucatan, ritual food for All Saints' festivities in October and November must be produced in new cooking pots, and San Jose potters produce these vessels only once a year prior to this occasion (Reina and Hill, 1978:142). Consumers continue to use the vessels after the annual ritual, but new pots must be made before the ritual occurs the following year. Organized community rituals elsewhere in Guatemala also require the use of new vessels (Reina and Hill, 1978:249). For family rituals like weddings, new vessels are part of the social etiquette (Reina and Hill, 1978:249) as are new pots for the Shipibo-Conibo girls' puberty ceremony (DeBoer and Lathrap, 1979:135).

The effect of ritual activities on demand is well illustrated by examining the production of ceramics in Amatenango, Chiapas. Nash (1961:187; Figure 6.6) found that pottery production drastically increased before major ritual occasions associated with local religious holidays. Production increases thus occur when there is the largest demand for pottery from visitors coming to a local fiesta (Nash, 1961:187).

A fourth ritual use of ceramics provided a demand for ceramics and sustained demand by removing the vessels permanently from further use. The native's reasons for this practice relate to the ideological system, such as a commitment to the societies' social and religious system, but on a deeper functional level, this practice also stimulated the production of ceramics leading to the development of more intensive specialization. The elimination of pottery from circulation ensured its scarcity and created and sustained a high value placed on it (see Flannery, 1968b:107-8; King, 1976:303). As a result, a significant demand emerged for these vessels and ensured a continued economic relationship with potters who supplied them. This effect created a new link between the technological and the belief and social structural system and some pots became the symbols of high status groups or individuals. These ceramic symbols thus tied in with the emergent social stratification that was evolving coincidentally with ceramic specialization.

There are several ritual practices which removed ceramics permanently from use. The first and most obvious of these practices is the placement of ceramics in burials. This cultural practice occurs widely in cultures throughout the world and is often found in areas with state level organization, such as nuclear America. Sometimes the burials themselves were placed in ceramic vessels as they were in Okinawa (Mizuo, 1974:65), Colombia (Bray, 1978:53), Peru (DeBoer, 1974:340; Lathrap, 1970:158-9, 163), Ecuador (Willey, 1971:302), Argentina (Willey, 1971:218-19, 223; Weber, 1981), Brazil (Willey, 1971:411-13), on the island of Murua (Woodstock Island–Seligman, 1910:731-2), in south-

Table 6.6 *Ceramic vessels per burial by period and style in the Moche Valley*
(From Donnan and Mackey, 1978)

Date	Period	Style	Burials	Mean ceramic vessels per burial
2200-1400 B.C.	Initial	- -	0	- -
1400-400 B.C.	Early Horizon	Cupisnique	0	- -
400 B.C-A.D.550	Early Intermediate	Salinar	5	3.4
		Gallinazo	2	1.5
		Moche I	1	3
		Moche II	0	0
		Moche III	4	2.5
		Moche IV	28	9.7
A.D. 550-900	Middle Horizon	Moche V	0	0
A.D. 900-1450	Late Intemediate	Early Chimu	31	1.9
		Middle Chimu	15	2.9
		Late Chimu	4	2.5
A.D.1450-1532	Late Horizon	Chimu Inca	11	1.8

eastern New Guinea (Egloff, 1972:145-63) and in the Trobriands (Lauer, 1974:238-9) in Melanesia.

In the Central Andes, the use of ceramics in burial has a long tradition. Except for one burial that contained ceramics in the Initial Period on the central coast, burials with ceramics as grave goods began on the coast of Peru in the Early Horizon (summarized in Donnan and Mackey, 1978:20, 23) and continued through the early Colonial Period. In the Moche valley, for example, the increased number of vessels per grave lot (Table 6.6) through time illustrates the importance of burials as an outlet for ceramics and suggests that a substantial portion of pottery made in the valley during the late Early Intermediate Period was going into burials. It is also likely that this practice created a significant demand for ceramics during this time.

Secondly, the deliberate breaking of ceramics in a ritual context was another important innovation that accelerated demand for ceramics by removing them permanently from use. This cultural innovation was used in the Ayacucho valley of Peru where the broken ceramics were used as room fill at the site of Conchopata-Chakipampa during the earliest phase of the Middle Horizon (Menzel, 1964). The ritual 'destruction' of offerings of jade, pottery and gold in the cenote at the Maya center of Chichén Itzá in Yucatan, Mexico, is an analogous practice. The ritual breaking of ceramic vessels is also reported among the Shipibo-Conibo in Peru (DeBoer and Lathrap, 1979:135). At the end of the girls' puberty ceremony, vessels accumulated for use during the ceremony would be ritually smashed during the drunken brawls which culminated the fiesta. The Shipibo-Conibo (DeBoer and Lathrap, 1979:135) and the Chacobo of Bolivia (Gil Prost, personal communication) also traditionally smashed the pottery of a deceased person immediately after his death.

Thirdly, the use of model churches and other ceramic objects on the tops of houses in the Ayacucho Valley of Peru is another way ceramics can be used ritually and eliminated from further use. These churches are made exclusively in the pottery making community of Quinua. Although potters now make them predominantly for the tourist trade, local inhabitants still use them in the traditional way by placing them on the roofs of new houses (Figure 6.7) or the new roofs of old houses. When builders finish the roof, a church (or less frequently a bull or other ceramic item) is placed in the center of the roof of the new house during a ceremony. When asked why ceramic churches are used in this way, people reply, 'it is our custom.' Litto (1976:43) suggests that the churches are a substi-

Figure 6.7 The ritual use of ceramic items on tops of houses in Quinua, Peru, provides one kind of demand for ceramics by removing them permanently from further use.

tute for crosses on the houses found elsewhere in central and southern Peru and serve as 'good luck' symbols to dispel evil. Neither of these explanations is particularly helpful, but this practice creates and sustains a demand for local ceramics by removing them from circulation and is the functional equivalent of placing a pot in a burial. This demand helps sustain production in Quinua and is significant for potters' livelihood since they live in such a marginal agricultural area and depend on ceramics to make a living (Arnold, 1975a; see Chapter 7). Thus, the use of ceramics in rituals which eliminate them from further use, provided a deviation amplifying effect on the intensity of the craft and culminated in the evolution of full-time ceramic specialization. The use of ceramics in ritual and its deviation amplifying effect on pottery production probably began with the use of ordinary utilitarian pottery for ritual before special pottery was produced for this purpose.

Finally, the existence of some distributive mechanism, such as markets, inter-regional or intra-regional trade networks, expands demand over a larger area and thus also has a deviation amplifying effect on ceramic production. Distribution mechanisms thus can act like urbanization in stimulating demand for pottery. In the Andes, for example, long distance trade via llama caravans makes distribution of pottery possible over long distances (Browman, 1974).

One example of how a distributive mechanism can act as a deviation amplifying mechanism is the relationship of pottery producing populations to central places. A pottery making community in or near a central place (see Christaller, 1966) has access to distribution and transportation networks which provide a deviation amplifying mechanism for ceramic specialization.

Contemporary pottery making communities which are large producers of ceramics and exist near large cities or have easy access to transportation systems suggest the deviation amplifying role of a central place in pottery production. Two of the important reasons that pottery making has flourished in Ticul, Yucatan, are its location on the main highway out of Yucatan to the southeast and its rail link to Mérida and the rest of Yucatan. Pots can be transported easily to all parts of the peninsula by highway or rail. Tepekán, another of the few surviving pottery making communities in Yucatan, is also in a favorable position along a branch of the highway from central Mexico to Mérida and along the main link of the railway system between the state capital of Mérida and Mexico City. A similar pattern exists for the flourishing pottery making communities (like Chinautla, Durazno and Sacojito) in the Valley of Guatemala. All of these communities lie within fifteen kilometers of Guatemala City. This easy access to the capital provides a readily available outlet for the ceramics, but more importantly, this location provides access to the national transportation network and facilitates the distribution of the pottery over much of the southwestern part of the country (Reina, 1960).

Similarly, one of the important reasons for the wide-spread distribution of Quinua pottery in the international tourist market is its proximity (about 30 km by an excellent road) to the Department capital of Ayacucho and its links by road to the rest of the Republic.

Being in or near a central place with access to distribution and transportation networks also helps explain the development of specialized pottery making communities in Melanesia. Several authors have argued that the emergence of communities making specialized pottery for trade is largely the result of their central place and its access to available trade routes. Tubetube, an island in the Kula ring (Brookfield and Hart, 1971:325-7; Hage, 1977), for example, developed specialized pottery production because of its central place. Similarly, Mailu (Irwin, 1974; Hage, 1977), an island south of New Guinea, also developed specialized pottery production and expanded its trade into the other areas in late prehistory because of its position as a central place (Irwin, 1974; 1978:39).

With the existence of water transport, however, it may not be as crucial to be located in a central place for demand to operate as a deviation amplifying mechanism. The Amphlett Islands in Melanesia rank relatively low in the central place hierarchy in the network as a whole (Irwin, 1978:29), but with respect to the Kula, they are conveniently enough located to have a virtual monopoly of the supply of pottery to the Trobriands, Marshall Bennetts and Northeastern Dobu (Irwin, 1978:29). While much of the Amphlett pottery was traded in these Kula districts, the majority of the pottery in the areas southeast of the Amphletts has recently come from Tubetube and Huari (Lauer, 1971). In response to this competition, Amphlett potters have expanded their pottery distribution into areas outside of the Kula (Goodenough Island and Fergusson Island) which were formerly hostile to the Kula (Lauer, 1970:165). Similarly, the Motu of Papua New Guinea distribute their pottery widely, making trading voyages to many parts of Melanesia from the coastal villages of Manumanu, Boera and Porebada carrying thousands of pots (Groves, 1960:8-10) annually. There are, however, no data concerning the positions of these villages as central places.

Relationship to other feedback mechanisms

Because of the low demand for pottery in societies of low population size, density and growth, the regulatory effects of weather and climate do not affect pottery making in these societies as much as in larger societies where the craft is economically more important. In places where weather and climate work as a regulatory mechanism to inhibit pottery making, a potter making a few pots would not be as affected by weather and climate as much as a potter who depended economically on the craft. It is not difficult to make a few pots during a brief dry period and carefully dry and fire them without being adversely affected by the regulatory aspects of weather. Societies in the tropical forest of South America, for example, live in a region of seasonally high rainfall which effectively prevents the production of much pottery during the rainy season. The occasional production of a few pots, however, would not be as affected by regulatory aspects of climate. A few pots can be made during a dry period, then easily stored in the house away from dampness and moisture prior to firing, and then fired during a subsequent dry period. Often pots are fired singly, and at most, only a few pots are fired at a time. This firing technique is adaptive for pottery production in the wet climate of the tropical forest because it significantly reduces risks of breaking groups of pots fired during wet weather by spreading firings out over a longer period. Problems can also be reduced by firing them inside the house, over the cooking fire if necessary. Furthermore, some North American societies that were very small and lived in a climate unfavorable for ceramic production (like the Eskimo) had a low demand and made pots in sufficiently small quantities that the regulatory aspects of climate did not affect their production. Conversely, the greater the demand for pottery, the more time necessary to make pots and the more limiting the deviation counteracting mechanisms of weather and climate.

7
Man/Land Relationships

Another feedback mechanism involves the relationship of a pottery making population to the land used for agricultural production. This mechanism is not as important for the origin of pottery making in all the societies of the world as the feedback processes of climate, resources, demand or scheduling. Rather, the man/land relationship is most relevant for the development of the craft among sedentary agricultural communities, the continuation of part-time production in certain of these communities and its evolution from a part-time activity to a full-time craft. This feedback mechanism favors the development of specialists who not only make pots for their own use, but are economically dependent on the craft to supplement or replace subsistence activities.

This feedback relationship can best be expressed as a general principle: when a population exceeds the ability of the land to sustain it (and thus exceeds its carrying capacity), there is movement into other occupations like pottery making. Expressed differently, as available land or the productivity of land for agriculture decreases per capita, people will increasingly turn to crafts like pottery. This mechanism, of course, is a general one which channels people into non-agricultural pursuits, but it does not specify that they must become potters. Rather, the other mechanisms mentioned in this book (like weather and climate, resources and demand) also come to bear on the development of the craft. The relationship of pottery making to a decreasing land base relative to population operates as a deviation amplifying feedback for pottery making, causing an increase in the numbers of potters, in the intensity of the craft and in its importance as an alternative subsistence technique.

Any factor that reduces the per capita return from agricultural land would set this deviation amplifying mechanism into operation. These 'kicks' fall into two major categories: (1) an increase in population with no increase in the amount or the productivity of agricultural land that is necessary to sustain the population, and/or (2) a decrease in the carrying capacity of the land base without a corresponding decrease in population. Both of these categories produce population pressure.

First of all, population growth with no increase in the amount of

168

agricultural land can produce dramatic population pressure. Population growth is a universal tendency among human societies. Whether this growth of population is realized, however, depends upon the balance of cultural and non-cultural factors like disease, warfare, and starvation (Dumond, 1965:320; 1972). Generally disease and warfare are insufficient in limiting population growth (Dumond, 1965:320). As groups expand, however, they put pressure on resources, causing great cultural changes (Dumond, 1965; 1972; Boserup, 1965; Spooner, 1972; Harner, 1970; Cohen, 1977) that are important in cultural evolution. Population growth and pressure, for example, stimulate cultural expansion and population migration and may also result in the intensification of agricultural practices (Boserup, 1965; Carneiro, 1970). This process makes more land available for agriculture, improves the productivity of existing land and results in increased food production which will in turn support a larger population (Dumond, 1965:320). Population pressure was one factor, for example, that produced intensification of agricultural practices from swidden to wet-rice agriculture in Indonesia (Geertz, 1968:32-7) and thus permitted the absorption of greater numbers of people. It was one factor that led to the development of terracing in Chiapas, Mexico (Turner, 1977) and to intensified agricultural practices in the towns around Lake Atitlán in Guatemala since 1945 (Hinshaw, 1975:150-1). (Hinshaw (1975:150-1) found that responses to population pressure included both manipulation of the resource base and population adjustments. Population adjustments included controlling frequency and number of births. Changes in the resource base included agricultural intensification and reduced consumption. Reduction in consumption involved: (a) a reduction in expenditure for ceremonial purposes and drinking as reflected in experimentation with alternative religious affiliations; (b) increased reliance on education for more lucrative employment; and (c) resorting to coastal migratory labor and military service.)

Other results of population pressure permit greater population growth. While population growth is favorable for social centralization and the tightening of social organization, social centralization also provides a stimulus to further population growth through increased stability and internal peace (Dumond, 1965). Population growth thus provides deviation amplifying feedback for cultural development because certain aspects of this development (like political centralization) increase the potential to absorb greater numbers of people.

When cultural development is impossible, population increases threaten the survival of a society and either of two choices must be made: limit the population or accept a lower living level with the threat of possible starvation (Dumond, 1965:320). Many societies have chosen the former and have built in regulatory mechanisms like infanticide, taboos in sexual relations and restrictive marriage rules which limit the growth of population (e.g., Meggers, 1971:103-10). These mechanisms commonly exist in environments where small populations are necessary to ensure the survival of the society. Small populations of limited size and growth, however, also affect cultural evolution by having less drive toward cultural complexity (Dumond, 1965:320).

The second kind of kick that can create population pressure is a decrease in the carrying capacity of the land. This can occur as the result of erosion of good agricultural land or by climatic change. Erosion has several adverse effects. First, it can completely destroy agricultural land by stream cutting. Second, it can decrease the fertility of the land by removing nutrient-rich top soil. Third, erosion can lower the water sources in irrigation systems, making agricultural land increasingly inaccessible to irrigation with the available technology. Decline in productivity inevitably results, along with possible population pressure.

The relationship between erosion and population pressure can be mediated by other factors. Decrease in fallow time due to increased population pressure can create the potential for erosion. On sloping terrain, the use of fallowed land for grazing can increase erosion potential. In the vicinity of Coyá, San Miguel Acatán in Guatemala, for example, grazing on fallowed land has reduced the vegetation cover and increased its potential for erosion. The result is a significant destruction of agricultural land.

Climatic change may reduce the productivity of the land per capita and produce population pressure. In the Andes, for example, where frost-sensitive maize agriculture is adapted to high altitude because of irrigation (Mitchell, 1976), a change in the number of frost free days could have drastic effects on the carrying capacity by lowering the upper limit of maize cultivation and thus reducing the amount of land for maize agriculture. Similarly, a decrease in the amount or frequency of rainfall or a shortened rainy season could also dramatically change the carrying capacity of the land.

Decrease in carrying capacity can also be caused by tectonic activity. Recent research in Peru by the *Programa Riego Antiguo* (Moseley et al., 1982) has demonstrated that tectonic uplift on the coast of Peru has caused a series of consequences that resulted in a great reduction of irrigated land in the Moche Valley. This uplift caused increased downcutting of streams and resulted in the mis-alignment of irrigation intake canals. Futhermore, feeder canals were no longer at a slope to carry water; in one case, canals which originally ran downhill developed an uphill orientation. All of these factors necessitated the rebuilding of the entire source and feeder canal system. As source canals were built further and further up the valley, the increased length of the irrigation system created more problems of seepage in the canals, with less water being available for agriculture at the end of the system. The result was a reduction in the amount of irrigated land and probably created population pressure (Moseley et al., 1982).

The decrease in carrying capacity relative to population size thus reduces the productivity per capita. Population pressure results when the population remains stable or increases and exceeds the limit imposed by the carrying capacity of the land.

Pottery making and population pressure

Besides increasing agricultural intensification and social centralization and complexity, population pressure may also lead to craft specialization like pottery making. The importance of population pressure and low agricultural productivity in developing and maintaining non-agricultural subsistence activities is well illustrated by pottery making communities in the valley of Guatemala north of Guatemala City.

The valley of Guatemala is an intermontane basin located in the Guatemala highlands. The chain of volcanoes bordering the southern part of the valley has produced ash and pumice which covers the valley floor and upland slopes in layers 200 m thick. Because of the friable nature of this ash, streams have cut steep-walled gorges through this easily eroded material (Figure 7.1). The northern part of the valley has been extensively cut with these gorges, producing a highly dissected landscape with occasional isolated mesa-like projections (Rice, 1977).

Seven pottery making communities (Chinautla, Sacojito, Durazno, La Ciénaga, Mixco, Sacoj and San Raimundo) occur in this part of the valley and lie on the poorest soils of the entire region. Around the pottery making communities of Chinautla, Sacojito and Sacoj, the highly eroded and dissected topography has resulted in a soil (the *áreas fragosas* or AF type) (Figure 7.2) derived from volcanic ash which is too poor to support permanent cultivation because of its shallowness, its lack of topsoil and its potential for erosion (Simmons, Tarano and Pinto, 1959:14, 33; see Table 7.1). The slope of the terrain does not permit much topsoil to form. The soil (the Chn or Chinautla-type) around the pottery making community of Durazno also has a very low fertility. This soil has formed from old igneous and plutonic rocks (Williams, 1960:Figure 2; Rice, 1978:424) and is shallow, very rocky and subject to erosion (McBryde, 1947:Map 5; Simmons et al., 1959:38). Other pottery making communities in the area like San Raimundo, La Cienaga and Mixco also lie on or very near poor soil (the GTp or sloping Guatemala-type soil) that can not support intensive cultivation because of its incline, lack of depth and great potential for erosion (Figure 7.2, Table 7.1). Although it is not as poor nor as extensive as the soils of the Chinautla and Durazno area, this soil is also derived from volcanic ash.

Ethnographic evidence indicates that population growth and population pressure have been a continuing feature of the area of Chinautla,

Table 7.1 *Soil types in Chinautla and Mixco areas of the Valley of Guatemala* (Compiled from Simmons et al., 1959; reprinted from Arnold, 1978a: 53, 55; Arnold, 1978b: 333)

Soil Type	Symbol	Dominant decline in %	Drainage through soil	Capacity to supply moisture	Level which limits root penetration	Erosion danger	Natural fertility	Problems
Áreas Fragosas	AF[1]	(erosion prohibits permanent agricultural use)						
Chinautla	Chn[2]	20 – 50	slow	low	Rocks to 40 – 50 cm.	very high	low	erosion
Cauqué	Cq	15 – 19	medium	high	none	high	high	combating erosion and maintaining organic materials
Guatemala	Gt	0 – 2	slow	very high	none	low	high	maintaining organic materials
Guatemala fase pendiente	Gtp[3]	(Eroded. Sloping Gt type soil of little depth)						

Notes

[1] CV, SA and AF type soils are areas of no dominant soil type or where some geological characteristic or other cause limit permanent agricultural use (Simmons et al., 1959:44).

[2] A soil of little depth over rock and not well adapted for intensive agricultural use (Simmons et al, 1959:33ff).

[3] Slope too inclined for intensive use (Simmons et al., 1959:33ff).

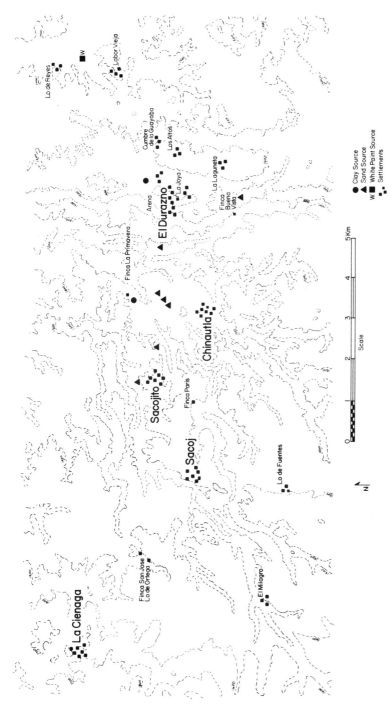

Figure 7.1 Map of the area around the pottery making settlements north of Guatemala City, showing the highly eroded land and deep gorges. The contour intervals are 100 meters (redrawn from Arnold, 1978b:Figure 1; used by permission).

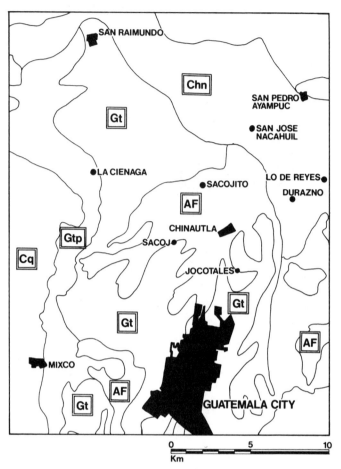

Figure 7.2 Soil map of the northern portion of the valley of Guatemala (map derived from Simmons et al., 1959; redrawn from Arnold 1978a: Figure 6 (used by permission); and Arnold 1978b: Figure 2, p. 334 (used by permission)). For explanation see Table 7.1.

Sacojito and Durazno. In his history of the area, Reina (1960:60; 1966:11) points out that the people of the Chinautla area have already faced population pressure in the past due to the scarcity of agricultural land and population growth. Between 1942 and 1946, there was a net population growth of 1064 in the *municipio* of Chinautla. This amounted to an annual growth rate of 5.6 per cent of the 1942 population (from data in Instituto Indigenista Nacional, 1948:39). Moreover, continued population growth has also been typical of the Guatemala Republic; between 1958 and 1964, it experienced a 3.2 per cent growth of population annually (Gonzales, 1967:25).

There is other evidence of population pressure in the Chinautla area. Only one-third of the families in the *municipio* of Chinautla possess land within the *municipio* (Instituto Indigenista Nacional, 1948:14). Slash and burn agriculture is the predominant agricultural pattern in the area and ethnographic studies indicate that a man generally cannot support his family by this means alone because of the scarcity of agricultural land and its poor quality (Instituto Indigenista Nacional, 1948:14; Reina, 1966:41-57; 1969:107). Thus, those families that do not have land or who have inadequate or poor land need to rely on other activities besides agriculture for subsistence (Instituto Indigenista Nacional, 1948:14). So, charcoal making (for the men) and pottery making (for the women) are important means of supplementing subsistence agriculture for a household (Reina, 1959:13; 1960:68; 1966:41-7; 1969:107; see also Instituto Indigenista Nacional, 1948:17). Indeed, in 1948 these two specializations represented the two most important economic activities in the *municipio* besides agriculture, with 75 per cent of the men making charcoal and 300 women (or 92 per cent of the women working in local occupations) making pottery (Instituto Indigenista Nacional, 1948:17, 20). This basic pattern was still predominant in 1970 with most Indian women making pottery and many men practicing slash and burn agriculture and making charcoal. The economic importance of pottery making in Chinautla is further reflected by the fact that skillful, hardworking potters will attract good husbands because pottery production is sufficiently lucrative that a potter working alone can support herself and her family if necessary (Reina, 1966:57). Potters thus make a significant contribution to the maintenance of the household in light of rather poor and insufficient agricultural land.

Population pressure continues to play an important role in the recent changes in the Chinautla region. One of the reasons that Chinautla men take jobs in the city is the lack of land available for slash and burn agriculture (a probable consequence of population pressure) and the lack of opportunity at home to earn a living or to acquire sufficient cash to meet basic necessities (Reina, 1960:74).

One of the main factors contributing to the process of population pressure given the population growth of the area is circumscription. In an area surrounded by natural barriers of non-agricultural land like mountains and deserts, population growth results in pressure on resources because access to new agricultural land is blocked by these barriers (Carneiro, 1970). Besides this environmental circumscription, the barriers may also be social and consist of groups which block the expansion of growing populations into nearby agricultural areas.

Circumscription and population growth are alleged to produce the intensification of agricultural techniques (Carneiro, 1970), but in the Chinautla area intensification is not really possible except in limited areas (like alluvial bottom land) because of the steepness of the terrain, the friable nature of the soil and, thus, its potential for erosion. The principal circumscribing mechanism in the area is not environmental since much of the surrounding land is excellent for agricultural purposes (the GT type soils, see Figure 7.2 and Table 7.1). Rather, the circumscription is of a social nature. Guatemala City consititutes a significant barrier to expansion onto the good agricultural soil to the south, but a more important circumscribing influence is the local *fincas* (farms) which lie in the best agricultural land of the region–the flat table land on the deep, rich Guatemala-type (GT) soils and the alluvial bottom land. Rather than the intensification of agricultural techniques, population pressure in this case has apparently led to specializations like pottery and charcoal making in order to supplement subsistence activities.

The role of pottery making as an alternative subsistence strategy under the conditions of population pressure also occurs in Tzintzuntzan, Mexico (Kemper, 1976:55-6). Tzintzuntzan has relatively poor agricultural land which is inadequate for the subsistence needs of its populace (Foster, 1967:37). Land is in short supply and except for limited lake shore fields of rich alluvial soil, fields are stony with steep slopes and soil of little depth (Foster, 1967:18,87). (This same pattern occurs elsewhere in the Tarascan area, where potters also live on marginal land where clay occurs (Margaret Hardin, personal communication).) The importance of alternative subsistence techniques in Tzintzuntzan is indicated by the fact that the percentage (more than 50 per cent) of family (or household) heads engaged in pottery making or pottery distribution exceeds the percentage of family heads (20 per cent) engaged in the subsistence categories of farming and fishing.

This pattern was probably established in the pre-conquest period when Tzintzuntzan was the center of the Tarascan heartland in the Patzcuaro Basin. Even in the proto-historic period, the agricultural and lacustrine resources in the Lake Patzcuaro Basin could not maintain the Tarascan population, and thus maize had to be imported through a combination of tribute and market exchange (Pollard and Gorenstein, 1980).

The role of population pressure in the development of alternative occupations besides farming and fishing in Tzintzuntzan is also evident in the recent period. For four centuries after the Conquest, the population of Tzintzuntzan stabilized, fluctuating around 1000 persons. In the 1930s, the improvement in health, and accessibility to adequate health care, brought a decline in the death rate (Table 7.2). As a result, the population has grown dramatically (Table 7.3). Up until 1940, the limited resources were sufficient to meet the requirements of the peasants (Kemper 1976:55-56). In the period 1940-75, however, the increase in population has not been matched by a growth of traditional occupational categories. In fact, Kemper (1976:56) points out that few traditional occupations except that of pottery middleman are profitable enough to permit life above the basic subsistence level. As a result, the population pressure has produced a shift to more lucrative occupations

Table 7.2 *Birth and death rates in Tzintzuntzan, 1935 to 1965*
(From Kemper, 1976:55; 1977:22)

	1935–45[1]	1945–55	1955–65
Birth rate per 1000	46.8	50.7	44.1
Death rate per 1000	29.8	16.8	8.7
Net increase in population	17.0	33.9	35.4

Note

[1] Foster, 1967:265.

Table 7.3 *Census of Tzintzuntzan, 1930-70*
(Data from Kemper, 1977:18)

	Mexican government census	
	Population	Percent increase
1930	1003	- -
1940	1077	.7
1950	1336	2.1
1960	1840	3.2
1970	2196	1.6

	Foster's ethnographic census	
	Population	Percent increase
1945	1231	1.4
1960	1877	2.8
1970	2253	1.8

and emigration to the large cities. In fact, the percentage of the population in traditional categories of potter, farmer and fisherman has declined in the last twenty-five years (Table 7.4) while day laborers and miscellaneous occupations have increased (Table 7.5).

In San Agustín Acasaguastlán, in the Montagua Valley in Guatema-

Table 7.4 *Percent of household heads engaged in pottery making as opposed to traditional subsistence categories in Tzintzuntzan* (Data from Kemper, 1976:56; 1977:23)

	1945 %	1960 %	1970 %
Occupation			
Potter	57.0	52.2	46.4
Pottery re-seller	4.5	4.4	4.7
Total	61.5	56.6	51.1
Farmer	11.0	12.2	7.5
Fisherman	6.0	5.0	3.6
Total	17.0	17.2	11.1
Total traditional	78.5	73.8	62.2
Other[1]	21.5	26.2	37.8
Totals (household heads)	292	320	360

Notes

[1] See Table 7.5.

Table 7.5 *Percentages of Tzintzuntzan household heads who are day laborers, employees and miscellaneous occupations* (From 'Other' category, Table 7.4,[1] Kemper, 1976:56; 1977:23)

	1945 %	1960 %	1970 %
Day laborer	6.0	11.6	14.7
Employees	2.0	3.1	4.7
Miscellaneous	1.0	4.4	9.4

Notes

[1] The remaining categories necessary to make 100% are storekeepers, construction personnel, and housekeepers – all of which fluctuated during the same period.

la, limited agricultural land and population pressure have produced a revival of pottery making (Reina and Hill, 1978:148). Land is poor and dry, rain is unpredictable, and if there is no rain, agricultural effort is wasted. If, however, the land does deliver one crop, fields must be left fallow for many years. Because of these factors, adults in the community make pottery in order to supplement their meagre and precarious subsistence activities (Reina and Hill, 1978:148).

Chatterjee (1975) noted population pressure as contributing to pottery making on the Island of Chowra. Chowra lies among the Nicobar Islands in the Indian Ocean and is the most densely populated of the group (Mathur, 1967:14). With a population of 1228 between 1964 and 1966 and an area of 10.7 square km, Chowra has a population density of 114.1 persons per square km. Chowra has neither enough coconut trees nor any other means of sustaining its economy, so the people of the island make pottery and canoes and export them in order to obtain food (Mathur 1967:14).

Population pressure may also have an important role in the development of pottery making in southwestern Guatemala. Ten of the twelve pottery production centers (the communities of Santa María Chiquimula, Santa Apolonia, San Pedro Jocopilas, Totonicapán, San Bartolomé, Comitancillo, San Miquel Ixtahuacán, Huehuetenango, San Cristóbal Totonicapán, and Sipacapa) mentioned by McBryde (1947:Map 15) are located in the areas with the highest population density (areas with more than 75 persons per square mile, McBryde, 1947:Map 8). Only the pottery making centers of Torlón and San Sebastián Huehuetenango are located outside these dense areas.

If the population pressure is responsible for the development of pottery specialization (and that of other crafts), potters would control a land base for agriculture that is declining both in quantity and quality. This process results in four kinds of empirical phenomena. First, potters (or other craftsmen) will use land for agriculture which is marginal in quality or insufficient in quantity. As a result, they must use their craft to supplement these marginal or insecure subsistence activities.

The supplementary role of pottery specialization in a land base that is declining in amount and carrying capacity is well illustrated by the Mossi, a group of farmer-herders that live in Upper Volta. The Mossi are primarily farmers, but grow their millet on a poor, thin, gravelly red soil which has little humus and lies just over a hard layer of ferruginous rock. Hammond (1966) explains the poverty of the soil in terms of the cycle of Mossi agricultural practices, which begins with overgrazing the land during the dry season. The fields are then burned prior to planting, but the manure from grazing and the ash from burning is insufficient to replace the loss of nutrients. Each new crop of millet thus removes more and more nutrients from the soil. The lack of humus provided by decaying organic matter causes still more evaporation and leaching from the soil, since decaying organic matter holds moisture. The result is drier and poorer soils which increasingly retard plant growth. When deeper, more fertile soils do form, the Mossi remove them to spread on sandy areas in poor fields or to make their gardens. As a result, the thin topsoil is totally removed, leaving areas of useless lateritic pan that must be abandoned. This practice increases the pressure on the already poor land that remains, forcing the Mossi to abandon old worn out and unproductive fields and search for new land to cultivate (Hammond, 1966:27-8). In this precarious agricultural situation, the Mossi are also craftsmen practicing metal working, basketry, pottery making, weaving, carpentry and house building. Hammond points out that all crafts are 'important to their material well being' and given the impoverished agricultural situation, crafts are a necessary supplement to a rather precarious and marginal subsistence (Hammond, 1966:59).

Potters in the town of Raqchi, in the Department of Cuzco, Peru, also live in marginal land. There are three factors which contribute to this marginality. First, Raqchi is located on the edge of a large lava flow from a nearby extinct volcano (Figures 7.3 and 7.4). Since there has been relatively little weathering and erosion of the lava, little agriculture is possible on the volcano slopes (Figure 7.4) and lava flow because of the rocky terrain. Second, the fields on the valley floor between the village

Figure 7.3 A large lava flow (center-left to right) south of Tinta, Peru. This flow probably originated from nearby volcanic cones (center and right center) and has been responsible for creating marginal agricultural land in this region. One pottery making community, Machacmarca, occurs at the foot of the flow in the center and right center. The village of Raqchi occurs beyond the extreme right edge of the flow.

Figure 7.4 The village of Raqchi nestled between a lava flow and the Vilcanota river. Agricultural land is restricted to: (1) the areas on the flood plain next to the river (foreground) which were swampy and waterlogged when this picture was taken (April 1973); (2) the sloping areas between the village and the flood plain which were the only locations where maize (visible here) was planted; (3) the land off the photo to the left (see Figure 7.6), (4) the swampy flat lands behind the village (see Figure 7.5) and behind the large structure on the extreme right center, and (5) the volcano slopes, which are limited to growing Old World grains.

and the Vilcanota River (Figure 7.4) are periodically flooded in the rainy season. Plots in a flat depression behind the community are swampy and also flooded (Figure 7.5). Finally, irrigation does not exist in the community for several reasons: (1) the lack of water sources during the dry season in the volcano and lava flow above; (2) a rocky and porous terrain which prevents the construction of irrigation canals; and (3) the variegated topography which makes adequate coverage of agricultural land by a gravity-fed irrigation system difficult if not impossible.

The lack of irrigation in the community contributes to the agricultural marginality in two ways. First, the lack of irrigation limits the crop repertoire, by excluding maize as a predominant crop. Maize cultivation is particularly important in the Andes because of its high value (see Gade, 1975:119), wide use for making beer (*chicha*) for religious ceremonies, and relative permanence during storage in comparison to root crops (Murra, 1973). Some maize is grown in the community (Figure 7.4), but it is grown only with rainfall and its success is limited. As a tropical grass, maize is frost sensitive and at higher altitudes, the grow-

Figure 7.5 Swampy land behind the village church in Raqchi. Low-lying flat land that is not swampy or waterlogged is scarce around the village. Some agriculture occurs on the slopes of the volcano in the distance (right center), but the crop repertoire is restricted and appears to be mostly Old World grains.

ing period increases and can exceed the length of the rainy season (see Mitchell, 1976). Since night frosts characterize the beginning of the dry season at the end of the rainy season, maize can be lost to frost before it matures. At an elevation of 3480 m (Gade, 1975:23), Raqchi lies just 120 m below the upper limit (3600 m) of maize cultivation (Gade, 1975:119). For the fields on the valley floor and on the lower slopes around the community, maize cultivation is possible, but it is still hazardous because of unseasonal frosts (Gade, 1975:119). Further down the valley at elevations below 3465 m (15 m below Raqchi), the risk of frost is considerably reduced. Thus, for extensive and secure maize cultivation at Raqchi, irrigation is mandatory.

The lack of irrigation further contributes to the marginality of the land by limiting its productivity in a more general way. Even without maize cultivation, irrigation permits planting of two crops of shorter maturity, one in the rainy season and another in the latter part of the dry season when the moisture is supplied by irrigation (e.g., see Mitchell, 1976). Without irrigation, only one crop can be planted and it must depend entirely on the moisture from rainfall. Therefore, in order to supplement agricultural productivity from marginal lands, each family in the community makes pottery from June to September. Nearby communities (Machacmarca, San Pedro, Qea) have similar problems (See Figures 7.3

Figure 7.6 The unirrigated land between Machacmarca and Raqchi. Much of this land was not in production in April 1973 (when this picture was taken). The little agriculture that was visible consisted of Old World grains and root crops. The clay source used by Machacmarca and Raqchi potters lies in the middle ground of the picture.

and 7.6) with marginal lands and are potters (Machacmarca), metal workers (San Pedro) or use their swampy land for grazing (Qea).

Potters in San Juanico, Santa María Canchesdá and Santiago Coachochiltán live on marginal land, the upper edges of the Temascalcingo valley in the mountainous terrain in the State of Mexico. The agricultural land of this region is poor because it is arid and eroded as a result of deforestation. Irrigation is not possible in the region because the water level of the natural water courses (like the Lerma River) is too far below the level of the fields and because of the way in which the river penetrates the rocky ranges (Papousek, 1974:1010). In this poor area, agriculture is insufficient for subsistence needs and thus three-fourths of the economically active population make pottery to supplement agricultural subsistence activities (Papousek, 1974:1010-11, 1015).

Potters in Quinua, Peru, also live in an agriculturally marginal environment. There are two major factors which contribute to this marginality. First, potters tend to live in the most sloping and highly eroded agricultural land in the community (Figure 7.7a and 7.7b; Arnold, 1975a). The Quinua terrain consists of sucessive layers of volcanic tuff and clays. While the gradual erosion of these layers has produced the gentle slopes of the region, streams fed by seasonal rains and lakes in the mountains have eroded deep ravines in the relatively soft beds of clay and tuff, often leaving fingers of land between deeply eroded gullies. In 1967, potters tended to live on or near this highly eroded area. By way of contrast, agricultural land further up the slope is flatter and far less eroded. The second factor contributing to the marginal land in the areas where the potters live is the reduced moisture available for agriculture. Several factors contribute to this relative lack of moisture. Firstly, potters live in the portion of the main agricultural zone in Quinua that gets the smallest amount of rainfall (Arnold, 1975a:189-90). The area they inhabit is in the lower part of the main agricultural zone and adjacent to the lower montane thorn steppe which except for the irrigated bottom land is too dry for much agriculture except for Old World grains like wheat (and a couple of minor Andean crops). Secondly, maize agriculture is not possible in this region without irrigation (Mitchell, 1976). In contrast to the land up the slope, irrigation in this area supplements moisture from rainfall during the wet season. In Quinua (as elsewhere in the Andes), maize is an important crop and is closely related to irrigation. In the higher region of the community (the upper portion of the lower montane savannah), it extends the growing season since the time needed for the maturity of the maize exceeds the length of the rainy season. In the lower part of the community, irrigation supplements rainfall which alone is insufficient for successful maize cultivation. Further up the slope, irrigation can also be used to grow two crops a year (other than maize), which is not possible in the area in which the potters live. Thirdly, less irrigation water is available for land down the slope than for that higher up. Potters tend to live further from the source of the

Figure 7.7 a. The highly sloping land on which potters live below the village of Quinua, Peru.

Figure 7.7 b. The highly eroded land on which potters live below the village of Quinua, Peru.

irrigation system, and since the canals are made of earth, a considerable amount of water seeps into the soil before the water arrives at its destination down slope (Mitchell, 1976). Furthermore, the section of the community in which the potters live (Lurinsayuq) has more land to

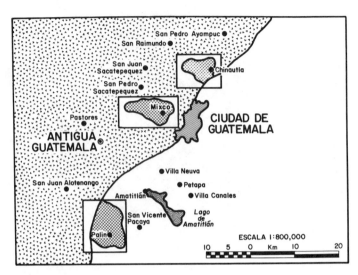

Figure 7.8 The three islands of the Pokomam language in the vicinity of Guatemala City (reprinted from Arnold, 1978a: Figure 1; used by permission).

irrigate and less irrigation water available than the other section of the community(Hanansayuq). This means that less water is available per capita in this section of the community than in the other and those that live at the lower end of the system get even less. Finally, some of the sloping, highly eroded land on which potters live in Lurinsayuq is inaccessible to the irrigation system because of the topography. Such land has a limited crop repertoire by excluding maize and a second dry season crop. Thus, land further up the slope is more productive, flatter and better watered than land located down the slope where the potters live.

Potters in Quinua, Peru, thus live in a marginal agricultural environment which is largely created through erosion, but is also a product of lesser rainfall, a reduced length of irrigation time and relative inaccessibility to the irrigation system. All these factors combine to produce a region of poorer agricultural potential than other areas of the community.

The relationship between marginal land with poor soils and pottery making can also be seen when one compares three small linguistic islands of the Pokomam language around Guatemala City: the Chinautla, Mixco and Palín areas (Figure 7.8). Pokomam (sometimes called Pokom in the Valley of Guatemala) is one of the Maya languages, and the dialect spoken in each of these three areas is very similar to that of the others, having a date of divergence approximately 1.2 centuries ago (Robles, 1962). Indeed, ethnohistoric evidence indicates that these people were part of the sixteenth-century Pokom State and thus have a similar culture history (Miles 1957:736-7; 1965). The Chinautla area has many potters and up until recently the Mixco area also had potters. (Pottery making disappeared in Mixco between 1970 and 1973. In the summer of 1970, Arnold found four potters there (Arnold, 1978a; 1978b), but by 1973, Reina and Hill (1978) report none were present.) No pottery making occurs in Palín.

The deviation amplifying effect of marginal land on pottery making in the Chinautla region contrasts with the other dialect areas of Pokomam. In contrast to the poor soils of the Chinautla dialect area (discussed earlier in this chapter), the soils of the Palín dialect area are deep, well watered and, in general, highly fertile even though they are subject to erosion (Simmons et al., 1959:33; see Figure 7.9, Table 7.6). Although clays are available in some of the soils of the Palín region (in the Escuintla (Es), Palín (Pl) and Morán (Mr) type–see Figure 7.9 and Arnold, 1978a:49), there are no potters there.

The Mixco dialect area represents a midpoint between the extremes of the Palín and Chinautla dialect areas. The soils are poorer than the soils in the Palín area, although they are not as poor nor as extensive as the AF (*áreas fragosas*) and Chn (Chinautla) type soils of the Chinautla area (compare Table 7.1 with Table 7.6 and Figure 7.2 with Figure 7.9). Soils

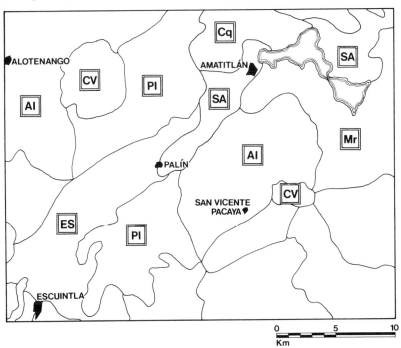

Figure 7.9 Soil map of the Palin area (map derived from Simmons et al., 1959; reprinted from Arnold, 1978a: Figure 7; used by permission). For explanation, see Table 7.6.

Table 7.6 *Soil types in Palín dialect area of the central Pokomam* (Compiled from Simmons et al., 1959; reprinted from Arnold, 1978a:54)

Soil type	Symbol	Dominant decline (in %)	Drainage through soil	Capacity to supply moisture	Level which limits root penetration	Erosion danger	Natural fertility	Problems
Alotenango	Al	12-40	very rapid	very low	none	high	moderate	combating erosion
Cauqué	Cq	15-19	moderate	high	none	high	high	combating erosion and maintaining organic material
Cimas volcánicas	CV[1]	'Volcanic cones' – no data provided						
Escuinta	Es	8-10	moderate	high	none	high	high	combating erosion
Morán	Mr	8-15	moderate	high	none	high	high	combating erosion and maintaining organic material

Table 7.6 (*Contd.*)

Soil type	Symbol	Dominant decline (in %)	Drainage through soil	Capacity to supply moisture	Level which limits root penetration	Erosion danger	Natural fertility	Problems
Palín	Pl	40-60	rapid	low	none	very high	moderate	Combating erosion
Suelos Aluviales	SA[2]	'Undifferated alluvial soils' – no data provided						

Notes

[1] CV, SA, and AF type soils are areas of no dominant soil type or where some geological characteristic or other cause limits permanent agricultural use (Simmons et al., 1959:44).

[2] SA soils have some valuable terrain for agriculture (Simmons et al., 1959:44), and this seems to be the case in the Palín area. See also Footnote 1.

in the immediate vicinity of Mixco are too poor to support intensive cultivation because of their incline, lack of soil depth and great potential for erosion (Figure 7.2, Table 7.1), even though soil within a three kilometer radius to the south-west and north-east of the community is excellent for agriculture (Figure 7.2, Table 7.1). Like the AF type soil of the Chinautla area, the GTp (sloping Guatemala) type soil of the Mixco area is derived from volcanic ash. In all of these respects, the Mixco region is identical to the environment of the Cakchiquel potters in La Ciénaga and San Raimundo. All three of these communities are located on or bordering the same kinds of poor soil (the GTp type).

Potters also live on poor agricultural land on the Huon Peninsula in New Guinea. Although Hogbin (1951) notes the importance of clay and other resources in accounting for the regional specialization around the Huon Gulf, he also notes that in comparison to other communities on the peninsula, pottery making villages lie in poor agricultural areas in which 'cultivation can be carried out only with difficulty' (Hobgin, 1951:81). Conversely, Basama, another village on the Gulf of Huon, 'has more agricultural land than is required to meet immediate needs and the people produce quantities of taro for export' (Hogbin, 1951:81). Some of this taro is traded to pottery making villages (Hogbin, 1951:70) in exchange for pots because potters must import food in order to survive. In fact, Hogbin notes that after making their wares, food shortages in potters' families cause them to travel to villages that specialize in taro or sago (Hogbin, 1951:89) in order to exchange pots for food.

A similar pattern exists in Chamula in Chiapas, Mexico, where potters are people who are 'land poor' or who live in areas of poor agricultural land (Howry, 1978). Potters tend to be concentrated in forested and mountainous areas where good agricultural land is scarce. This terrain is remote and steep and has limited fertility, but it is cheaper than good agricultural land and better for its fuel potential than equivalently priced farmland (Howry, 1978:242-3). Both men and women potters tend to be from households which possess very limited agricultural land. Male potters typically have little land in proportion to their household size and subsist by purchasing staples of corn and beans.

Marginal agricultural land also occurs in the area around the Motu speaking potters of Papua New Guinea (Groves, 1960). The Motu live mostly along a narrow strip of relatively infertile coast which extends for about 112 kilometers along a barren, sunbaked shore. The land consists of:

little more than the beach and the seaside slopes that immediately overlook it, together with some coral reefs, sand-spits and arid islets. (Groves, 1960:5)

It receives the lowest annual rainfall recorded in Papua New Guinea.

The Motu area is far less fertile than the other tribal lands surrounding it and the Motu have never been able entirely to live off their land.

Several kilometers inland, behind the coastal hillsides on which the Motu cultivate garden plots, richer grasslands watered by the Laloki River sustain the agricultural Koita (Groves, 1960:5). In the rain forests further inland, the Koiari, the Doura and the Gabadi peoples clear garden plots which yield a substantial surplus above local subsistence requirements. Although the Motu agricultural lands consist mostly of the arid slopes along the coast, some Motu do have access to good agricultural land (Groves, 1960:7). In contrast to the remainder of the Motu area, the village of Manumanu, for example, owns and cultivates rain-forest clearings on the banks of the Vanapa and Veimauri Rivers. In recent years, the Motu people in Rea Rea, Porebada, Hanuabada and Pari have obtained usufructuary rights in the more productive Koita domain between the coast and the Laloki River by means of inter-marriage with Koita (Groves, 1960:7). Nevertheless, famine has been endemic among the Motu. The yam crop often fails entirely and leaves the Motu short of food the whole year round (Groves, 1960:7). In the villages of Boera, Porebada and Hanuabada, located at the feet of arid seaside hills, famine usually follows drought while at Manumanu, situated on low-lying land at the mouth of a large river estuary, famine usually follows flood (Groves, 1960:7).

The Motu thus lack an adequate means of subsistence and must obtain food through trade (Groves, 1960:7). Although the Motu trade fish and crabs to neighboring groups, these items alone can not assure them of a regular nor adequate staple. First, a large catch of fish depresses the market value so that the amount of items received in exchange for the fish is less. Second, fish are perishable and cannot be easily transported to distant markets without spoilage. Finally, fish are not a reliable resource: people cannot count on good catches whenever they need them. In order to obtain enough food to supplement that from their poor agricultural and subsistence resources, the Motu make pottery and trade it locally and over long distances for food (Groves, 1960:7-8).

The relationship of poor agricultural land and pottery making also occurs on the Amphlett Islands which lie off the coast of eastern New Guinea. The Amphlett Islands consist entirely of lava and agglomerate. They are barren, steep and rocky (with seldom more than 15-25 cm of soil) and are thus relativley poor for agriculture (Lauer, 1970:165). Out of the twenty-eight islands in the group, only four are inhabited, with a total population of 230. Gardens are cultivated on all the inhabited islands and a number of the uninhabited islands (Lauer, 1970:165). Because the gardens are on rocky ground on steep slopes, retaining walls of rocks and sticks have to be erected to prevent surface material from being eroded (Lauer, 1970:165). Tubers never grow to a large size and the yield is not very satisfactory (Lauer, 1970:165). Although copra is produced for cash income, the inhabitants are dependent on making pots which they exchange to surrounding islands to supplement their sparse food supply (Malinowski, 1922:46; Fortune, 1932:208; Lauer, 1970:169; 1973). All girls under fourteen and all married women are potters (Lauer, 1970:165). Each household makes six pots per month with 300-350 vessels as the monthly production of the entire population (Lauer, 1970:166). The total amount of food imported for these pots is 3000-3500 kg per month with each individual receiving 13-24 kg, which is one third of the individual's needs (Lauer, 1970:169).

There are many other examples of potters utilizing marginal or insufficient land for agriculture. In the pottery making community of Bailén, Spain, the land is poor and rocky and used for olive groves and wheat. Fields are supplemented by tiny household gardens which supply a few additional vegetables, peppers and herbs (Curtis, 1962:487). Potters in the vicinity of Coyá, Acatán, Guatemala, also live on marginal land. The soil is naturally fertile, but it is shallow with rock underneath at 30-40 cm, cannot hold moisture, and has great potential for erosion because of the steep incline (Simmons et al., 1959:135). Kresz (1975:197) also noted the relationship of poor soil and crafts in Hungary. Potters in Tenango, Chiapas, explain that they need to make pottery because they need the money to supplement the products of their insufficient lands (Blom and La Farge, 1927:382). Similarly, further south in Chiapas, Amatenango potters also have a limited land base (Nash, 1961:190). The potters at Tokoname in Japan live on the barren and sandy Chita Peninsula (Rhodes, 1970:154-9). Although Rhodes (1970:159) explains the existence of potters by the excellent and abundant clay deposits on the peninsula, the marginal agricultural land was presumably also a factor. Similarly, potters in Catacaos on the extreme northern Peruvian desert live on land that is agriculturally poor due to an insufficient water supply (Spahni, 1966:19). Finally, Murray (1972) noted that the location of pottery making villages among the Ibo in Nigeria corresponded to the lack of productive soil for agriculture and thus pottery making significantly supplemented subsistence activities (Murray, 1972:149).

The association of many pottery making communities with marginal agricultural land is not necessarily a universal phenomenon. Rather, the relationship is probably due to the fact that marginal agricultural land has a lower carrying capacity with a lower threshold of population size and density than good land. With an expanding population, agricultural intensification may not be possible because the factors responsible for making the land marginal for agriculture can not be mitigated or changed with the available technology. Thus, movement into crafts like pottery making is another consequence of population pressure when agricultural intensification is not possible. With population growth, movement into crafts would be sooner in marginal land than in more fertile areas. In more productive areas, the carrying capacity is higher and can support more people. Population pressure will not occur until the population reaches a density much higher than on marginal agricultural land.

The second empirical phenomenon one would expect from population pressure is the end product of such pressure: people without land for agriculture. As population pressure on agricultural land continues, some land will become increasingly marginal (because of erosion), and increasing numbers of people will have progressively less agricultural land. Also, potters already living on eroded marginal land will experience an increasing decline in fertility and witness the progressive destruction of their land until it becomes totally useless. While it is not always possible to document the relationship of population pressure and pottery making, population pressure does explain why some potters are landless. There are several examples of landless potters in the literature. In San Nicolas in the province of Ilocos Norte in the Philippines, Scheans (1965:9) found that twenty-two out of the thirty potters he interviewed had no family land holdings and thus pottery earnings contributed significantly to their income. Similarly, potters in Chirag Dilli, India are also landless and few of their relatives have land (Gupta, 1969:21).

It is not unusual that pottery making and other crafts are a secondary choice to agriculture and resorted to by people with poor quality, insufficient or no land. While agriculture provides food directly to a family, craft production does not, but requires additional labor and greater risks than agriculture. The agriculturalist takes risks with weather, disease and thievery which may cause damage and loss to his crop, but the potter also takes risks in the forming of the pottery and the production of fired pots (elaborated in Chapters 2 and 3). Unlike the farmer, however, who can eat the results of his labor, the potter cannot eat pots and they must be exchanged or sold to obtain food. There must be sufficient demand for the pots and the potter must be in step with the demand if he is to survive. Furthermore, the potter may often have to travel to exchange his pottery and the longer the distance he travels, the greater the risk of loss due to breakage. While agriculture thus provides food directly to a family, pottery making adds some extra steps between the labor invested and food received. These steps require more labor, energy and risks than farming alone. It is not unusual, then, that pottery making, as an indirect subsistence technique, is the result of population pressure and not a desirable occupation for most farmers (Netting, 1974:40).

The third type of empirical data one would expect if population pressure was a deviation amplifying mechanism for pottery making is that once there is a better living with agriculture or more secure or steady work, pottery making is abandoned. Foster points out that potters prefer agriculture to making pots and become farmers when they have the opportunity (Foster, 1965: 47), a conclusion also reached by Netting (1974:40). In San José, Michoacán, for example, potters who acquire enough animals or wealth to support an extended family or who have access to land will abandon the craft (Margaret Hardin, personal communication). In Riotenco San Lorenzo, Mexico, pottery making is dying out because most of the men have become farmers and only the most destitute continue to be potters (Rendón, 1950:255). Foster (1965:46) also reports that non-potter husbands from Tzintzuntzan and other villages also often become potters if they have no other means of support. In his survey of pottery making in the south Indian states of Andra Pradesh, Madras, Kerala and Mysore, Behura (1967:36) found that when families of potters acquired some land, they switched to agriculture for a livelihood while others would be willing to take employment in agriculture, commerce, government, factories or cattle farming. Similarly, in his survey of pottery making villages in Orissa, eight per cent of the families in the traditional potters' caste have given up pottery making in recent times in favor of other occupations (Behura, 1978:221) such as agriculture, minor trade, government or private services or agricultural wage labor, but they generally avoid activities associated with the unclean sub-castes below them. Employment opportunities with government or private organizations are outside the traditional caste categories, but they are difficult to obtain since competition is high (Behura, 1978:222). Agriculture is also practiced as a part-time occupation by many potters because it does not affect their caste status, provides sustenance wholly or partly, and does not require prolonged training nor substantial capital investment like trade or commerce does (Behura, 1978:223). These data suggest that potters who are dependent on their craft for a living make pottery only out of economic necessity, and that when better economic opportunities exist they abandon the craft.

Another example of the probable abandonment of pottery making in favor of agriculture or other activities comes from analyses of historical documents concerning the economics of pottery making during the Middle Ages in Britain (Patourel, 1968). In the early Middle Ages, the majority of potters were cottagers with 1.5 to 5 acres of land (Patourel, 1968:106, 123). It is not clear from the data whether this amount of land was sufficient for the potter's sustenance or not, but some potters began investing their profits in acquiring more agricultural land (Patourel, 1968:107). At Harlow (Essex), this practice increased through the early fourteenth and up to the fifteenth centuries (Patourel, 1968:106-7,109). A second phenomenon that suggested the abandonment of pottery making when potters acquired sufficient agricultural land was the cessation of the payment for clay. In the mid-fourteenth century, the payment for clay ceased because no one wanted it (Patourel, 1968:109). This change may have also occured because of the high fee for clay. In Cowick, Yorkshire, England, the payment climbed so high (twenty shillings by A. D. 1373) that the potters subsequently abandoned the craft (Patourel,

1968:115). Clay acquisition probably required a fee because its excavation destroyed agricultural land (see Figure 7.6). Nevertheless, the cessation of payment suggested that either the potters had enough land to obtain clay, that land for agriculture was abundant or that there were fewer potters. It is likely that all three factors were involved since the Black Death produced a general depopulation during the early fourteenth century and reduced the numbers of potters as well (Patourel, 1968:108). At least one community of thirteen potters was completely wiped out. A third phenomenon that suggested that the acquisition of agricultural land led to the abandonment of pottery making in the Middle Ages comes from court records. At Harlow (Essex, England) during the fourteenth and fifteenth centuries, potters with large land holdings were hauled into manorial court on charges which were largely agricultural: cows and pigs which were loose in the lord's woods, the neglect of fencing a common field and the existence of sheep and cattle in the communal lands (Patourel, 1968:110). In summary, then, Patourel (1968:109) argues that adequate holdings of land were preferred to the hazards of potting at any time before the fifteenth century.

A fourth kind of empirical data that one would find if population pressure were a force in the development of pottery specialization is the occurrence of potters that are poor and marginal in the society. In his survey of the pottery making groups in twenty-two villages of south India, Behura noted that all were economically marginal or below the subsistence level. In one village, 89 per cent (16/18) of the potters were in debt (Behura, 1967:32). In the state of Orissa in east India, Behura (1978:227) also points out that an average potter using traditional techniques has a meagre income that is below the subsistence level. He is hardly able to make ends meet. In Acatlán, Mexico, potters are also poor (Lackey, 1982:41) with an income that is 'miserably low'. One family of potters in Acatlán that Lackey studied is not as poor as some, but she noted that they live from day to day and almost from hour to hour. Any unexpected expense brings great financial loss. Sometimes, the family must give up their possessions as a security for a loan or must strain the limits of credit, friendship, or *compadrazgo* bonds (Lackey, 1982:41). The economic marginality of potters is further suggested by the potters in the municipality of Temascalcingo in Mexico. Potters go to Mexico City during the rainy season to find work as *albañiles* (masons) or itinerant merchants because of the limiting effect of weather and climate on pottery making and because there is little else they can do in the rainy season at home (Papousek, 1974:1032). Fulani potters are socially and economically marginal (David and Hennig, 1972:27). The craft is carried on by the relatively poor and especially by those without a husband or close male relatives to supply them with tea, kerosene and other minor luxuries (David and Hennig, 1972:4). Thus, only women who already know the craft and otherwise are unable to supplement their income by other means become potters (David and Hennig, 1972:25).

In summary, then, population pressure serves as a deviation amplifying mechanism for the development of pottery specialization in a population, for potters' continued economic dependence on the craft and, finally, for the evolution of a full-time specialization. Seeing the development of pottery specialization as a response to population pressure helps to explain the abundant examples of potters who are landless or who farm marginal or insufficient agricultural land. Without sufficient return from agriculture to feed the family, farmers must turn their attention to alternate economic strategies like pottery making.

The relationship of population pressure and social structure

The existence of population pressure as a feedback mechanism for the development of pottery specialists is further reflected in their social position. If pottery specialization is, in part, the result of population pressure on agricultural resources forcing people into alternative non-agricultural occupations like pottery making, and people become specialist potters only out of necessity, then one would expect these potters to have a low social position.

There is some evidence that potters have a low social position (Foster, 1965) in societies with hierarchically arranged social groups. They have a low status in Quinua, Peru (Mitchell, 1979). In Ticul, Yucatan, Mexico, they are near the bottom of the social scale in wealth and prestige (Thompson, 1974:121, 123, 130). Similarly, in Chirag Dilli (India) potters have a relatively low social position institutionalized by a rigid caste system that will not allow them to rise above their present level (Gupta, 1969:21). Papousek (1974:1015) mentions that the Mazahua potters constitute the lowest socio-economic class in the Temascalcingo area of Mexico. This may result from the fact that all the potters are indians (Papousek, 1974:1018). The low social value of pottery making in this area (see Papousek, 1976) is further confirmed by Iwanska (1971:95) who noted that the Mazahua concept of human 'badness' was illustrated by one Mazahua village which gave up agriculture (which is the only 'real work' for a good Mazahua) for pottery making and made 'good money this way without having to work at all' (Iwanska, 1971:95). Potters in Acatlán, Mexico, are also in the lowest position in the town (Foster, 1965:46; Lackey, 1982:36-9,42).

Likewise, N. K. Behura in his survey of seven pottery making villages in the Indian state of Orissa, found that potters always occurred in the lowest *varna* or caste grouping called *shudra*. Within this grouping, potters were always in the lowest ranking 'clean' sub-caste grouping along with other sub-castes like carpenters, weavers and blacksmiths (Behura, 1978:32-6). In his survey of twenty-two villages in southern India,

Behura (1967:23) also noted that potters also occurred within this lowest caste grouping (*shudra*) but their rank within the sub-caste relative to other craft specialists was not uniform from village to village. In Assam (Gait, 1897:5) potters rank below those members of castes whose occupation has been traditionally purely agricultural.

The low social position of potters is not restricted to modern societies with hierarchically ordered social groups. Although solid data are lacking, Hodges (1974) argues largely from circumstantial evidence that the medieval potter occupied a low social position because of the utilitarian nature of the pottery and the fact that the few surviving craft handbooks have little to say about it.

Foster (1965) tries to explain the low status of potters by the 'dirtiness' of the work. Gupta (1969:21) also reflects this view by noting that potters in India are of a low status because they work with clay and dung–both of which are dirty. Papousek (1974) disputes the relationship of the low social position of potters to the dirtiness of their work by saying that other occupations (like that of automobile mechanic) are dirtier but have a higher status than potters. Rather, he argues that the potter's low social position is a product of the social and economic structure (like the patron–client relationship, see Foster, 1963) which exploits potters by favoring those who have more money.

Potters, however, do not always have a low social position. Potters have a high social position in Chinautla, Guatemala (Reina, 1966:33), Veracruz, Mexico (Krotser, 1974:134-5), and among the Papago in the U. S. Southwest (Fontana et al., 1962:30). Rhodes (1970:111) reports that in Japan potting is an occupation considered no better or worse than farming or vending. The high status of potters can be explained primarily by contextual factors. First, the high status of women potters in Chinautla, for example, generally results from several factors: (1) In the rather precarious agricultural position of Chinautla, any source of a steady income (like pottery making) can be an asset to a family with poor quality, little or no agricultural land; (2) since potters are women, the income that they bring into the family is extra and above that of the main breadwinner for the family since generally their time is not as economically valuable as that of the husband (see Tax, 1941:25). In Pereruela, Spain (Cortes, 1954:145), the pottery made by women is a necessary contribution to the household income. In other societies with social classes, women potters could be in a similar position and probably the high status of women potters can be explained by one of these factors. Another factor leading to the high status of potters in some areas results from the wealth acquired through their trade or from the production of some highly valued item–such as a vessel of great mythological significance. Hodges (1974) noted that the medieval Islamic potter of the Middle East probably enjoyed higher status than his European counterpart, because he produced tiles which were needed for the decoration of mosques. Likewise, Lackey (1982:37) notes several modern potters in the industrial world who have become famous because of the artistic quality of their work. The socio-economic position of potters in Japan described by Rhodes (1970) may also be explained by this factor.

Potters can become wealthy making pottery. Smith (1967:9) reports that pottery has made Yabob in New Guinea an extremely wealthy village. Indeed, Mitchell (personal communication) reports that the social position of potters in Quinua (Peru) has increased because of the increased wealth generated from the booming tourist demand for their pottery. Furthermore, potters who become artists and make desirable items can also become wealthy and achieve considerable fame.

The relationship of potters to a hierarchical social structure is thus dependent on two factors besides population pressure. The first factor concerns the sexual division of labor. In agricultural societies where men are potters and are dependent on the craft for a livelihood, it is likely that the potters will have a low social position until they begin making highly valued items. When women are potters, however, their position is relatively high because they supplement primary subsistence activities. A second factor involves the demand for pottery. When the demand for pottery involves mythical, religious or social structural symbols, potters that produce this pottery will have a high social position.

Relationship to resources

In cases where the 'kick' towards decreased carrying capacity of the land is produced by erosion, another deviation amplifying mechanism for pottery production may occur to stimulate the craft towards full-time specialization. Erosion and weathering destroy topsoil and reduce the productivity of the land, but they have advantageous effects on the development and exposure of ceramic resources. The processes of weathering not only create some clays (Shepard, 1956:10-11), but erosion, a much faster weathering process, also exposes a wide variety of geological strata which may contain ceramic resources. In the northern part of the valley of Guatemala, for example, erosion has created the poorest land of the area, but it has also been responsible for exposing clays which lie under a substantial overburden of volcanic ash. In the Chinautla area particularly, the clays used for pottery making lie at the base of an ash deposit which has a thickness of approximately 100-300 meters. Without erosion, these excellent clays for making pottery would lie unexposed, and hence could not be utilized by local populations. Similarly, in the areas in which potters live around Quinua, Peru, erosion has created a rather marginal environment for agriculture, but it has exposed a wide variety of ceramic resources like clays, tempers, slips and paints. Thus, erosion and weathering constitute important environmental processes affecting the resource potential for ceramic production, and it is understandable that highly eroded and thus poor agricultural land sometimes co-occurs with pottery making communities. Conversely, since erosion causes a decline in agricultural productivity, good agricultural land and land producing good ceramic resources would not be expected to co-occur. Furthermore, the quarrying and extraction of ceramic resources like temper and clay may themselves destroy agricultural land (see Figure 7.6).

Adaptations combining the advantages of both pottery making and agriculture can be made by groups living in marginal agricultural areas to maximize their economic productivity. In the northern part of the valley of Guatemala, for example, pottery making and charcoal production are excellent adaptations to poor agricultural land. Weathering and erosion both create and expose ceramic resources like clays, temper, slips and paints, but charcoal making is also an excellent adaptation to this poor land because forests can grow where crops cannot or where crops are relatively unproductive. So, while the land may be poor for agriculture, it provides the most important resource for charcoal production–i.e., trees, and has the added benefit of providing the fuel for pottery firing (Arnold, 1978b).

Relationship to demand

The man/land feedback mechanism is closely related to demand. Population pressure (due to several factors) has already been implicated as the primary driving force in this feedback mechanism and this factor can be closely related to the demand mechanism. If population pressure results from population growth or urbanization, these factors provide an increasing outlet for ceramics. In areas where potters must depend heavily on their crafts to make a living, agricultural producers on non-marginal land must be able to support intensified agricultural production at a level which will permit the exchange of food supplies for pots. Thus, although the potter can not raise enough food for his own subsistence, he must rely on the supplies of others to exchange for pots.

As population growth continues, it progressively eliminates the agricultural base of some of the population, and people will need to turn to crafts to provide subsistence for their families. In order to obtain food for their craft products, traders engaged in commerce will emerge to exchange ceramics outside of the immediate area. The increasing population thus provides a ready market for potters who are forced to rely on their craft for subsistence. With more demographic pressure, the greater the potters' dependence on ceramics and trade, the more intensive their specialization, and the more demand for craft products that are necessary to sustain the craftsman.

The traditional explantion for the development of craft specialization and subsequent trade postulates that these phenomena developed as the result of highly localized and unequally distributed resources. This explanation may seem plausible when dealing with resources that are highly localized like obsidian, jade or turquoise. Clays, however, are widely distributed, but their occurrence alone does not account for the existence of the potter's craft (Arnold, 1978a).

If localized resources were responsible for the development of craft specialization, why was it important to exploit these resources to begin with? When compared with subsistence, any craft (particularly ceramics) requires more risks and more effort than agriculture between production and meeting basic subsistence needs. An agriculturalist grows his own food and the effort and energy inputs between harvest and consumption are small. Potters, on the other hand, run the same risks with weather and climate that agriculturalists do, but have the additional risk of firing. Once production is completed, however, they face the problem of turning their pots into food. This problem is solved through exchange, trade, markets and/or other distributive mechanisms which convert craft products into items needed for subsistence. It follows, then, that except for those who make pottery only for their own use, people probably would not choose to become potters if the subsistence (e. g. agricultural) base was adequate. Since craft specialization is dependent upon extensive distributive mechanisms, these factors need to develop simultaneously, and this suggests that the processes that led to the development of craft specialization are also responsible for the development of trade and distributive mechanisms. Thus, an inadequate subsistence base relative to population is one of the important causative factors of extensive methods of distribution as well as of the development of craft specialization.

This second explanation for the development of crafts and distributive mechanisms is supported by the ethnographic literature. For example, an inadequate subsistence base (as indicated by insufficient and poor quality land relative to population) explains the importance of commerce in Mitla in Mexico (Parsons, 1936) where people have turned to non-agricultural pursuits since the land base is too limited to provide an adequate livelihood. Although Mitla is an agricultural town, the land around the town is arid and unproductive; there is a shortage of water for agriculture in the valley and the weather is variable. Because of these factors, farming is an occupation with little appeal and was associated with poverty and drudgery (Leslie, 1960:6). As a result, people turned to trading and the community became known for its commerce. Most significant in the movement away from agriculture, however, was the fact that fifty-two per cent of the families in the community were landless (Parsons, 1936:55) and thus required some alternative occupation besides farming. Similarly, an inadequate subsistence base also explains the development of trade in certain villages in Brazil. Gross et al. (1979) compared four villages in Brazil and found that intense trade was linked to those villages in which great amounts of time were necessary for subsistence activities, caused by low soil productivity and lack of the traditional (and necessary) movement to new areas.

Similar ethnographic examples come from Melansia. The islands of Mailu and Tubetube were both important pottery making centers which traded their wares over many parts of Melanesia because of their strategic location as a central place. Both islands, however, have powerful ecological inducements for alternative subsistence techniques like pottery making and the development of trade. Mailu's carrying capacity was far below its population and it had to export pots and exchange them for food (Irwin, 1974:269); there was not much garden land (Irwin, 1974:270). Population pressure, then, was as important for the development of distribution mechanisms to exchange pots for food as for the development of pottery making itself.

8
Technological
Innovations

The feedback mechanisms described in previous chapters had rather direct relationships with the pottery making process. This chapter concerns the effect of technological innovations on the process. Some of these innovations create new feedback mechanisms. Others mitigate the effects of previously mentioned regulatory mechanisms and free the craft from the adverse effects of negative feedback. The result is that these innovations provide deviation amplifying feedback for part-time specialization, its expansion into new areas and its evolution into a full time craft.

One innovation that has profound consequences for the evolution of full-time ceramic specialization is the development of forming techniques which speeded vessel fabrication and thus increased production. These techniques also help reduce the negative feedback of weather and climate. The first such technique is molding which permits a vessel to be made in two vertical halves. With techniques like modeling (or hand molding), coiling or paddle and anvil forming, pottery is often made in several stages which require drying after each stage so that the partial vessel will not sag or crack when more clay is added. In the village of Yabob in Papua New Guinea, for example, potters must spend one half-hour a day for a week to properly shape a vessel using a hand molding and a paddle and anvil technique (Smith,1967:12). Saraswati and Behura (1966:84-7) mention several techniques in India that require drying time between stages and thus extend forming time. With the vertical-half molding technique, clay can be pressed into each mold and then made into a vessel with only a brief drying period—enough to allow the clay in each half of the mold to dry slightly before pressing the two halves of the mold together. The result is that pottery can be made faster, with less drying time during fabrication. In cases where pottery is made in several stages, vertical-half molds can cut several days from drying time.

Because of the drying time between stages, the amount of pottery produced by traditional techniques like coiling, modified coiling and the paddle and anvil is relatively small in comparison to the vertical-half

202

Figure 8.1 A potter in Chinautla, Guatemala, in the early portion of the second stage of making a water carrying jar. The first stage (turned upside down in the background) is molded on a discarded jar and must dry at least one day. After the mold-made base of a jar has dried sufficiently, it is scraped and thinned before large coils are added and drawn up to form the body.

molding technique. In Sacojito, Durazno and Chinautla, Guatemala, for example, vessels are made in a series of stages (see Figure 3.2 and Figure 8.1) using a combination of molding (for the base) and modified coiling. Each stage requires as much as one day's drying time. For some vessels like water carrying pots, fabrication of one vessel requires three to four days because of drying time necessary during the fabricating process. Few pots except tiny toys and very small vessels can be completed in a single day. As a result, each Chinautla potter can only make about twenty medium water carrying vessels (*tinajas*) or four to five large water storage jars (*tinajeras*) per week (Reina and Hill, 1978:41). On Buka Island (Melanesia), pottery made with a modified coiling and a paddle and anvil technique requires long drying periods between stages of fabrication and a potter may have as many as 20-4 vessels in various stages of completion at one time. One potter took two weeks to finish twelve medium sized vessels. Since pottery making ceases during the wet season (December-April), Specht (1972:128,135) suggests a maximum output of 150 vessels per potter per year.

Production rates using similar technologies in other areas are also low. In the the village of Wagholi, India, a pot with a mouth of 35 cm, a height of 70-105 cm and a diameter of 40 cm is formed using a combination of a modeling and a paddle and anvil technique and requires a fabrication time of 2 hours and 20-50 minutes stretched over five days (Gupta, 1966:70-1). Using a combination of a paddle and anvil and molding technique, one Nasioi potter on the island of Bougainville in Melanesia completed one vessel approximately 25 cm high in 39 minutes and a small vessel in 25 minutes with a six hour drying time (Ogan, 1970:88). Fewkes (1944:94-5) reported that a Catawba potter (from eastern North America) using a combination of a modeling and a coiling technique required a total of 2 hours and 5 minutes to fabricate a vessel interspersed with a total of 41 hours' drying time between stages. For a large vessel, fabrication may require 6 hours. Using a coiling technique, Tarahumara potters require 1 hour to 3-4 hours to fabricate a pot. Small cooking pots, bowls and elliptically shaped corn poppers each require about an hour to produce. Working a long day, a Tarahumara potter can complete 2-4 medium water storage pots (Pastron, 1974:105). Thompson (1958) reported that using a modified coiling technique, a Yucatec potter may produce only 4-6 water carrying jars (*cantaros*) per day. Similarly, a Diola potter from West Africa produces 8-10 pots per day using coiling and a paddle and anvil technique (Linares de Sapir, 1969:4). In three weeks, a potter will produce 200 vessels of different sizes. A Tangkhul Naga potter produces one medium sized bowl with a constricted mouth and a handle in 50 minutes using modeling and rolling (Betts, 1950:117). Using a combination of modeling and drawing coils up from a vessel on a turntable, a Pereruela potter (Spain) can produce a low open bowl (a *cazuela*) in 15 minutes with a total of 26 possible in one day (Cortes, 1954:152-4). Among the Shipibo-Conibo of eastern Peru, production of even small pots by coiling will take several hours (Table 8.1) and the process may go on for days on end because of the need for adequate drying time. Amphlett Island potters require 2.3 hours to construct and decorate a bowl (Lauer, 1974:151,162) with a slightly constricted neck, a mean height (N=36) of 22.55 cm, a mean mouth diameter of 18.04 cm and a mean maximum width of 20.78 cm (Lauer, 1974:162) using a combination of a modified coiling and a paddle and anvil technique (Lauer, 1974:144).

By way of contrast, potters using a vertical two-piece mold in the municipio of Temascalcingo, Mexico, can complete a pot in 10-20 minutes depending on the size of the vessel and the experience of the potter (Papousek, 1974:1025). Working seven hours a day, potters produce a maximum of 36-42 vessels a day—roughly the amount of vessels it would take a Chinautla woman two weeks to produce. While women potters in the Chinautla area probably do not work seven hours a day like the male potters in Temascalcingo because of household responsibilities, there is no doubt that the vertical-half mold technique is faster since a Temascalcingo potter can complete a minimum of 3 vessels per hour and in 7 hours exceed the weekly production of a Chinautla potter.

Table 8.1 *Time needed to produce coiled vessels among the Shipibo-Conibo*
(Data from DeBoer and Lathrap, 1979:120)

Type of vessel	Actual time spent[1]		Elapsed time		
	Hours	Minutes	Days	Hours	Minutes
Serving vessel	9	52	7	7	14
Food bowl	4	37	5	1	0
Medium cooking pot	4	3	3	22	18
Small cooking pot	3	15	3	22	18
Large jar	14	55	7	0	35

Notes: Table 8.1

[1] Includes firing time because each vessel is fired singly.

He can also produce 6 vessels in the time it takes the Catawba potter to produce one vessel and in four hours complete the semi-monthly production of a Buka Island potter. The increased efficiency of vertical-half molds is further supported by Charlton and Katz (1979:47), who reported that Tonalá pottery was made with mushroom molds until the mid-twentieth century when potters switched to vertical-half molds partly because they found production using the new technique less time-consuming. Thus, the two-piece mold technique cuts forming and drying time substantially and potters can produce pottery much faster.

A second advantage of the mold-made technique is that it requires less skill than modeling, coiling, modified coiling or paddle and anvil techniques. In Ticul, Yucatan, the lesser amount of skill required by the vertical-half mold is illustrated by the speed and ease with which adult potters learn this technique in contrast to the long apprenticeship necessary with traditional techniques. Ticul potters produce traditional pots by adding large coils to the vessel and drawing them up with the fingers first and then with a calabash rind scraper. In the last twenty-thirty years, however, there has been a great market for molded items like banks made in shapes such as pigs, dogs, chickens and cartoon characters (like Mighty Mouse). In contrast to the simple skills needed to make these molded items, fabricating the traditional vessels requires great skill in certain motor habit patterns. These skills include scraping and shaping the crude vessel, rotating the vessel support with the hand or foot, co-ordinating the movements of each hand and those of the hands and feet, knowing how long each stage must dry, and knowing how much clay to add to the unfinished vessel.

Since a considerable number of motor habit patterns and skills are involved in making traditional Maya pots of Ticul, it takes many years to become a competent potter using traditional techniques. These skills are more easily and more effectively learned during childhood. If children begin to learn pottery making around six or seven years of age, they can be accomplished potters by fifteen or sixteen. (This long learning period of motor habit patterns is not unusual. Wahlman (1972:315) notes that many years are necessary to perfect pottery making skills among the Yoruba.) Although adults can learn pottery making (usually through marriage to a potter), they may never become as competent as one who has learned the craft during childhood. Still, many adults do become potters and do so rapidly in Ticul, but they rarely learn the full range of traditional techniques like those a potter learned as a child. Rather, these new adult potters most often learn to make pottery using vertical-half molds and often produce this kind of pottery exclusively (Figure 8.2). Molded items require far less skill to produce, can be made quickly and have much less investment of time and labor. Furthermore, the work of an amateur is virtually indistinguishable from that of a master potter. Mold-made vessels can thus be marketed easily and immediately without a lengthy apprenticeship period during which the novice produces items of poor or mediocre quality or those that require only rudimentary skill.

Mold-made techniques produced deviation amplifying feedback for pottery production in Quinua, Peru, by reducing drying time during fabrication and reducing the time necessary to learn the craft. This latter factor placed pottery making within the reach of more people. From February to July 1967, there were no vertical-half molds used for pottery production. If used at all, molds were used to impress faces on certain items of pottery. Except for the government-sponsored artisan school in the village and local ceramic items for sale in stores in the community, pottery making was a relatively invisible craft. By way of contrast, a brief visit to the community in 1978 revealed that pottery making was very much in evidence with pottery workshops and stores along the highway selling a wide range of tourist wares. Except for some traditional pottery and ceramic churches (which can not be made with a mold technique), some potters have switched to making mold-made objects, and it appears that the pottery making industry has grown tremendously (William Mitchell, personal communication), in part because of tourism and the ease of transportation to central places (see Chapter 6).

In the archaeological record, it was probably the development and use of the vertical-half molds (see Donnan, 1965) during the Early Intermediate Period (200 B. C.-A. D. 600) which permitted the development of full-time potters in the Moche culture on the north coast of Peru. By greatly reducing drying time, mold-made pottery speeded and increased production. Furthermore, it could have permitted full-time ceramic production to develop in the cloudy, foggy and damp season

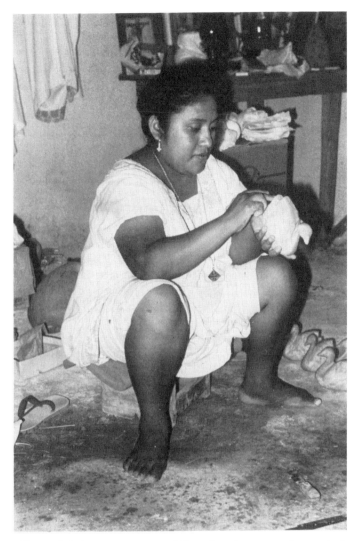

Figure 8.2 A woman potter obliterating the seam of a vertical half-molded object in Ticul, Yucatan, Mexico. Vertical half-molds require less fabrication and drying time than traditional techniques such as coiling, modeling, paddle and anvil or modified coiling, and require less skill. This woman formerly had no knowledge of pottery making, but learned the molding technique and other aspects of the craft that require little skill after she married a Ticul potter.

when pottery making was not otherwise possible in parts of the coast. Chimu pottery was also made with vertical-half molds in the Late Intermediate Period (A. D. 1000-1476) even though no evidence of potters has been found at Chan Chan, the Chimu capital (Michael Moseley and Carol Mackey, personal communication). The use of two-piece molds during this time continued the high production rate of pottery begun in the Moche culture.

The second fabrication innovation (besides vertical-half molds) which increased efficiency and thus speeded production was the development of the potter's wheel. The use of a wheel has even more of an advantage than the vertical-half mold since pieces can be made at one sitting and then allowed to dry without any drying time between stages like that necessary with modeling, coiling, the paddle and anvil technique or other hand forming techniques.In the household factories in Bailén, Spain, one workman using a wheel claimed that he could produce 100 small pieces an hour and that five or six hundred pieces of assorted shapes would not be an unusual day's work for a good master potter (Curtis, 1962:493). A small shop of two wheels, one kiln, two master potters and two apprentices turned out an estimated 100,000 smaller and less expensive pieces such as mortars, flower pots and small pitchers in a single season, while a larger shop of three kilns, twelve wheels and twenty employees reportedly turned out an estimated 300,000 pottery vessels in a season (Curtis, 1962:488). With approximately 183 days (April to September) available during the dry season for making pottery, the small shop thus produced 1926 small vessels per wheel per week and the larger shop produced 962 vessels per wheel per week. These values are three to four times the weekly production of a Temascalcingo potter using a vertical-half mold. In Totonicapán, Guatemala, a potter can produce 50 bowls per hour using the wheel (Bock, 1970:15) and over a three week period, three potters in a single workshop can produce 5000 such wheel-made bowls. In India, Saraswati and Behura (1966:54) and Behura (1978:154) found that using a wheel, a potter completed a medium pot in a mean time of no more than three minutes and 22.6 seconds (Table 8.2). Five different potters of the same age produced the same pot in a mean time of approximately three minutes and 38 seconds. With an estimated two minutes necessary to place the clay on the wheel and remove the completed vessel, these potters could produce 10-11 pots of this size per hour. This rate is one-third to one-sixth the time necessary for a Temascalcingo potter to complete a vessel using a two-piece mold, and far faster than the Chinautla, Buka Island or Catawba potters. In Dera Ismail Khan, Pakistan, one potter produced 40-80 wheel-made vessels per day with as many as 250 water jars per week and an average weekly production of 75-100 such jars (Rye and Evans, 1976:52-3). A potter from Shahbaz Ahmed Khel, Pakistan, produced 100 large unde-corated wheel-thrown bowls or 500 small bowls each day (Table 8.3). He can also produce 80 vessels per day in the form either of a water vessel with handles or of a water pitcher with a handle and spout. These rates of production, however, cannot be maintained because the potter must spend time digging and preparing clay, firing, selling the finished vessels and maintaining his workshop (Rye and Evans, 1976:49). Thus, these

Table 8.2 *Mean times for production of wheel-made pottery in India*

| Vessel size (in cm) | | | | N | Comment | Mean throwing time | | Standard Deviation in seconds | Source | Group |
Mouth	Bottom	Height	Circum-ference			Minutes	Seconds			
19	22	33.5	82.5	5	same potter	2	52	7.07	Behura, 1978:154	Bathuli (Orissa)
20	23.5	36	86.5	5	same potter	3	22.6	3.63	" " "	Bathuli (Orissa)
20	22.5	47.5	91.5	5	same potter	3	11.2	10.03	Saraswati & Behura, 1966:54	not mentioned
20	22.5	47.5	91.5	5	different potters	3	38	17.88	" " "	" "

data are maximum rates and apply only when the potter has clay already prepared and works throughout the day. Nevertheless, daily production rates still surpass those of the Temascalcingo potter (36-42 vessels per day) with the vertical-half mold technology and indicate that the wheel is a faster production technique than vertical-half mold technique.

In actual fact, however, the production of a potter using the wheel varies greatly and does not always seem to have an advantage over a two-piece mold production. In Kharmathu, Pakistan, one workshop produced approximately 50 vessels per person per week (Rye and Evans, 1976:41), while in Bannu, Pakistan large vessels were thrown in batches of 30-50 each morning with no pots made in the afternoon (Rye and Evans, 1976:45). Furthermore, the time necessary to produce decorated wheel thrown pots was far longer than that for wheel-made undecorated pottery (Table 8.3), so decorating a vessel slows down wheel production considerably. Thus, the potential for increased production of wheel-made ceramics, in comparison to the vertical-half mold, is possible but not always fully realized.

In summary, one important factor affecting the production rates of pottery is related to the efficiency of the forming techniques. Production rates of different techniques are difficult to compare precisely because of the variation in hours worked, amount of drying time and lack of complete data on the time needed to complete a vessel. Nevertheless, the

Table 8.3 *Production rates for undecorated and decorated wheel-produced pottery by one potter in Shahbaz Ahmed Khel, Northwest Frontier Province* (Rye and Evans, 1976:49)

Decoration	Type	Size (cm)		Production, no. per day
		Height	Diameter	
Undecorated	Bowl with solid foot	11	23	100
	Small bowl with solid foot	5	10	500
Decorated with incised or impressed patterns	Water vessel with handles	25	27	80
	Water pitcher with handle and spout	28	19	80
Decorated with black pigment brush mark	Milk vessel with lid	22	24	80
Decorated with red slip and black pigment over the slip	Large dish for serving food	–	38	40
	Three large dishes for for kneading bread dough	–	33	40
		–	43	40
		–	54	40

data available do indicate that hand forming techniques are the least efficient, with vertical-half molds next in efficiency and the wheel technique (i. e. a technique that uses the centrifical force of the wheel) being the most efficient. Efficiency of molds and the wheel, however, may be more limited than is indicated here because more time and/or capital must be invested in their purchase and/or fabrication than with techniques not using these devices.

A second class of technical innovations is the use of drying facilities. These innovations mitigate the regulatory effects of weather and climate and thus provide deviation amplifying feedback for ceramic specialization. In many parts of the world, the regulatory effects of climate limit ceramic production to the dry season (see Chapter 3). In parts of the Old World, however, where ceramics are ancient and highly evolved, communities have adapted to this problem by using elaborate drying facilities. In the modern ceramics industry, for example, factories have controlled temperature/relative humidity driers that utilize hot gases from the kiln. These gases enter the drier at one end and pick up moisture and lose heat as they move through it. At the other end, the moist, cooler air exits from the drier. Pottery wares pass through this drier on drier cars with the wet product entering the cool end and leaving dried at the hot end. This technique reduces the uneven drying and cracking of the ware so that it dries and shrinks evenly (Arthur White, personal communication).

Innovations in the drying process need not be as obvious or elaborate as the controlled temperature and relative humidity driers of the modern ceramics industry. Sometimes even small innovations can mitigate the regulatory effects of weather and climate. First, use of sheets of polyethylene plastic to cover pottery during the drying process is a simple innovation of recent origin, but one with profound consequences. By protecting the pottery during the rainy season, these sheets keep rain and moisture off the pottery and thus help prevent damage due to damp weather. Plastic sheets are used in Ticul, Yucatan, especially for this purpose, and thus lessen the limiting effects of weather and climate on the pottery making process. In warmer and drier climates, potters can use sheets of plastic to slow drying (Lackey, 1982:110). Delaying drying is particularly important with large vessels because they can crack if they are dried too quickly. This innovation has dubious significance for ancient potters, but other materials (like palm leaves) could have been used to produce a similar effect.

A second simple drying innovation is drying pottery on or near a fire. In order to accomplish drying successfully, however, the clay/temper ratio must be such as to avoid cracking and excessive shrinkage of the vessel. This technique is widely used in the tropical forest of South America. In his summary of the pottery technology of South America, Linné (1925:121) mentioned that in northwestern Brazil pottery was dried on a platform near the fire (and occasionally in it) before being dried in the sun. On the island of Chiloé (in Chile), vessels were dried in the smoke of the fire (Fonck, 1870:291).

This technique is also used in other wet climates. In Nigeria, Willett and Connah (1969:138) note that after some drying and before firing, pottery is stacked onto a wood platform approximately 130 cm off the ground over a slow burning and smokey fire of split and dried plantain stems. Among the Madang in Papua New Guinea, vessels are dried in the shade for two weeks and then brought inside the house and hung to dry for a month over the fire (Kakubayashi, 1978:139). The potters of Santa Apolonia, Guatemala (Arrot, 1972:24; Reina and Hill, 1978:63), dry their pottery inside a shed on a rack which is suspended about 150 cm over a series of slowly burning logs. Potters first dry their pottery for twelve hours on the rack and then on the fuel. On Tiree, the outermost island of the Inner Hebrides, a pot is dried by placing it near a fire for 24 hours (large vessels require 2-3 days) and it is then placed in the hot ashes after the fire has died down (Holleyman, 1947:209). An identical technique is reported by Murray (1972:165) among the Ibo of Nigeria on the evening before firing. The next morning the pots are dried further by revolving them directly over the fire immediately prior to firing.

This drying technique is also effective in cold Arctic areas. The Ingalik Eskimo (e.g., Osgood, 1940:147) dry their pottery next to the fire. Without this drying innovation, pottery probably could not dry effectively in the cold Arctic areas (see Figure 3.6). As it is, however, it takes three days to complete a pot for cooking.

Although effective for drying pottery in a wet climate, drying pottery in or near a fire also limits the number of vessels that can be dried to a very few and is unsuitable when ceramic production expands greatly. Full-time potters or potters engaged in making many pots would find this technique too costly and too slow, but this innovation may have been crucial for the original development of the craft in some areas.

A third simple drying innovation is using unheated driers, buildings or open drying sheds for drying pottery away from the wind and rain. The extra capital required for this innovation may be excessive for specialist potters since they are already poor (see Chapter 7), but the same effect can be gained by drying pottery in their home. For example, the Yekuaná and Guinaú of South America dried their vessels in their huts (Linné, 1925:121). Lauer (1973:72) notes that the Miadeba of Normanby Island in Melanesia dried their vessels in their houses two to three weeks before firing. (Kilns can also serve as heated driers. Potters in Bailén, Spain, dry their pots in the rear of the fire box of the kiln while a small fire of olive branches burns in the opening (Curtis, 1962:493-4)). In spite of these innovations, however, warping and cracking, although lessened in comparison to sun drying, are still more of a problem than with the elaborate driers of the modern ceramics industry (Arthur White, personal communication).

A third class of technological innovations which also mitigates the regulatory effects of weather and climate is the use of kilns. Kilns, of course, retain heat, permit higher firing temperatures and permit control of draft and firing atmosphere (Shepard, 1956:75). It is primarily the insulating qualities of the kiln (which prevent heat losses during firing) and the greater control that the potter has over the firing process that makes the kiln a more evolved and more effective innovation for ceramic production than other firing methods. The control of the process is accomplished through choices of fuel, the control of access of air to the fuel, the rate at which the potter supplies fuel to the fire and the duration of firing (Rye and Evans, 1976:164). In the elaborate divided updraft kilns of Pakistan, for example, vessels are placed in one chamber near the top of the kiln while the fuel burns in a separate chamber. Flames travel upward from the fire through holes in the floor of the upper chamber, around the vessels, and then are vented through flues at the top of the kiln. This type of kiln affords the potter great control over the firing process. First, he can partially close off the flues in the top of the kiln in order to control the draft. He can control the amounts of fuel and air during the firing and can terminate the process by ceasing to add fuel and/or closing off air access. Finally, he can close up the openings in either or both chambers with bricks, sherds or tiles to conserve heat (Rye and Evans, 1976:164).

Because of greater insulation and greater control of the fire, kilns produce higher temperatures than other firing techniques and thus produce pottery of more lasting quality (Shepard, 1956:75, 83). More importantly, the kiln protects the firing process from rain and moisture and thus permits the potter to fire during conditions which would make firing ordinarily difficult or impossible. Saraswati and Behura (1966:128), for example, noted that in Darbhanga and Champaran, India, potters use a subterranean vertical kiln only during the four months of winter to maximize control of the fire in the face of gusts of wind. Similarly, production of glazed ware in Zahkel Bala, Pakistan, continues year around with an elaborate updraft kiln. Nevertheless, potters work less in winter because periods of inclement weather increase firing costs and delay the drying of the pottery.

By way of contrast, open firing is more susceptible to the deviation counteracting effect of rain than oven or kiln firing. The problems of open firing are closely related to the weather and climate.

During rainy days, pots can not be fired in the open, and while firing, if it rains, a good number of pots are damaged. Sometimes all the pots are not uniformly fired if there is a strong wind.... (Saraswati and Behura, 1966:112; used by permission of the Anthropological Survey of India)

Rye and Evans (1976:77-8) noted similar problems in Zakhel Bala in the

Northwest Frontier Province of Pakistan where potters fire unglazed pottery in a corner of a courtyard with a low mud wall forming the third side. In the winter, production of this ware ceases because the openness of the firing creates a great danger of damage to the pottery during rainy or cold periods.

Potters cannot control open firing as much as kiln firing (Saraswati and Behura, 1966:112). When fuel and vessels are placed together either in open firing or in partially enclosed walls, the potter has more limited control over the process than with kiln firing. Control is restricted to the initial choice of fuel and the arrangement of the fuel and pottery before the firing process begins. Furthermore, the potter can not alter the access of air to the fuel during firing.

The duration of firing is determined by the amount of fuel set in place before the beginning the firing, since no fuel is added during firing. The rate of heating, and evenness of heating throughout the setting, is also determined before firing by the type, amount, and evenness of distribution of fuel. In many versions of this type of firing some degree of insulation is provided during setting to retain the heat. A layer of sherds, earth, stone, wet straw, or thick layers of fuel may be placed over the setting as insulation. Naturally, if this insulating layer is combustible it burns away as the firing progresses. (Rye and Evans, 1976:164)

Ovens represent a more evolved firing method than open firing, but are not as complex nor sophisticated as an elaborate updraft kiln. Ovens have the advantage of a permanent or semi-permanent structure which insulates the firing process, but potters cannot control draft or fuel consumption after the initial arrangement of fuel and pottery as they can with kilns. In India, oven firing conserves heat better than open firing and higher temperatures are possible with ovens than with open firing. Ovens also prevent cold drafts of air from getting inside the structure and causing damage to the pots (Saraswati and Behura, 1966:119).

The increasing degree of firing control from open firing to oven and finally kiln firing suggest that progressive fuel efficiencies may exist for each of these three types. Rye and Evans (1976:165) show that the different firing techniques in Pakistan could be ranked according to the insulating and air supply sophistication of the techniques with the greatest insulation and control of the air supply being the most efficient. The data for the ratios of pottery to fuel (by weight) for various firing techniques other than that of the elaborate updraft kiln confirm this generalization (Table 8.4). The values for updraft kilns, however, are relatively inefficient compared to other firing methods. This apparent inefficiency may be due to several factors: (1) Rye and Evans' data (1976:165) were approximate (by their own admission) and based on potters' own estimates of the weight of fuel and pottery; (2) other factors need to be taken into consideration such as firing temperature and degree of breakage (Rye and Evans, 1976:165); and (3) the increased amount of control in firing with an updraft kiln does not come without

Table 8.4 *Ranking (from least to most) of firing processes according to insulation and degree of control of the process in Pakistan showing the relative efficiency of each type in ratio of pottery to fuel* (Rye and Evans, 1976:165)

Firing type	Name	Location	Ratio (by weight) of body to fuel
Open pit used for firing	āvī	Shahdiwal	3.1
Oven (pit with walls)	pajā	Dir	2.8
Oven (pit with walls)	pajā	Musazi	2.5
Kiln/oven with stoking/air intake hole	kūp	Gurjat	2.0
Elaborate updraft kiln	-	Zakhel Bala	3.2
Elaborate updraft kiln (glazed pottery)	-	Gurjat	2.6

increased energy costs. The cost of being able to control firing and thus to fire during otherwise marginal or unfavorable weather requires increased energy in building the kiln and firing it and thus large updraft kilns are theoretically less efficient in the short term than simpler methods. In return for this energy cost, however, the potter can fire more pots with more control (and presumably less loss), at higher temperatures and for a greater number of days during the year.

The role of ovens and kilns as a mitigating effect on the negative feedback of weather and climate is well illustrated by the correspondence of the distribution of kilns and ovens in India and the areas which have the largest number of wet months in the yearly cycle. These devices tend to be concentrated in south India, east India and Kashmir—all of which have eight to nine months with rainfall and preciptitation exceeding 50 mm (Figure 8.3). Open firing, on the other hand, is widespread, but it constitutes the exclusive firing technique in central, north central and western India, where there are only four to five months with more than 50 mm of rainfall and thus seven to eight months with less than 50 mm (Saraswati and Behura, 1966:103, 112, 120 compared with Ginsberg, 1970:140). These data also correspond to the data from Rye and Evans (Table 8.5) which tend to show that firing technologies that do not use elaborate kilns are associated with seasonal pottery production.

The combination of drying facilities and the use of kilns has permitted ceramic production to occur in areas where pottery making would ordinarily not be possible. The modern ceramics industry in such climatically unfavorable areas as northern Europe and the northern United States, for example, utilizes elaborate drying chambers (e.g., see Shepard, 1956:74) and kilns to dry and fire pottery with energy sources such

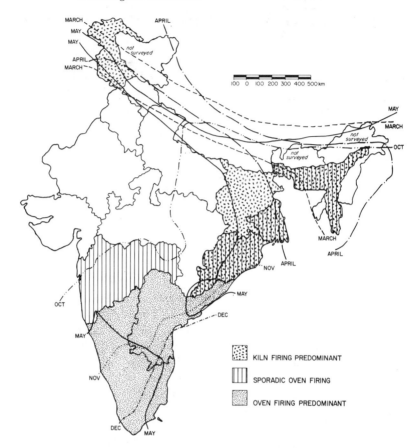

Figure 8.3 Distribution of oven and kiln firing in India plotted with monthly isolets of 50 mm. January and February are dry months with less than 25 mm while June to September are wet. Eastern and southern India tend to have more months of rainfall that exceeds 50 mm than central or western India. (Produced by projecting isolets from Ginsberg, 1970:140, on the map of India in Saraswati and Behura, 1966. Base map used by permission of the Anthropological Survey of India and isolets used by permission of George Philip and Son Limited.)

as coal or petroleum products which do not require drying like wood or dung. Similarly, it is probably the use of drying sheds and kilns that has made the manufacture of highly specialized pottery possible in humid and rainy Japan. Japan is a particularly hostile environment for making pottery, but the Japanese potters have developed an elaborate kiln and drying technology to adapt to the less than ideal weather.

The Japanese kiln is one example of such an adaptation. One kind of Japanese kiln is a long tube 32-45 meters long that is partially buried in the earth, covered with a roof and built on an upward slope of about 30

Table 8.5 *Production variation according to firing type in Pakistan*

Production time	Firing type	Location	Bibliographic Source: Rye and Evans, 1976
seasonal	small open pit	Bomboret Valley	7, 12
seasonal	open	Chitral Valley	13, 16
seasonal	open	Zakhel Bala (unglazed pottery)	36, 78
seasonal	pajā (open pit)	Dir	17, 23-4
seasonal	pajā (open pit)	Swat	27, 29
all year[1]	pajā, but similar to āvī (pit)	Musazi	31, 34
all year[2]	āvī (pit)	Dera Ismail Khan	54
no data	āvī (open pit)	Shadiwal	61
no data	āvī (pit)	Shadarah	55-6
all year[2]	āvī (pit)	Kharmathu	38-9, 41
no data	open kiln	Prang	38
all year[1]	simple updraft	Bannu	44, 47
all year[1]	updraft (glazed)	Zakhel Bala	77, 83
all year	large updraft (elaborate)	Multan	89, 104-7
all year	kūp (elaborate open kiln)	Gurjat (Garhi Magbulabad)	56, 58-9
all year	large updraft kiln	Ahmedpar East	62, 65-6
all year[1]	large updraft kiln	Hala, Sind	107, 110-14

Notes

[1] Production decreases slightly from February to April because of the difficulty of drying pottery on rainy days.

[2] Results are best in summer because of lower losses or potters make only small vessels in winter when firing is more difficult.

degrees (Rhodes, 1970:119; Peterson, 1974:73). This elaborate kiln may have as many as five distinct, interconnected chambers (each with 104 cubic meters of space) with many doors and stoking holes (Rhodes, 1970:120; Petersen, 1974:73). The long kiln with an upward slope provides a strong draft permitting rapid burning and thus high temperatures (Rhodes, 1970:121). The kiln area also serves as a drying area for wood since wood can conveniently be placed under the roof on top of the kiln. These technological adaptations help free the pottery industry from the limiting factors of climate, thus causing a deviation from the regulatory effects of weather and climate.

In pre-industrial societies without kilns or elaborate drying facilities, weather and climate can have a profound effect on pottery making by preventing or slowing drying, increasing susceptibility to breakage, and preventing or inhibiting firing (see Chapter 3). Since there are no known pottery kilns of Precolumbian origin in the New World, New World potters were more affected by weather and climate during firing than many of their Old World and industrial counterparts. Pit firing, however, like that which occurs today on the north coast of Peru (Spahni, 1966:26, 28-9; Litto, 1976:15) would mitigate some of the limiting effects of weather and climate and retain the heat better than open firing. Linné (1925:125) reports that Brünig (1898) found archaeological evidence of fire-hardened pits on the north coast of Peru that suggests that pit firing had a Precolumbian origin. Bordaz (1964) found three Precolumbian horizontal fire-baked pits at Peñitas, Nayarit, Mexico, with ceramic evidence that indicated that they were used to fire pottery. Although these pits, like those from the north coast of Peru, provide more heat retention than open firing, they do not permit control over the process like that possible with many Old World kilns (like the elaborate updraft kiln of Pakistan) and thus do not totally counteract the regulatory effects of climate in these areas.

Another small but profound innovation that mitigates problems of weather and climate involves utilizing a firing location that maximizes environmental factors like wind to help ensure a successful firing. Potters of the high altitude Altiplano around Lake Titicaca in Peru and Bolivia (4000 m above sea level) have two innovations to increase the firing temperature in this cold area. The best time for producing pottery in this region is during the dry season (May-September) when frequent night frosts and cold temperatures make this period the coldest of the year. Potters must thus maximize every opportunity to increase firing temperature. At Urania (southeast of La Paz) and Pucarani (northwest of La Paz), for example, potters use *huayra* furnaces to fire their pottery and place them at appropriate altitudes to get maximum wind for them (David Browman, personal communication). Furnaces help retain heat in cold high altitude areas and their placement to catch the wind helps increase temperature. Even in areas of the Altiplano where no furnaces are used for firing, potters fire on the tops of hills and knolls (Tschopik, 1950; Spahni, 1966:41,44) so that prevailing winds can increase temperature and burn the fuel more efficiently. Potters also maximize firing temperature in the Altiplano by using llama dung (Tschopik, 1950), a fuel which has superior burning qualities over straw or wood (Winterhalder et al., 1974).

The Shipibo-Conibo along the Ucayali river in eastern Peru also use a firing innovation that helps retain heat during firing. The Shipibo-Conibo place a ceramic vessel over the fire in which a smaller vessel is fired (Linné, 1925:126; DeBoer, 1974:336; DeBoer and Lathrap, 1979:105, 120). A similar technique occurs among the Curaray and the Sarayacu Quichua of eastern Ecuador (Rye, 1975:13; Kelley and Orr, 1976:22). This innovation also helps mitigate the effects of weather and climate and provides more heat retention than open firing, but it does not provide the control possible with the elaborate updraft kiln of the Old World. (It is not, however, a functionally equivalent alternative of the Old World kiln.) Furthermore, it provides deviation counteracting feedback for increased production leading to full-time specialization because only one small vessel can be fired at one time. Not all Shipibo-Conibo vessels are fired using this device, however (DeBoer and Lathrap, 1979:120), but generally no more than a few at a time are fired when this device is not used (Ronald Weber, personal communication).

Even with the use of kilns, however, potters are still affected by weather and climate because they must dry fuel and pottery prior to firing and rain can still adversely affect kiln firing. In Quinua, Peru, potters use cylindrical open-topped kilns approximately 150 cm high, but this innovation is unsuccessful in mitigating the regulatory effects of weather and climate because potters must dry both fuel and pottery prior to firing and, during periods of inclement weather, moisture can easily enter the top of the kiln and damage the pottery.

Elaborate oven or kiln technology requires more investment in capital and labor for building the kiln and obtaining the fuel to fire it than open firing. Little capital or extra labor is required for firing in the open and the potter can fire anywhere and modify the firing area according to the size of his production. In India, for example, potters use readily available materials like cattle dung, husks, straw, refuse, dry leaves and brush wood with open firing. In contrast, oven firing requires more wood than open firing and kiln firing requires still more wood (Saraswati and Behura, 1966:119). Kiln firing and some oven firing thus requires more investment of capital and labor than open firing (Saraswati and Behura, 1966:119, 122, 128). By investing labor and capital in fuel and firing facilities, the potter achieves greater control over the firing process and helps mitigate if not eliminate the negative feedback of weather and climate. The investment of labor and capital in the craft, then, feeds back into the intensity of the craft as a deviation amplifying mechanism.

The process of innovation

The process by which innovations enter a society is closely related to the socio-economic position of the innovator. Using a tripartite scheme, Silver (1981) found that the highest and lowest categories of wood carvers in West Africa regularly innovate although each group specializes in a different kind of innovation.

In general, the decision to innovate is economically illogical. In order for innovations to be successful, they must be saleable. So, unless trial pieces can be sold, there is no economic reward for innovation. In order to make a decent income, full-time carvers must produce dozens of objects per week. Since cash is accumulated through volume with a small profit per item, taking time away from producing readily saleable items requires a measure of economic risk. This risk is accepted by higher status carvers who create indigenous innovations that do not violate community norms. The only market for these innovations is store owners who are brokers for new ideas and have made their money outside of carving. They buy attractive and 'trendy' items from higher status carvers who have a good reputation for selling innovative items because prestige comes from being a 'patron' or seller of new artistic trends. This market for innovations, however, is economically very limited so that higher status carvers gain little from their innovations except increased prestige. Low status carvers, on the other hand, innovate for quite different reasons. Many of these are relatively new, unskilled or semi-skilled carvers that are marginal to the society. They innovate to survive and produce more radical innovations. Carvers in the middle rank, however, do not innovate. These data conform to Homans' (1961) model of innovation that high status individuals innovate to maintain their distinctiveness while low status individuals innovate in hope of beating the system that provides them with few rewards.

The 'kicks' that turned technological innovations in pottery production into deviation amplifying mechanisms were probably the result of feedback processes like population pressure and increased demand for ceramic vessels. The adaptive advantage of these technological changes occurred in an environment where weather and climate produced negative feedback for pottery making and where increased efficiency of the craft was necessary. When women are the potters and subsistence is based upon agriculture, efficiency is not important because women's time in the home does not contribute economically to agriculture. Thus, time is not viewed as being part of the production cost. She can, however, make pots and supplement subsistence returns by using her craft. Whether it takes her ten minutes or ten hours to make a pot, her time is not economically crucial. When subsistence returns decrease through population pressure, however, and men turn to the craft because of diminishing farmland and agricultural returns, relatively inefficient forming techniques can not support a family, and more efficient technologies like the vertical-half molds become more attractive and more adaptive because they provide greater returns for equal effort. The negative feedback of weather and climate also places limits on the amount of time during which pottery can be made, so as dependency on the craft increased, so did the need for producing more vessels during the period of favorable climate in order to make an adequate living from the craft. Furthermore, some of the forming technologies (such as the vertical-half mold technique) can be learned easily with less time and effort than traditional technologies. Thus, as population pressure forced more males into the craft, it provided fertile ground for innovations that increased efficiency. The acceptance of these devices thus led to the initiation of deviation amplifying feedback for pottery production which could eventually lead to its development into a full-time craft.

Barriers to innovation and cultural change

There are several barriers that may act as deviation counteracting mechanisms and prevent the acceptance of an innovation. First, the motor habit patterns of the innovation may be incompatible with the motor habit patterns already existing in the society. The wheel, for example, may be resisted because the traditional motor habit patterns may not conform to those required by this innovation. As Spier (1967:63-4) noted, motor habit patterns are rather rigid and difficult to change. Foster (1948) found that the introduction of the wheel in many areas of Mexico was only successful in two kinds of situations: (1) when non-potters were trained to use the wheel, and (2) when mushroom molds were used to make the bottom of the vessel and hand forming (by revolving the vessel and pinching strips of clay in place) was used to make the top of the vessel. With this latter technique, Foster (1948:368-9) says that the introduction of the potter's wheel was not entirely new, but an improved modification of an already existing method. The key, Foster argues, is the compatibility of the motor habits of the two techniques. The result is often a combination of a mushroom-molded base and a wheel-made top. By way of contrast, Foster (1948:369) argues that the resistance to the wheel in Tzintzuntzan is due to the incompatibility of the motor habit patterns of the vertical-half mold system (the traditional technique of Tzintzuntzan) and those required by the wheel technique. A probable further factor, however, is that wheel-made pottery requires a greater development of certain motor habit patterns than the rudimentary skill required for using vertical-half molds. It is also likely that the wheel may not offer an adequate time advantage over the vertical-half mold technique that it does over hand-forming techniques, given the lesser skill required for a vertical-half molding technology.

A similar resistance to the wheel occurred in Ticul, Yucatan. Potters reported that, during the nineteen-forties, the wheel technique was introduced in Ticul in order to improve pottery production in the community. Although Yucatec potters make their pots using a circular motion with a movable pottery support (Thompson, 1958), the motor habit patterns necessary for using the wheel were incompatible with the traditional Ticul patterns. Ticul potters make their pottery in a squatting position seated on a low stool with the legs drawn up to the body but spread apart (see Figure 8.2). Occasionally, the potter will use his bare feet to turn the turntable upon which the pot rests in order to free both hands to work on the vessel. In contrast, the wheel required a seated position about a meter off the ground with the legs outstretched with one used to propel the flywheel. It is also likely that the potter would have to wear some kind of foot protection to prevent scrapes and abrasions to his foot while propelling the wheel. In 1965, only one elderly male potter still had a wheel which he used as a platform for making pottery using vertical-half molds.

Second, the organizational patterns of pottery making (including the sexual division of labor) may be inconsistent with those necessary for the innovation. The introduction of the wheel in Guatemala, for example, was incompatible with the organizational patterns associated with traditional pottery making in the society. In Guatemala, pottery is made by women on a part-time basis between household tasks. Men may help fire it and take it to market (Tax, 1941:25). In Spain, however, pottery was wheel-made and produced primarily by male specialists who worked in workshops in towns (Tax, 1941:25). Because of the vastly different organizational patterns of the craft in the two areas, the wheel made virtually no impact on traditional pottery in Guatemala: Indian potters still used their traditional methods from the Spanish Conquest up until the present day. Nevertheless, the wheel was introduced into Guatemala as a separate industry from the traditional Indian craft and was performed by men (as in Totonicapán–see Bock, 1970; Reina and Hill, 1978:273). The wheel, however, was apparently unable to compete with traditional methods because the wheel, in recent years at least, was not used to produce the traditional shapes which were tied to traditional economic values in the country (see Chapter 6). Furthermore, women potters could still make traditional pots between household tasks using time-consuming methods, and the prices could be competitive since her time was not figured into the cost of production.

A third factor that acts as a deviation counteracting mechanism and thus inhibits innovation and change is the economic marginality of potters. Since potters are poor and have limited resources, any innovation that requires capital investment will not be accepted. This limitation on potters is suggested by Whitaker and Whitaker (1978:27, 30) in their broad survey of Mexican potters. Few potters, they say, can afford the capital investment for a covered storage shed just for drying pottery.

Moreover, the reason that Ticul potters gave for rejecting the wheel was its high cost (500 pesos) which the potters could not pay. For the poor, then, the only commodities available for investment are time and labor, and any innovation that requires investment in anything other than these will not be successful.

A final barrier to innovations and cultural change is the attitudes and beliefs of the society in which the potter works. These are often the most difficult to relate to an ecological point of view. One of the most important beliefs that creates a deviation counteracting mechanism for innovation and change is the 'image of limited good', an attitude found in corporate peasant communities of Latin America (Wolf, 1955) such as the pottery making community of Tzintzuntzan, Mexico. The 'image of limited good' is the belief that almost all of the desired things in life like wealth, friendship, land, health, money, honor, manliness, power, influence, security and prestige exist in absolute limited quantities that can not meet even the minimal needs of a population (Foster, 1967:123). Furthermore, there is no way to increase the available supplies in their social, economic and natural universe (Foster, 1967:124). Thus, an individual or a family can improve its position only at the expense of others (Foster, 1967:124). The community then uses negative sanctions as regulatory mechanisms to minimize the deviations.

The role of traditional belief systems in limiting change is illustrated in the attitudes that prevented a farmer and a potter from continuing their innovations in Chinautla, Guatemala, during the 1950s (Reina, 1963; Reina and Hill, 1978:253-69). The inhabitants of Chinautla believed that members of the community should practice traditional occupations and not innovate. For the potter, this meant strict adherence to traditional shape categories. Strong informal sanctions were brought to bear on the farmer and potter for their innovations and prevented the finalization of their marriage plans until they abandoned their innovations. In 1970, however, the resistance to change in vessel shapes had changed greatly, and there were at least four households in Chinautla (out of about fifteen that were visited–see Arnold, 1978b:361) which produced innovations like those abandoned by one potter fifteen years earlier. Some of these innovations were religious figures, others were censers used for burning incense during religious ritual (see Arnold, 1978b:361) while others included pottery and animals with elaborate plastic decoration. In 1975-6, these innovations were even more in evidence, with a total of ten families devoted exclusively to this pursuit (Reina and Hill, 1978:253-69). This innovative ware was oriented primarily to the urban market in Guatemala City and reflected more individuality in shape, decoration, and technology than the traditional pottery. This ware was more reflective of the national *ladino* culture than the traditional indian roots of the craft. This change created the internal differentiation of potters, with the innovative potters having more prestige, social recognition and education like the higher class *ladinos* than the lower class indian potters who produced the traditional shape categories in the time-honored way.

What caused the change between the 1950s and 1976? Reina and Hill (1978:260) list several factors that caused this change. National inflation, lack of capital and the scarcity of productive land in the area were all responsible for creating difficult economic conditions for families (Reina and Hill, 1978:260). Moreover, metal and plastic vessels were replacing ceramic ones. This process occurred more slowly because of the traditional economic values associated with ceramic vessels (see Chapter 6), but replacement still took place. The ultimate effect was reduced demand for traditional pottery and thus less income for Chinautla potters. It is also likely that continued population growth in Chinautla continued to put pressure on local agricultural land which was already too poor and insufficient for the local population (see Chapter 7). Because the income of a Chinautla potter is often crucial for the support of the household, potters must change the vessel shapes they produce in order to respond to demand if the craft is going to continue to supplement male subsistence activities. Regardless of the reasons the potters themselves give (see Reina and Hill, 1978:262-9), changes in vessel shape repertoire are thus a response to the changing demand for pottery and local population pressure.

The role of population pressure in creating changes in the culture's ideological sub-system has been noted elsewhere. Lawless (1975) found that population pressure on local resources in northern Luzon created a change in the practice of divination. The decline of game animals in the area created a need for more hunting dogs. Formerly, the supply of hunting dogs was largely dependent on divination using the dogs' nipples at about the age of one year. Whether a dog was killed and eaten or used as a hunting dog depended on this practice (Lawless, 1975:25). The need for more hunting dogs in turn created a change in these divination practices to allow a larger portion of the dog population to be perceived as hunting dogs. Concurrently, omens that had formerly curtailed travel in the area also changed due to pressure on resources in order to permit wider ranging trips to obtain food and game. Thus, when subsistence returns are threatened, the strongly conservative values in a society that resist change are challenged and changed.

9
Conclusion

So far, this book has emphasized the processual aspects of ceramic production. These aspects are not concerned with the historical *event* of the origin of the craft. It most certainly began through innovation or diffusion. The significant question is not *how* pottery making began, but what were the cultural and ecological processes which favored or limited its appearance and subsequent development into a full-time craft. Previous chapters, in conformity with a systems terminology, referred to these processes in terms of feedback mechanisms and emphasized their effect on the origin and evolution of the craft.

As the feedback mechanisms have progressed throughout this work, they have become more complex with an increasing number of relationships with other feedback processes. Furthermore, processes like demand, man-land relationships and innovations do not apply in the same way to all societies that make pottery. While the intention of this work was to describe those diachronic processes that cross-cut the types of socio-cultural evolution, it is now necessary to utilize a set of synchronic categories in order to specify the conditions under which the feedback processes operate. The evolution of the craft from its earliest development to complex full-time specialists can not be described diachronically without reference to these categories because different processes have operated differently at different times in the past. Peacock (1981) has provided a such a set of synchronic categories (based on the earlier work of Van der Leeuw (1976)) which he calls 'modes of production'. These modes cross-cut the feedback processes developed in this work and provide a set of changing structural arrangements in the evolution of ceramic production. Since some of the feedback processes developed here account for the change from one mode to another, these synchronic categories, then, are system 'states' that represent the systemic processes of ceramic evolution in points of time (see Van der Leeuw, 1981). The total number of these states that are possible is not necessarily restricted to those described here.

The first system state of ceramic production is household production, where pottery production is located exclusively within the household.

The technological and utilitarian advantages of pottery and at least partial sedentariness of the society in a location with favorable resources and climate provide deviation amplifying feedback for the origin of the craft. Each household makes pottery for its own use and mechanical solidarity characterizes the society; there are no specialists and no division of labor except by sex. Since females are tied to the household by reasons of child care and nursing, potters in this system state are females. All adult females have learned the craft and have the same potential to make pots.

The next system state of ceramic production is the household industry and results, in part, from the "kick" of population pressure (Chapter 7) which is reducing the per capita returns from agriculture and/or other primary subsistence activities. This change marks the beginning of specialized production. Females may be potters in this system state because of their ties to the household, but men may also be potters or assist women depending on the yearly climatic pattern and if the optimum weather for pottery production does not conflict with significant male subsistence responsibilities. Having females produce pottery, however, reduces the risk of possible subsistence losses that may occur if men were diverted from agriculture or other primary subsistence activities. Pottery production is part-time due to a woman's household responsibilities and because the weather (rainfall) necessary for subsistence (such as agriculture) may provide regulatory feedback for the craft. If potters are male and have some agricultural land, however, agriculture would be a deviation counteracting mechanism for the increased intensity of the craft since pottery making must be interrupted to perform agricultural tasks (as in Tonalá (Diaz, 1966:173)).

Women potters in the household industry often utilize time-consuming forming techniques that have limited efficiency. When men are involved in subsistence activities like agriculture, women's time is otherwise under-utilized and it does not contribute directly to subsistence. Thus, their contribution to household income is supplementary and fabrication time is not viewed as part of the cost of production.

The social position of potters in the household industry is related to population pressure and the sexual division of labor. When women are potters, the craft may be valued because a woman can supplement her husband's income from subsistence activities. When male subsistence activities are eliminated, however, and the amount of agricultural land diminishes, scarce land is highly valued and land ownership becomes a source of power and prestige (Harner, 1970). Population pressure forces men into the craft and the social position of the potters thus decreases because of their limited access to or ownership of agricultural land.

Population pressure may have a further effect on access to agricultural land. Besides decreasing land and productivity per capita and eliminating the land base, population pressure also forces farmers to go further and further away to obtain suitable agricultural land. Part-time potters could either move or intensify their craft. At a distance of 7-8 kms (see Chapter 2; Table 2.7), travel to their fields becomes uneconomic and people may prefer to exploit resources like ceramic raw materials closer to their homes.

With the progressive elimination of primary subsistence activities like agriculture because of population pressure, marketing strategies must develop in order to turn pots into food if ceramic production is to serve as an alternative to direct food production. Thus, a potter may utilize extensive networks of exchange, trade and distribution to exchange pots for food. Pottery producing centers near high level central places provide access to one kind of distribution system.

The development of increased demand is also important for the household industry mode of production. Demand provides both regulatory feedback and a 'kick' for deviation amplifying feedback for the craft. If there is no demand for the potters' wares, there is no need to make pottery. For strictly utilitarian pottery, the most significant increase in demand is closely related to the increase in the number of households although population growth through natural fertility would create some significant demand in populations over 1000. New uses for these vessels, however, still create a limited increase in demand for pottery. When population pressure eliminates agriculture for subsistence, potters are largely dependent on their craft to make a living, and innovations which tie ceramics to the social structural and ideological subsystems of culture are necessary to provide the deviation amplifying feedback for intensifying the craft. These innovations involve making pottery which reflects mythical or religious themes and using ceramic vessels for ritual and burial.

Pottery making in the household industry mode of production is thus an adaptation of a population to specific kinds of non-agricultural resources; it is an adaptation to land which is limited or poor agriculturally, but which has ceramic resources. This explanation accounts for the occurrence of many potters in the Chinautla dialect area in Guatemala and why none are found in the Palín dialect area even though both have similar culture history and both have clays available. It also explains the the presence of potters on the marginal land in Mixco and the Cakchiquel communities of San Raimundo and La Ciénaga in the Valley of Guatemala, among the Mossi, in Raqchi and in Quinua, Peru, and in Chamula and the Temascalcingo Valley in Mexico.

Although new uses for ceramics created deviation amplifying feedback for the household industry mode of production, such innovations were crucial for the evolution of the next mode of ceramic development—the workshop industry and the emergence of pottery making into a full-time craft. In the workshop industry, population pressure has largely, if not completely, eliminated agriculture as a subsistence base for the potters. Subsistence activities do not conflict with pottery making and thus males are potters since they have no alternative means of subsistence.

Once direct food production ceases, the potter's family is dependent on the craft for a living, and the risks inherent in making pottery must be reduced in order to have a reliable income. In the household industry, this risk reduction is accomplished by having females make pots. Reducing risks in the workshop mode, however, involves having more control over the craft by increasing its efficiency and mitigating the negative feedback of weather and climate. Increased efficiency means that potters can make more pots in the same amount of time. (The absolute amount of energy invested in the craft, however, may be greater than that invested in earlier system states or modes of production.) The negative feedback of climate is largely eliminated by innovations in vessel forming techniques (like vertical-half molds) that shorten drying time and those (like drying sheds and an elaborate kiln technology) that extend the length of time that pottery can be made during the year. If ceramic production occurs in an area where climate does not adversely affect pottery production, technical innovations will consist of vessel forming techniques which reduced the time required to make each vessel and thus increase production. Increased control over the pottery making process thus permits the potter to make more pots for a longer period during the year.

In order for the potter to realize increased control over the process, capital investment in innovations is necessary (such as constructing a shed for forming and drying pottery, building a kiln, and buying or making molds or a wheel). Because potters in the household industry are poor and economically marginal, most potters cannot afford the capital investment that these innovations require and are therefore forced to hire themselves out to those who have them. In some cases, potters in the workshop industry can not support themselves with their craft without innovations designed to increase production. This change removes pottery production from the household and thus totally eliminates women from the pottery making process because of their ties to household and child care responsibilities.

Since pottery making is a low status occupation (for males) in the household industry, potters do not usually utilize any capital they accrue to intensify their craft, but rather use it to increase their status. For example, potters in Tonalá, Mexico, spend any capital they generate on religious rituals or hospitality, while others purchase land or cattle which will bring more prestige. A potter in Tonalá may also try to increase his status by becoming a middleman who buys pottery from potters and resells it in the markets of the area. Middlemen who were formerly potters try hard to avoid involvement in the actual production of pottery (Diaz, 1966:188-9). Reina and Hill (1978:276) also note that many *ladino* potters in Guatemala are ready to leave pottery making if another alternative offers more rapid economic and social advancement.

This same phenomenon occurred in Ticul, Yucatan, Mexico, with a potter named José Kab (a pseudonym). Between 1965 and 1970, José made at least three trips to the U.S. to work with anthropologists at three different universities. When he returned to Ticul, the money he earned in the U. S. was not used to intensify his craft. Instead, he added two rooms to his father's house. By 1970, he had purchased a house near the plaza of one of the *barrios* of Ticul and opened a store in it. His brother-in-law, who was also a potter, but lived in a less favorable location, built a structure next to his house and opened a store there also. This behavior was clearly an attempt by both potters to raise their own status by becoming merchants. Similarly, other potters in Ticul who have abandoned pottery making have either left it completely or become middlemen. Some middlemen who were formerly potters have begun workshops. Potters were hired to fabricate pottery for a regular wage. Often the owners no longer made pottery themselves, but only supervised the work and traveled to different parts of the Yucatan to sell the pottery.

The failure of potters to invest capital in their craft helps explain the evolution of a more intensive craft in a workshop context. Because of the low status of pottery making and the economic marginality of potters in a household industry, potters often do not choose to develop a more intensive craft, but rather prefer to enhance their status. They may ultimately abandon pottery making for a more prestigious and lucrative occupation as a middleman or the owner of a pottery workshop. Thus, the development of a workshop mode of production with capital investment (needed for obtaining innovations and paying workers on a regular basis) is a pattern initiated by higher status individuals who are either outside of pottery making completely or socially and economically marginal to the craft.

Since potters make pots out of economic necessity in the household and workshop industries, the degree of innovation practiced by them will be geared more to demand than to artistic urge. In fact, with pottery making providing only minimal returns, the potter probably will not choose to innovate by producing a new shape or design. This kind of innovation is too risky unless he is a new potter, has nothing to lose, and/or his returns are threatened because of changing demand. He has no reason to take a chance to produce a possibly unsaleable innovative item when he can use the production time to make an item that he knows will sell.

The technological innovations that led to greater efficiency of the craft, however, were probably introduced and accepted first by the low status potters who were under economic pressure. They had little to lose and could succeed in producing more pottery for their effort. On the other hand, innovations such as new uses for pots and new designs came from higher status potters. They could afford to experiment with innovations in shape, design and and use and they (like West African carvers—see Silver, 1981) could gain prestige by producing such an item. Thus, the social differentiation of potters into higher and lower positions probably preceded the acceptance of innovations by potters and the development of a workshop industry.

In a workshop context, the potter is freed from the direct economic consequences of the vicissitudes of demand. He does not need to assume the risks of innovation (such as reduced income) and is freed from the deviation counteracting effects of producing innovative but unsaleable pots. The workshop owner, then, assumes the economic risks of innovation, and may ask his workers to make specific innovative items. In Yucatan, Mexico, for example, Ticul potters were hired to make pots in a workshop at one of the tourist hotels at the nearby ruins of Uxmal (Hacienda Uxmal). Potters were paid a regular wage, but the owner of the souvenir shop in the hotel required them to produce specific innovations. In some cases, potters copied ancient shapes, whereas in other cases they created new ones or used commercial paint to make new designs on traditional vessels. One innovation consisted of figurines for Christmas creche sets; some of the figurines had Yucatec facial features and were painted to show traditional Yucatec clothing. Another innovation was a black ware obtained by burning a heavy smoke-producing wood during the last stage of firing and closing up the door of the kiln.

A similar example of the workshop owner assuming the risks of innovation is the artisan school in Quinua, Peru. Although most of the potters worked in their own households in the rural portions of the community in 1967, three potters worked at the artisan school in the village and were paid a regular wage by the Peruvian government to teach pottery making to any student who wanted to learn. Since wages were paid whether the pottery was sold or not, the potters at the artisan school had opportunities to experiment in ways that did not adversely affect their wages. As a result, they developed an innovative clay filter and produced a number of experimental and non-traditional items of pottery consisting of new vessel shapes and non-traditional combinations of vessel shapes and slips (or lack of them). Thus, in this case as well, innovations developed when the potter was freed from the potential economic risks of those innovations.

In the workshop mode of production, innovations in design, in more efficient forming techniques, and in items that increased the amount of time during which pottery could be made created 'kicks' that set deviation amplifying feedback into motion for the continued evolution of the craft. These innovations, however, required capital investment and created many economic risks that few, if any, potters working alone in their household could afford.

The last system state of ceramic production is what Van der Leeuw

(1976) termed large-scale industry. It is characterized by substantial capital investment in production for a maximum output and minimal cost per unit (Van der Leeuw, 1976:397). The regulating effects of weather and climate are totally eliminated by extensive capital investment in drying chambers and kilns. Innovations have accrued which have maximized efficiency. Thus, production is full-time for the entire year. Since potters must be full-time, there are no scheduling conflicts with subsistence activities. Since production is removed from the household, women are totally eliminated from the production process because of their ties to household and child care responsibilities, and potters are men. In order to ensure demand to support continued production, pottery must have uses outside of cooking, service or utility uses with ties to the ideological and social structural system. Furthermore, full-time production requires extensive distribution of pottery to provide remuneration for the potter to buy food.

Implications for archaeology

The preceding feedback processes in Chapters 2-8 were presented as a series of generalizations which not only showed relationships between two or more classes of phenomena, but helped explain why those relationships exist. This processual approach to ceramics can reveal a number of insights for the archaeologist. Firstly, it gives insight into the evolution of ceramic specialization. It is no longer necessary to refer to such monocausal mechanisms as 'leisure time' or 'surplus' that led to the development of pottery making and its evolution into a full-time craft. Rather, the multicausal systemic explanations developed here are more comprehensive and more definable archaeologically. Secondly, ceramics are not the simple products of 'culture' in an analytically isolated sense but have significant interrelationships with the environment. Thirdly, ceramic production is not universal nor potentially so. The occurrence of ceramic production and its evolution through time thus does not reflect a simple culture-history model, but rather reflects certain cultural and environmental conditions which have favored or limited ceramic development. Some of these factors exist independently of cultural historical forces. Fourthly, the processes elaborated in this work provide guidelines to interpret ancient ceramics without resorting to ethnographic analogy. All of these feedback relationships eventually build upon the chemical and physical characteristics of clays. These characteristics provide the basis for understanding the relationship of ceramics to environment and culture apart from any ideological or social structural factors. The cross-cultural generalizations formulated from these relationships can be applied to any culture of the past whenever the environmental factors are known. This approach to ceramics can thus provide a basis for modeling the past and developing inferences about social, political and economic structures independently of direct historical connection of the ancient and modern societies and apart from ethnographic analogy.

From the comparison of the local geology with mineralogical studies of local ceramic pastes, it is possible to determine whether pottery was made at a site or not. Most pottery communities obtain their primary resources of clay and temper within 1 km of their residence and may go as far as 6-9 km. Beyond this distance, the procurement of these raw materials is generally (but not always) too costly to make pottery. From the analysis of ancient weather and climate, it is possible to predict when pottery making was scheduled during the year. When these data are combined with the analysis of the subsistence pattern, archaeologists can determine whether the ancient potters were men or women using the guidelines described in Chapter 3. The analysis of the use of pottery in ritual contexts and the presence of mythical themes on pottery can provide some indications of the demand for pottery outside of technological and utilitarian advantages. Furthermore, this approach can give some indication of the dependency of potters on their craft that may be necessary to supplement their subsistence. Reconstruction of ancient land use, population density and settlement patterns can determine if population pressure was present and can suggest whether potters were specialists because of their positions in cities or their location on marginal agricultural land. These reconstructions can be used to formulate hypotheses of local and long distance trade utilized by ancient social and political structures. These hypotheses can be tested using mineralogical and trace element analysis of the pottery fabric so long as the distance between sites is at least 12-18 km.

Probably one of the most interesting archaeological implications of these processes is the relationship between agriculture and the origin of pottery making. These two phenomena are often linked together in antiquity. Cohen (1977) has argued that the development of agriculture resulted from population pressure on extant resources. As resources from hunting and gathering decreased, man turned to utilizing specific plants which culminated in food production through agriculture. During the process of domestication, the crops that man consistently chose for use were probably those which survived disease and insect and animal predation. Man's selection was subsequent to natural selection by these factors, and some plants responded over time with larger yields or other culturally appropriate characteristics like taste or color (see Johns, 1982).

The reason for the survival of these plants was their toxic constituent, which protected the plant against insect and animal predation. This substance, however, was often toxic to humans and had to be removed in order to make the plants fit for human consumption. Baskets can be used for detoxifying plant products by soaking and/or stone boiling, and in some cases, the toxic constituent of both wild and domesticated plants can be removed without using any vessel at all. The California Indians, for example, had a variety of techniques for detoxifying acorns by removing the tannic acid in them. While some of these techniques used baskets, some groups utilized detoxifying methods (like burial or roasting) which used no vessel of any kind (Gifford, 1951). In the Andes, toxins in root crops are also leached out of root crops without the use of any vessel by placing the tubers in streams (Johns, 1982).

A more versatile and more universal way of adapting to the problem of toxins in plant foods was the use of fired clay vessels. Ceramic vessels provided convenient, durable containers made of a fairly universal raw material that permitted a variety of detoxification and food preparation processes (like direct and sustained heating, toasting and soaking with caustic substances) that were not possible with vessels of wood, hide or basketry. Further, they provided vermin-proof containers for storage of agricultural produce. This advantage was most important in the tropics where insects, animals and fungus were more of a threat to stored food than in temperate areas. Because of the existence of toxins in the most important domesticated food plants and the significant role of pottery in detoxifying processes, it is unlikely that there was substantial reliance upon domesticated food plants without the use of pottery. Thus, the origin of pottery was probably facilitated by the necessity to detoxify plant foods.

Leopold and Ardrey (1972) tried to show that the toxic factor found in food plants was an important reason why early man developed fire, since cooking often destroys the toxins. Plant toxicity, however, only became an adaptive problem for human populations under conditions of population pressure when few animal resources were available and man had to be more dependent on a restricted range of plant resources that survived animal and insect predation. Otherwise, man could have used animals or non-toxic plant materials for subsistence. In the latter case, he would have competed with other animals for food. A further problem with the Leopold and Ardrey (1972) hypothesis is that almost all the research that they cite has concentrated on domesticated plants grown in an agricultural context, and thus does not provide a valid analogy with the food habits of early man before the development of agriculture.

There are several other implications of this work for archaeology. First, the persistence of motor habit patterns required for using pottery such as water carrying jars suggests that the extent of large populations can be traced in space by mapping vessel shapes that required identical motor habit patterns for their use. Shifts in these populations can be noted in time, and population growth, migration and conquest could be inferred. Moreover, target populations for trade pottery can be identified and the intensity of that trade can be assessed. Hypotheses concerning trade relationships can be developed using this method and then tested using mineralogical and trace element data.

How can the generalizations developed here be applied to the study of cultural process in the past? Regulatory feedback mechanisms show why cultures do not change. Deviation amplifying mechanisms, on the other hand, are those mechanisms that stimulate development and produce change. How can these mechanisms be identified from ceramics in the archaeological record? Ceramic analysis, classification and typology by themselves may be inadequate to answer questions of cultural process. Because these approaches to ceramics are based upon an analytical paradigm, ascertaining processual relationships after analysis rather than before it may eliminate many questions that can be answered by using ceramic data. The key is knowing the questions one wants to ask and then developing a system of classification that helps answer those questions. Processes of ceramic change need to be understood with reference to tangible units of behavior. Many ceramic typologies consist of analytical units which are ripped out of behavioral contexts and reassembled into abstractions like types that have limited significance outside of chronologies. Rather, the unit of ceramic behavior most useful in the identification of cultural process is not the abstract type, but the vessel shape. Vessel shapes are behaviorally significant to a culture and can provide important behavioral data about the society. Cultural change can be identified in a society when new shapes enter or leave the ceramic repertoire through time. New shapes suggest new utilitarian or religious uses for ceramics which provided a 'kick' for deviation amplifying feedback for the craft. If these were imported, they reveal economic relationships with other areas that require certain structures for integration into the society. The development of new ceramic designs that are not purely abstract and the use of ceramics in new ritual contexts may mark the beginning of a deviation amplifying mechanism of demand and may also suggest the development of an increasingly institutionalized religion and perhaps the emergence of a state religion. The sudden appearance of mythical themes from the site of Tiahuanaco in Bolivia in the ceramics of the Ayacucho Valley of Peru about A. D. 600, for example, produced a 'kick' that created a deviation amplifying affect on the craft during the Middle Horizon Period (A. D. 600-800). This feedback resulted in a proliferation of new mythical and ritual pottery during this time. Furthermore, the widespread distribution of pottery with related mythical themes in Peru during the Middle Horizon suggests the existence of a state religion.

An emphasis on vessel shapes may seem like a difficult or impossible task for the archaeologist when most of the ceramics he finds occur in the form of sherds. Vessel shapes obviously can be reconstructed from sherds and often single sherds can identify particular vessel shapes. But vessel shapes can be reconstructed even before ceramic analysis begins.

This may seem like an onerous task, but it was successfully accomplished at the George C. Davis site in Texas (Newell and Krieger, 1949) where ceramic types were based upon reconstructed vessel forms. The time it takes for such an approach may be no greater than that for the sorting, coding, and analysis of sherds used in other typological methods. The art historical approach used by the Berkeley school for Peruvian pottery (e. g. Menzel, Rowe and Dawson, 1964; Proulx, 1968; Roark, 1965; Menzel, 1976, and others) is a classification scheme that provides much potential in identifying cultural process in the past because vessel shapes are studied in their entirety. In this approach, vessels rather than sherds form the basis for study, and changes in designs through time are understood in terms of the shapes on which they occur. Up to this time, this approach has concentrated on chronological and historical rather processual concerns, but the approach has the potential to infer cultural process from ceramic data. A unique approach within this tradition (Raymond, DeBoer and Roe, 1975) described the design fields and design units on particular vessels shapes, formulated grammatical rules for the production of the design and then compared these data between the ceramic assemblages at each of two sites. These comparisons revealed that while shape, design fields and design units were similar between sites, the grammatical rules used for generating the designs were not. The different grammatical rules were most likely the product of different populations of potters. More recently, Weber (1981) has used a similar approach to infer basic social organization from the analysis of designs on Santa María burial urns from northwest Argentina. Another way to increase the potential for using ceramics to study cultural process is to highlight the most significant behavioral attributes of the ceramics such as the forming technique and vessel shape (Derricourt, 1972) in the classification of sherds. There are undoubtedly other classification methods that also emphasize vessel shapes. The results of using shapes will be far more useful in identifying cultural changes that provided deviation amplifying feedback for ceramic production than the use of abstract attributes or types alone.

Besides vessel shapes, their uses, their behavioral contexts and the religious designs on them, there is other information derived from ceramic data that can identify processes involved in prehistoric culture change. Forming techniques are related to specific motor habit patterns which are culturally based and difficult to change. Reina and Hill (1978:204-6) found that each language area in Guatemala used specific forming patterns which differed from language area to language area. Behura (1978:22) found that forming patterns used by potters in India varied from population to population even within the same language group. Gifford (1928) found that in the U. S. Southwest, certain Yuman, Piman and Shoshonean groups used the paddle and anvil technique while the Pueblos used a coiling technique. There are additional ethnographic data that suggest a relationship between the forming techniques of a pottery making population and the linguistic affiliation of that population (see Arnold, 1981). Since forming patterns and their associated motor habit patterns are probably the most conservative aspect of a ceramic complex, they can be used to identify macro-populations in time and space. Furthermore, the identification of such patterns (with reference to particular vessel shapes) can provide information about population stability, movement and change, particularly in areas with a great diversity of such techniques (such as New Guinea). The approach can also be used to identify trade or exchange between macro-populations in such locations. This approach has limited utility, however, in areas where a particular forming technique was widespread (like coiling in certain areas of North America). Nevertheless, the approach can be used to separate large populations in ceramic assemblages in certain areas (such as the Southwest) and to generate hypotheses of exchange or population movement which can be tested with other kinds of data. Often, forming techniques can be identified by inspection of sherds themselves or by breakage patterns, but petrographic thin section (Woods, 1982) and X-ray radiography (Rye, 1977) can also be used to reveal such forming patterns. Since two different techniques may be used to make the same vessel, analyses of several parts of the vessel along a vertical dimension should be made. Persistent lack of change of forming patterns through time suggests the continuity of a particular pottery producing population. Rapid change in such patterns with new vessel shapes indicates a replacement of one ceramic producing population by another. The addition of new vessel shapes made with new forming techniques indicates the addition of a new pottery making population or new economic relationship with another population.

Ceramics are related to the area in which they were made primarily through the material used for the pottery fabric. The identification of the minerals present in the paste is the most valid approach to the location of manufacture, but when supplemented by trace element analysis, more precise locational data can often be obtained. Changing compositions in space and time show how populations have adapted to local clay sources by using different clays and tempers. They do not necessarily reveal a cultural change other than technological change. Different compositions may reveal different pottery making populations in different locations. By comparing the relative frequency of vessel shapes with the composition of the fabric of these shapes, the archaeologist can assess the relative economic dominance of a pottery making community in an area. Since such areas are relatively small, with a maximum radius of 9 km, fabric analysis can provide important information about ceramic distribution patterns and accompanying economic relationships in an area. Thus, with the identification of the location of ceramic production by paste analysis, the identification of new and discarded vessel shapes in time and the identification of forming patterns, it is possible to use ceramics to identify cultural processes that have operated in antiquity as a reflection of major demographic shifts. If the source location of a particular paste can be identified by mineralogical and trace element analysis, changes in forming patterns may mean a total replacement of a population by warfare or conquest. If such patterns remain the same in time, but the ceramic paste changes, a population has merely changed the source location of its raw materials.

Because of the incompatibility of motor habit patterns of traditional and innovative forming techniques, and differences in the social organization of pottery making, new methods of ceramic production may lead to the independent establishment of a pottery making population apart from traditional contexts. Thus, two independent populations of potters may exist simultaneously in a society. In Guatemala, for example, traditional pottery is made by women in a household industry, but a male-dominated workshop industry based on the wheel was started separately from the existing patterns probably because of the incompatibility with existing patterns. Thus, a conquering population may establish a new pottery tradition alongside of the old traditional techniques of the conquered population (unless it is wiped out) rather than replacing or modifying traditional production. Expressed differently, two different modes of ceramic production may exist in the same society and reflect different aspects of that society (e. g. the 'state' versus a peasant or folk tradition). Each mode of production may produce pottery for a different segment of the population.

The tie of ceramic vessels to food detoxification and preparation indicates that these vessels form an important link to the adaptation of a population to the local environment. These vessels probably change the least over time as long as the population is exploiting the same environment. Continuity of the same utilitarian shapes over time will reveal the continuity of the same basic population, whereas great changes in these vessels (in repertoire, shape and mineralogical composition) may reveal the addition of a new population (if new utilitarian shapes are added to the repertoire of old ones) or the replacement of an old population with a new one (if the old utilitarian vessel shapes are replaced with new ones).

In conclusion, ceramic classification needs to reflect behavioral significance in a way that can be used to identify cultural process in the past. The archaeologist thus needs to tie his classification primarily to vessel shapes, and also to forming patterns. (Mineralogical analysis of the pottery fabric is less important, but primarily related to the geological location of ceramic production.) Furthermore, he needs to identify the context of pottery uses. This approach will put ceramics into their proper behavioral context and make inferences about the non-material aspects of society easier and more valid. It will also provide a behavioral base for inferring cultural processes through time that cannot be identified using ethnographic analogy alone.

BIBLIOGRAPHY

Adams, R. McC. 1972. Patterns of urbanization in early southern Mesopotamia. In *Man, settlement and urbanism*, ed. P. J. Ucko, R. Tringham, and G. W. Dimbleby, pp. 735-49. Boston, Schenkman.

Adams, W. Y. 1979. On the argument from ceramics to history: a challenge based on evidence from Medieval Nubia. *Current Anthropology* 20:727-44.

Allen, W. L. and J. B. Richardson, III. 1971. The reconstruction of kinship from archaeological data: the concepts, the methods, and the feasibility. *American Antiquity* 36:41-53.

American Ceramic Society Bulletin. 1961. Tunisian potter plies ancient craft. Vol. 40:543.

Arnold, D. E. 1971. Ethnomineralogy of Ticul, Yucatan potters: etics and emics. *American Antiquity* 36:20-40.

Arnold, D. E. 1972a. Native pottery making in Quinua, Peru. *Anthropos* 67:858-72.

Arnold, D. E. 1972b. Mineralogical analyses of ceramic materials from Quinua, Department of Ayacucho, Peru. *Archaeometry* 14:93-101.

Arnold, D. E. 1975a. Ceramic ecology of the Ayacucho Basin, Peru: implications for prehistory. *Current Anthropology* 16:183-205.

Arnold, D. E. 1975b. Some principles of paste analysis: a preliminary formulation. *Journal of the Steward Anthropological Society* 6(1):33-47 (Fall, 1974).

Arnold, D. E. 1976. Ecological variables and ceramic production: towards a general model. In *Primitive art and technology*, ed. J. S. Raymond, B. Loveseth, C. Arnold and G. Reardon, pp. 92-108. Archaeological Association, Department of Archaeology, University of Calgary, Alberta, Canada.

Arnold, D. E. 1978a. Ceramic variability, environment and culture history among the Pokom in the Valley of Guatemala. In *The spatial organization of culture*, ed. I. Hodder, pp. 39-59. London, Gerald Duckworth.

Arnold, D. E. 1978b. The ethnography of pottery making in the Valley of Guatemala. In *The ceramics of Kaminaljuyu*, ed. R. Wetherington, pp. 327-400. University Park, The Pennsylvania State University Press.

Arnold, D. E. 1981. A model for the identification of non-local ceramic distribution: a view from the present. In *Production and distribution: a ceramic viewpoint*, ed. H. Howard and E. Morris, pp. 31-44. BAR International Series 120.

Arnold, D. E. and B. F. Bohor. 1977. An ancient clay mine at Yo' K'at, Yucatan. *American Antiquity* 42:575-82.

Arrot, C. R. 1967. Ceramica actual de (Mixco Nuevo) Guatemala. *Antropología e Historia de Guatemala* 19(1):65-70.

Arrot, M. 1972. A unique method of making pottery: Santa Apolonia, Guatemala. *Expedition* 14:17-26.

Ascher, R. 1961. Analogy in archaeological interpretation. *Southwestern Journal of Anthropology* 17:317-25.

Beckett, T. H. 1958. Two pottery techniques in Morocco. *Man* 58:185-8.

Behura, N. K. 1967. Sociology of pottery among certain groups of potters in south India. *India Anthropological Survey Bulletin* 13:19-38.

Behura, N. K. 1978. *Peasant potters of Orissa*. New Delhi, Sterling.

Benedict, R. 1934. *Patterns of culture*. Boston, Houghton Mifflin.

Bertalanffy, L. V. 1968. *General system theory*. New York, George Braziller.

Betts, F. N. 1950. Tangkhul Naga pottery making. *Man* 50:117.

Birk, Y. 1969. Saponins. In *Toxic constituents of plant foodstuffs*, ed. I. E. Leiner, pp. 169-210. New York, Academic Press.

Birmingham, J. 1967. Pottery making in Andros. *Expedition* 10:33-9.

Birmingham, J. 1975. Traditional potters of the Kathmandu Valley: an ethnoarchaeological study. *Man* 10:370-86.

Bivins, J., Jr. 1972. *The Moravian potters in North Carolina*. Chapel Hill, University of North Carolina Press.

Blair, T. A. 1942. *Climatology, general and regional*. Englewood Cliffs, Prentice-Hall.

Blinman, P., J. Mehringer, Jr and J. C. Sheppard. 1979. Pollen influx and the deposition of Mazama and Glacier Peak Tephra. In *Volcanic activity and human ecology*, ed. P. D. Sheets and D. K. Grayson, pp. 373-426. New York, Academic Press.

Blom, F. and O. La Farge. 1927. *Tribes and temples*, Vol. 2. New Orleans, Middle American Research Institute.

Bock, L. 1970. Folk pottery of Guatemala. *Ceramics Monthly* 18 (February):12-15.

Bohannan, P. 1954. *Tiv farm and settlement*. London, Her Majesty's Stationery Office.

Bohannan, P. and L. Bohannan. 1958. Three source notebooks in Tiv ethnography. Unpublished manuscript. New Haven, Human Relations Area Files.

Bordaz, J. 1964. Pre-columbian ceramic kilns at Peñitas, a Post-Classic site in coastal Nayarit, Mexico. Ph. D. Dissertation in Anthropology, Columbia University. Ann Arbor, University Microfilms Publication No. 67-09325.

Boserup, E. 1965. *The conditions of agricultural growth: the economics of agrarian change under population pressure*. Chicago, Aldine.

Boulanger, G. R. 1969. Prologue: what is cybernetics? In *Survey of cybernetics*, ed. J. Rose, pp. 3-9. New York, Gordon and Breach.

Bray, W. 1978. *The gold of El Dorado*. London, Times Newspapers Limited,

Broad, W. J. 1979. Paul Feyerabend: science and the anarchist. *Science* 206:534-7.

Brookfield, H. C. and D. Hart. 1971. *Melanesia: a geographical interpretation of an island world*. London, Methuen.

Browman, D. L. 1974. Pastoral nomadism in the Andes. *Current Anthropology* 15:188-96.

Browman, D. L. 1976. Demographic correlations of the Wari conquest of Junin. *American Antiquity* 41:465-77.

Browman, D. L. 1981. Prehistoric nutrition and medicine in the Lake Titicaca Basin. In *Health in the Andes*, ed. J. W. Bastien and J. M. Donahue, pp. 103-18. Special Publication of the American Anthropological Association No. 12.

Brown, C. H. 1977. Folk botanical life-forms: their universality and growth. *American Anthropologist* 79:317-42.

Brown, J. K. 1970. A note on the division of labor by sex. *American Anthropologist* 72:1073-8.

Brünig, H. H. 1898. Moderne töpferei der indianer Perus. *Globus, Illustrierte Zeitschrift für Länder- und Völkerkunde* 74(1):259-60.

Brush, J. E. and H. E. Bracey. 1955. Rural service centers in southwestern Wisconsin and southern England. *Geographical Review* 45:559-69.

Brush, S. R. 1977. *Mountain, field, and family: the economy and human ecology of an Andean valley*. Philadelphia, University of Pennsylvania Press.

Buck, P. H. 1938. *Vikings of the sunrise*. New York, Frederick A. Stokes.

Buckley, W. 1967. *Sociology and modern systems theory*. Englewood Cliffs, Prentice-Hall.

Bullard, W. R., Jr. 1960. Maya settlement patterns in northeastern Peten, Guatemala. *American Antiquity* 25:355-72.

Bunzel, R. L. 1929. *The Pueblo potter: a study of creative imagination in primitive art*. New York, Columbia University Press.

Burton, M. L., L. A. Brudner and D. R. White. 1977. A model of the sexual division of labor. *American Ethnologist* 4:227-51.

Butler, J. and D. E. Arnold. 1977. Tzutujil maize classification in San Pedro la Laguna. In *Cognitive studies of southern Meso-america*, ed. H. L. Neuenswander and D. E. Arnold, pp. 182-205. Dallas, SIL Museum of Anthropology.

Butt, A. J. 1977. Land use and social organization of tropical forest peoples of the Guianas. In *Human ecology in the tropics: symposia of the Society for the Study of Human Biology*, Vol. XVI, ed. J. P. Garlick and R. W. J. Keay, pp. 1-18. New York, Halsted Press.

Cardew, M. 1952. Nigerian traditional pottery. *Nigeria* 39:188-201.

Cardew, M. 1969. *Pioneer pottery*. New York, St Martin's Press.

Carneiro, R. 1956. Slash-and-burn: a closer look at its implications for settlement patterns. In *Men and cultures, selected papers of the 5th ICAES*, ed. A. F. C. Wallace, pp. 229-34. Philadelphia.

Carneiro, R. 1970. A theory of the origin of the state. *Science* 169:733-8.

Carter, W. E. 1969. *New lands and old traditions: Kekchi cultivators in the Guatemalan lowlands*. Latin American Monographs (second series) No. 6. Center for Latin American Studies, University of Florida, Gainsville.

Casson, S. 1938. The modern pottery trade in the Aegean. *Antiquity* 12:467-73.

Chapman, K. 1977. *The pottery of Santo Domingo Pueblo: a detailed study of its decoration* (reprint of the 1938 edition). Albuquerque, University of New Mexico Press.

Charlton, T. H. 1976a. Modern ceramics in the Teotihuacan Valley. In *Ethnic and tourist arts*, ed. N. H. H. Graburn, pp. 137-48. Berkeley, University of California Press.

Charlton, T. H. 1976b. Contemporary central Mexican ceramics: a view from the past. *Man* (n.s.) 11:517-25.

Charlton, T. H. and R. R. Katz. 1979. Tonalá Bruñida Ware: past and present. *Archaeology* 32:45-53

Chatterjee, B. K. 1975. Comment on 'Ceramic ecology of the Ayacucho Basin, Peru: implications for prehistory' by D. E. Arnold. *Current Anthropology* 16:194-5.

Chicago Tribune 1980. Ash cloud from Mt St Helens volcano leaves trail of fallout. Wednesday, May 21, 1980, pp. 1,5.

Chisholm, M. 1968. *Rural settlement and land use*. London, Hutchinson.

Chomsky, N. 1957. *Syntactic structures*. The Hague, Mouton.

Christaller, W. 1966. *Central places in southern Germany*. Translated by C. W. Baskin from the 1933 edition. Englewood Cliffs, Prentice-Hall.

Christensen, R. T. 1955. A modern ceramic industry at Simbilá near Piura, Peru. *Chimor, Boletín de Museo de Arqueología de la Universidad Nacional de Trujillo*, Ano 3, pp. 10-20.

Christenson, A. L. 1982. Maximizing clarity in economic terminology. *American Antiquity* 47:419-26.

Clarke, D. L. 1977. Spatial information in archaeology. *Revista Mexicana de Estudios Anthropologicos* 13:31-57.

Clarke, W. C. 1971. *Place and people: an ecology of a New Guinean community*. Berkeley, University of California Press.

Clemen, R. T. 1976. Aspects of prehistoric social organization on Black Mesa. In *Papers on the archaeology of Black Mesa, Arizona*, ed. G. J. Gumerman and R. C. Euler, pp. 113-35. Carbondale, Southern Illinois University Press.

Cohen, M. N. 1977. *The food crisis in prehistory: overpopulation and the origins of agriculture*. New Haven, Yale University Press.

Cohen, R. 1960. The structure of Kanuri society. Ph. D. Dissertation in Anthropology, University of Wisconsin. Ann Arbor, University Microfilms Publication No. 60-986.

Cohen, R. 1967. *The Kanuri of Bornu*. New York, Holt, Rinehart and Winston.

Collier, D. 1959. Pottery stamping and molding on the north coast of Peru. *Actas del XXXIII Congreso Internacional de Americanistas*, Vol. 2, pp. 421-31. San Jose, Costa Rica, Editorial Antonio Lehman.

Conklin, H. C. 1953. Buhid pottery. *Journal of East Asiatic Studies* 3:1-12.

Cortes, L. L. 1954. La alfarería en Pereruela (Zamora). *Zephyrus* 5:141-63.

Cortes, L. L. 1958. Alfarería femenina en Moveros (Zamora). *Zephyrus* 9:95-107.

Crowfoot, G. M. 1932. Pots, ancient and modern. *Palestine Exploration Quarterly* (no vol.):179-87.

Curtis, F. 1962. The utility pottery industry of Bailén, Southern Spain. *American Anthropologist* 64:486-503.

David, N. and H. Hennig. 1972. The ethnography of pottery: a Fulani case seen in archaeological perspective. *Addison Wesley Modular Publications*, No. 21, pp. 1-29. Reading, Mass., Addison Wesley.

DeBoer, W. R. 1974. Ceramic longevity and archaeological interpretation: an example from the upper Ucayali, Peru. *American Antiquity* 39:335-43.

DeBoer, W. R. and D. W. Lathrap. 1979. The making and breaking of Shipibo-Conibo ceramics. In *Ethnoarchaeology: implications of ethnography for archaeology*, ed. C. Kramer, pp. 102-38. New York, Columbia University Press.

Deetz, J. 1965. *The dynamics of stylistic change in Arikara ceramics*. Urbana, University of Illinois Press.

Deetz. J. 1967. *Invitation to archaeology*. Garden City, The Natural History Press.

Densmore, F. 1929. *Chippewa customs*. Washington, U. S. Government Printing Office.

Derricourt, R. M. 1972. Ware analysis of ceramic assemblages. *South African Archaeological Bulletin* 27:144-9.

Diaz, M. 1966. *Tonalá: conservatism, responsibility and authority in a Mexican town*. Berkeley, University of California Press.

Dillon, B. D. 1977. *Salinas de Los Nueve Cerros: preliminary archaeological investigations*. Ballena Press studies in Mesoamerican art, archaeology and ethnohistory no. 2, ed. J. A. Graham. Socorro, New Mexico, Ballena Press.

Dixon, W. J. and F. J. Massey. 1969. *Introduction to statistics*. New York, McGraw-Hill.

Dobbs, H. R. C. 1897. The pottery and glass industries of the north-west provinces and Oudh. *The Journal of Indian Art and Industry* 57:1-6.

Dole, G. E. 1974. Types of Amahuaca pottery and techniques of its construction. *Ethnologische Zeitschrift Zürich* (Festschrift Otto Zerries) 1:145-59.

Donnan, C. B. 1965. Moche ceramic technology. *Ñawpa Pacha* 3:115-34.

Donnan, C. B. 1971. Ancient Peruvian potters' marks and their interpretation through ethnographic analogy. *American Antiquity* 36:460-6.

Donnan, C. B. 1978. *Moche art of Peru: pre-columbian symbolic communication*. Los Angeles, University of California, Museum of Cultural History.

Donnan, C. B. and C. Mackey. 1978. *Ancient burial practices of the Moche Valley, Peru.* Austin, University of Texas Press.

Doran, J. 1970. Systems theory, computer simulations and archaeology. *World Archaeology* 1:289-98.

Doxiadis, C. A. 1970. Ekistics, the science of human settlements. *Science* 170:393-404.

Driver, H. E. 1969. *Indians of North America,* 2nd edition. Chicago, University of Chicago Press.

Driver, H. E. and W. C. Massey. 1957. Comparative studies of North American indians. *Transactions of the American Philosophical Society* 47:165-456.

Ducey, P. R. 1956. Cultural continuity and population change on the isle of Skye. Ph. D. Dissertation in Anthropology, Columbia University. Ann Arbor, University Microfilms Publication No. 60-17, 51.

Dumond, D. E. 1965. Population growth and cultural changes. *Southwestern Journal of Anthropology* 21:302-24.

Dumond, D. E. 1969. The prehistoric pottery of southwestern Alaska. *Anthropological Papers of the University of Alaska* 14(2):19-42.

Dumond, D. E. 1972. Population growth and political centralization. In *Population growth: anthropological implications,* ed. B. Spooner, pp. 286-310. Cambridge, Mass., The MIT Press.

Dumont, L. 1952. A remarkable feature of south Indian pot making. *Man* 52:81-3.

Egloff, B. J. 1972. The sepulchral pottery of Nuamata Island. *Archaeology and Physical Anthropology in Oceania* 7:145-63.

Egloff, B. J. 1973. Contemporary Wanigela pottery. In *Occasional Papers in Anthropology, Anthropology Museum, University of Queensland,* Vol. 2, ed. P. K. Lauer, pp. 61-79.

Ellen, R. F. and I. C. Glover. 1974. Pottery manufacture and trade in the central Moluccas. *Man* 9:353-79.

Environmental Data Service. 1968. *Climatic atlas of the United States.* Washington, U. S. Dept. of Commerce, Environmental Services Administration (reprinted in 1977 by the National Oceanic and Atmospheric Administration).

Evans-Pritchard, E. E. 1949. *The Sanusi of Cyrenaica.* Oxford, Clarendon Press.

Facts on File. 1980. Mount Saint Helens erupts: blast devastates 1200 square mile area. Vol. 40(2063):382.

Farabee, W. C. 1924. The central Caribs. *The University of Pennsylvania Museum Anthropological Publications,* Vol. 10.

Fewkes, V. J. 1944. Catawba pottery making with notes on Pamunkey pottery making, Cherokee pottery making, and coiling. *Proceedings of the American Philosophical Society* 88(2):69-124.

Flannery, K. V. 1968a. Archaeological Systems Theory and early Meso-America. In *Anthropological archaeology in the Americas,* ed. B. J. Meggers, pp. 67-87. Washington, D. C., The Anthropological Society of Washington.

Flannery, K. V. 1968b. The Olmec and the valley of Oaxaca: a model for inter-regional interaction in formative times. In *Dumbarton Oaks conference on the Olmec,* ed. E. P. Benson, pp. 79-110. Dumbarton Oaks Research Library and Collection, Trustees for Harvard University, Washington, D. C.

Fonck, C. 1870. Die Indier des südlichen Chile von sonst und jetzt. *Zeitschrift für Ethnologie, Organ der Berliner Gesellschaft für Antropologie, Ethnologie und Urgeschichte* 2:284-94.

Fontana, B. L., W. J. Robinson, C. W. Cormack and E. E. Leavitt, Jr. 1962. *Papago indian pottery.* Seattle, University of Washington Press.

Forde, D. 1964. *Yako studies*. International African Institute and Oxford University Press.

Fortune, R. F. 1932. *Sorcerers of Dobu*. New York, E. P. Dutton.

Foster, G. M. 1948. Some implications of modern Mexican mold-made pottery. *Southwestern Journal of Anthropology* 4:356-70.

Foster, G. M. 1955. Contemporary pottery techniques in southern and central Mexico. *Middle American Research Institute Publication* No. 2.

Foster, G. M. 1960a. Life expectancy of utilitarian pottery in Tzintzuntzan, Michoacan, Mexico. *American Antiquity* 25:606-9.

Foster, G. M. 1960b. Archaeological implications of the modern pottery of Acatlan, Puebla, Mexico. *American Antiquity* 26:205-14.

Foster, G. M. 1962. *Traditional cultures and the impact of technological change*. New York, Harper and Row.

Foster, G. M. 1963. The dyadic contract, II: patron-client relationship. *American Anthropologist* 65:1280-94.

Foster, G. M. 1965. The sociology of pottery: questions and hypotheses arising from contemporary Mexican work. In *Ceramics and man*, ed. F. R. Matson, pp. 43-61. Chicago, Aldine.

Foster, G. M. 1967. *Tzintzuntzan: Mexican peasants in a changing world*. Boston, Little, Brown.

Foster, G. M., assisted by G. Ospina. 1948. *Empire's children: the people of Tzintzuntzan*. Smithsonian Institution, Institute of Social Anthropology Publication No. 6.

Friedman, L. and S. I. Shibko. 1969. Adventitious toxic factors in processed foods. In *Toxic constituents of plant foodstuffs*, ed. I. E. Liener, pp. 349-408. New York, Academic Press.

Friedrich, M. H. 1970. Design structure and social interaction: archaeological implications of an ethnographic analysis. *American Antiquity* 35:332-43.

Fruchter, J. S., D. E. Robertson, J. C. Evans, K. B. Olsen, E. A. Lepel, J. C. Laul, K. H. Abel, R. W. Sanders, P. O. Jackson, N. S. Wogman, R. W. Perkins, H. H. Van Tuyl, R. H. Beauchamp, J. W. Shade, J. L. Daniel, R. L. Erikson, G. A. Sehmel, R. N. Lee, A. V. Robinson, O. R. Moss, J. K. Briant, W. C. Cannon. 1980. Mount St Helens ash from the 18 May eruption: chemical, physical, mineralogical, and biological properties. *Science* 209:1116-25.

Fürer-Haimendorf, C. von. 1962. *The Apa Tanis and their neighbours*. New York, The Free Press of Glencoe.

Gade, D. W. 1975. *Plants, man and the land in the Vilcanota Valley of Peru*. Biogeographica Vol. 6. The Hague, W. Junk B. V.

Gait, E. A. 1897. The manufacture of pottery in Assam. *Journal of Indian Arts and Industries* 7:5-7.

Gayton, A. H. 1929. Yokuts and western Mono pottery making. *University of California Publications in American Archaeology and Ethnology* 24(3):239-55.

Geddes, A. 1955. *The isle of Lewis and Harris: a study in British community*. Edinburgh, Edinburgh University Press.

Geertz, C. 1968. *Agricultural involution: the processes of ecological change in Indonesia*. Berkeley and Los Angeles, University of California Press.

Geijskes, D. C. 1954. De Landbouw bij de Bosnegers van de Marowijne. *De West-Indische Gids* 35:135-53.

Gifford, E. W. 1928. Pottery making in the Southwest. *University of California Publications in American Archaeology and Ethnology* 23:352-73.

Gifford, E. W. 1951. Californian balanophagy. In *The California Indians: a source book*, ed. R. F. Heizer and M. A. Whipple, pp. 237-41. Berkeley and Los Angeles, University of California Press.

Gifford, J. C. 1960. The type-variety method of ceramic classification as an indicator of cultural phenomenon. *American Antiquity* 25:341-7.

Ginsberg, N., consulting editor. 1970. *Aldine university atlas*. Chicago, Aldine.

Golson, J. 1972. Both sides of the Wallace Line: New Guinea, Australia, Island Melanesia and Asian Prehistory. In *Early Chinese art and its possible influence in the Pacific Basin*, ed. N. Barnard, pp. 353-595. New York, Intercultural Arts Press.

Gonzalez, A. 1967. Some effects of population growth on Latin America's economy. *Journal of Inter-American Studies* 9:22-42.

Gould, R. A. 1980. *Living archaeology*. Cambridge, Cambridge University Press.

Grieder, T. 1975. The interpretation of ancient symbols. *American Anthropologist* 77:849-55.

Grim, R. E. 1962. *Applied clay mineralogy*. New York, McGraw-Hill.

Grim, R. E. 1968. *Clay mineralogy*. New York, McGraw-Hill.

Gross, D. R., G. Eiten, N. M. Flowers, F. M. Leoi, M. L. Ritter, D. W. Werner. 1979. Ecology and acculturation among native peoples of central Brazil. *Science* 206:1043-50.

Groves, M. 1960. Motu pottery. *Journal of the Polynesian Society* 69:3-22.

Gupta, J. D. 1966. The potters' craft in Poona City. *India Anthropological Survey Bulletin* 11:67-74.

Gupta, S. P. 1969. Sociology of pottery: Chirag Dilli, a case study. In *Potteries in ancient India*, ed. B. P. Sinha. pp. 15-26. Patna, Department of Ancient Indian History and Archaeology, Patna University.

Guthe, C. 1925. *Pueblo pottery making, a study at the village of San Ildefonso*. Phillips Academy, Papers of the Southwest Expedition no. 2. New Haven, Yale University Press.

Hage, P. 1977. Centrality in the Kula ring. *Journal of the Polynesian Society* 86:27-36.

Hambly, W. D. 1937. *Source book for African anthropology*, part II. Field Museum of Natural History, Publication 396.

Hammond, N. D. C. 1972. Locational models and the site of Labaantun: a classic Maya center. In *Models in archaeology*, ed. D. L. Clarke, pp. 757-800. London, Methuen.

Hammond, N. D. C. 1974. The distribution of late classic Maya major ceremonial centers in the central area. In *Mesoamerican archaeology: new approaches*, ed. N. D. C. Hammond, pp. 313-34. Austin, University of Texas Press.

Hammond, P. B. 1966. *Yatenga: technology in the culture of a west African kingdom*. New York, The Free Press.

Handler, J. 1963a. Pottery making in rural Barbados. *Southwestern Journal of Anthropology* 19:314-34.

Handler, J. 1963b. A historical sketch of pottery manufacture in Barbados. *Journal of the Barbados Museum and Historical Society* 30:129-53.

Hankey, V. 1968. Pottery-making at Beit Shebab, Lebanon. *Palestine Exploration Quarterly* 100:27-32.

Hanson, N. R. 1958. *Patterns of discovery: an inquiry into the conceptual foundations of science*. Cambridge, Cambridge University Press.

Harner, M. 1970. Population pressure and the social evolution of agriculturalists. *Southwestern Journal of Anthropology* 26:67-86.

Harris, M. 1968. *The rise of anthropological theory*. New York, T. Y. Crowell.

Harris, M. 1979. *Cultural materialism: the struggle for a science of culture*. New York, Random House.

Hatch, E. 1973a. The growth of economic, subsistence and ecological studies in American anthropology. *Journal of Anthropologial Research* 29:221-43.

Hatch, E. 1973b. *Theories of man and culture*. New York, Columbia University Press.

Hay, H. 1973. *Clay pot cooking*. Brattleboro, Vermont, Stephen Greene.

Heizer, R. F. and M. A. Whipple. 1951. *The California indians: a source book*. Berkeley, University of California Press.

Henderson, J. W., J. M. Heimann, K. W. Martindale, R.-S. Shinn, J. O. Weaver and E. T. White. 1971. *Area handbook for Burma*. Washington, U. S. Government Printing Office.

Henne, M. G. 1977. Quiche food: its cognitive structure in Chichicastenango. In *Cognitive studies of southern Meso-america*, ed. H. L. Neuenswander and D. E. Arnold, pp. 66-91. Dallas, SIL Museum of Anthropology.

Higgs, E. S. and C. Vita-Finzi. 1972. Prehistoric economies: a territorial approach. In *Papers in economic prehistory*, ed. E. S. Higgs, pp. 27-46. Cambridge, Cambridge University Press.

Hill, J. N. 1970. *Broken K Pueblo: prehistoric social organization in the American Southwest*. Anthropological Papers of the University of Arizona, No. 18. Tuscon, University of Arizona Press.

Hill, R. K. 1975. A practical system of clay evaluation. *Journal of the Australian Ceramic Society* 11:14-19.

Hill, W. W. 1937. *Navaho pottery manufacture*. University of New Mexico Bulletin, Vol. 2, No. 3, Whole number 317.

Hinshaw, R. E. 1975. *Panajachel: a Guatemalan town in thirty-year perspective*. Pittsburgh, University of Pittsburgh Press.

Hobson, S. 1970. Ceramist's odyssey of clay: the Palau Islands. *Craft Horizons* 30:16-17.

Hodder, I. R. 1972. Locational models and the study of Romano-British settlements. In *Models in archaeology*, ed. D. L. Clarke, pp. 887-909. London, Methuen.

Hodges, H. 1964. *Artifacts: an introduction to primitive technology*. New York, Frederick A. Praeger.

Hodges, H. 1974. The medieval potter: artisan or artist? In *Medieval pottery from excavations*, ed. V. I. Erison, H. Hodges and J. G. Hurst, pp. 33-40. London, John Baker.

Hogbin, H. I. 1951. *Transformation scene: the changing culture of a New Guinea village*. London, Routledge and Kegan Paul.

Holdridge, L. R. 1947. Determination of world plant formations from simple climatic data. *Science* 105:367-8.

Holleyman, G. A. 1947. Tiree Craggans. *Antiquity* 21:205-11.

Homans, G. C. 1961. *Social behavior: its elementary forms*. New York, Harcourt Brace and World.

Hopkins, K. D. and G. V. Glass. 1978. *Basic statistics for the behavioral sciences*. Englewood Cliffs, Prentice-Hall.

Howry, J. C. 1978. Ethnographic realities of Mayan prehistory. In *Cultural continuities in Meso-america*, ed. D. L. Browman, pp. 239-57. The Hague, Mouton.

Huntingford, G. W. B. 1950. *Nandi work and culture*. Colonial Research Studies No. 4. London, His Majesty's Stationery Office.

Hurault, J. 1959. Etude démographique comparée des Indiens Oayana et des noirs réfugiés Boni du Haut-Maroni (Guyane Française). *Population* 14:509-34.

Ikawa-Smith, F. 1976. On ceramic technology in east Asia. *Current Anthropology* 17:513-15.

Instituto Indigenista Nacional. 1948. *Chinaulta, síntesis socio-económica de una com-*

unidad indígena. Guatemala, Publicaciones Especiales del Instituto Indigenista Nacional, No. 4.

Instituto Nacional de Planificación. 1969. *Atlas historico, geográfico y de paisajes Peruanos*. Lima.

Irwin G. J. 1974. The emergence of a central place in coastal Papuan prehistory: a theoretical approach. *Mankind* 9:268-72.

Irwin, G. J. 1978. Pots and entrepôts: a study of settlement, trade and the development of economic specialization in Papuan prehistory. *World Archaeology* 9:299-319.

Irwin, G. 1978. Chieftainship, Kula and trade in Massim prehistory. *University of Auckland, Department of Anthropology Working Papers in Anthropology, Archaeology, Linguistics, Maori Studies*, No. 52.

Isbell, W. H. 1977. *The rural foundations for urbanism: economic and stylistic interaction between rural and urban communities in eighth century Peru*. Urbana, University of Illinois Press.

Isbell, W. H. and K. J. Schreiber. 1978. Was Huari a state? *American Antiquity* 43:372-89.

Iwanska, A. 1971. *Purgatory and utopia: a Mazuhua indian village of Mexico*. Cambridge, Mass., Schenkman.

Jaffé, W. G. 1969. Hemagluttinins. In *Toxic constituents of plant foodstuffs*, ed. I. E. Liener, pp. 66-101. New York, Academic Press.

Jaffé, W. G. 1980. Hemagluttinins. In *Toxic constituents of plant foodstuffs*, second edition, ed. I. E. Liener, pp. 73-102. New York, Academic Press.

Jarman, M. R. 1972. A territorial model for archaeology: a behavioral and geographical approach. In *Models in archaeology*, ed. D. L. Clarke, pp. 705-33. London, Methuen.

Jarman, M. R., C. Vita-Finzi, and E. S. Higgs. 1972. Site catchment analysis in archaeology. In *Man, settlement and urbanism*, ed. P. J. Ucko, R. Tringham, and G. W. Dimbleby, pp. 61-6. Boston, Schenkman.

Jeffreys, M. W. D. 1940. A musical pot from southern Nigeria. *Man* 40:186-7.

Jenni, D. A. and M. A. Jenni 1976. Carrying behavior in humans: analysis of sex differences. *Science* 194:859-60.

Johns, T. 1982. Domestication processes in Andean tuber complex. Paper presented at the 10th Annual Midwest Conference on Andean and Amazonian Archaeology and Ethnohistory, Ann Arbor, Michigan, February 28.

Kakubayashi, F. 1978. A study on the pottery-making and its economic function around Madang, Papua New Guinea. *Minzokugaku Kenkyu* (Japanese Journal of Ethnology) 43(2):138-55.

Kahn, M. C. 1931. *Djuka: the Bush Negroes of Dutch Guiana*. New York, Viking Press.

Katz, S. H., M. L. Hediger and L. A Valleroy. 1974. Traditional maize processing techniques in the New World. *Science* 184:765-73.

Kelley, I. and A. Palerm. 1952. *The Tajín Totonac: Part I, history, subsistence, shelter and technology*. Smithsonian Institution, Institute of Social Anthropology Publication No. 13.

Kelley, P. and C. Orr. 1976. *Sarayacu Quichua pottery*. SIL Museum of Anthropology, Publication No. 1. Dallas, Summer Institute of Linguistics.

Kemper, R. V. 1976. Contemporary Mexican urbanization: a view from Tzintzuntzan, Michoacan. *Atti XL Congreso Internazionale Delgi Americanisti* 4:53-65. Genova, Italy, Tilgher Genova.

Kemper, R. V. 1977. *Migration and adaptation: Tzintzuntzan peasants in Mexico City*. Sage Library of Social Research, Vol. 43. Beverly Hills, Sage Publications.

Kempton, W. 1981. *The folk classification of ceramics: a study of cognitive prototypes.* New York, Academic Press.

Kennedy, J. 1981. Lapita colonization of the Admiralty Islands? *Science* 213:757-8.

Key, C. A. 1968. Pottery manufacture in the Wanigela area of Collingwood Bay, Papua. *Mankind* 6:653-7.

King, C. 1976. Chumash intervillage economic exchange. In *Native Californians: a theoretical perspective*, ed. L. J. Bean and T. C. Blackburn, pp. 289-318. Socorro, New Mexico, Ballena Press.

Klejn, L. S. 1977. A panorama of theoretical archaeology. *Current Anthropology* 18:1-42.

Koeppe, C. K. 1931. *Canadian climate.* Bloomington, Illinois, McNight and McNight.

Kolb, C. C. 1976. The methodology of Latin American ceramic ecology. *El Dorado: Newsletter-Bulletin on South American Anthropology* 1(2):44-82.

Kresz, M. 1975. 'Comment' on 'Ceramic ecology of the Ayacucho Basin, Peru'. *Current Anthropology* 16:196-7.

Kroeber, A. L. 1928. *Peoples of the Philippines.* American Museum of Natural History Series, No. 8, second edition.

Krotser, P. H. 1974. Country pottery of Veracruz, Mexico: technological survival and culture change. In *Ethnoarchaeology*, ed. C. B. Donnan and C. W. Clewlow, Jr, pp. 131-48. Monograph IV, Institute of Archaeology, University of California, Los Angeles.

Kuhn, T. S. 1962. *The structure of scientific revolutions.* Chicago, University of Chicago Press.

Lackey, L. M. 1982. *The pottery of Acatlán: a changing Mexican tradition.* Norman, University of Oklahoma Press.

Lagacé, R. O. 1977. *Sixty cultures: a guide to the HRAF probability sample files.* New Haven, Human Relations Area Files.

Landes, R. 1937. *Ojibwa sociology.* New York, Columbia University Press.

Lanning, E. P. 1967. *Peru before the Incas.* Englewood Cliffs, Prentice-Hall.

Laszlo, E. 1972. *Introduction to systems philosophy.* New York, Gordon and Breach.

Lathrap, D. W. 1970. *The upper Amazon.* New York, Praeger.

Lathrap, D. W. 1973. The antiquity and importance of long-distance trade relationships in the moist tropics of pre-Columbian South America. *World Archaeology* 5:170-86.

Lauer, P. K. 1970. Amphlett Islands' pottery trade and the Kula. *Mankind* 7:165-76.

Lauer, P. K. 1971. Changing patterns of pottery trade to the Trobriand Islands. *World Archaeology* 3:197-209.

Lauer, P. K. 1973. Miadeba pottery. *Records of the Papua New Guinea Museum*, No. 3, pp. 63-77.

Lauer, P. K. 1974. The technology of pottery manufacture on Goodenough Island and in the Amphlett group, S. E. Papua. In *Occasional Papers in Anthropology, Anthropology Museum, University of Queensland*, vol. 2, ed. P. K. Lauer, pp. 125-60.

LaVallee, D. 1967. La poterie de Aco (Andes Centrales du Pérou). *Objets et Mondes* 7(2):103-20.

Lawless, R. 1975. Effects of population growth and environment changes on divination practices in northern Luzon. *Journal of Anthropological Research* 31:18-33.

LeFree, B. 1975. *Santa Clara pottery today*. School of American Research Monograph No. 29. Albuquerque, University of New Mexico Press.

Leopold, A. C. and R. Ardrey. 1972. Toxic substances in plants and the food habits of early man. *Science* 176:512-14.

Leslie, C. L. 1960. *Now we are civilized: a study of the world view of the Zapotec indians of Mitla, Oaxaca*. Detroit, Wayne State University Press.

Lewis, I. M. 1955. *The peoples of the Horn of Africa: Somali, Afar, and Saho, north eastern Africa*, Part I. Ethnographic Survey of Africa, ed. D. Forde. London, International African Institute.

Liener, I. E. 1969. Miscellaneous toxic factors. In *Toxic constituents of plant foodstuffs*, ed. I. E. Liener, pp. 409-48. New York, Academic Press.

Liener, I. E. and M. L. Kakade. 1969. Protease inhibitors. In *Toxic constituents of plant foodstuffs*, ed. I. E. Liener, pp. 8-68. New York, Academic Press.

Liener, I. E. and M. L. Kakade. 1980. Protease inhibitors. In *Toxic constituents of plant foodstuffs*, second edition, ed. I. E. Liener, pp. 7-71. New York, Academic Press.

Linares de Sapir, O. 1969. Diola pottery of the Fogny and Kasa. *Expedition* 11(3):2-11.

Lindblom, G. 1969. *The Akamba in British East Africa*. New York, Negro Universities Press (reprint of the 1920 edition).

Linné, S. 1925. *The technique of South American ceramics*. Kungl. Vetenskaps- och Vitterhets-Samhälles Handlingar, Fjärde följden, Band 29, No. 5. Göteborg.

Linné, S. 1965. The ethnologist and the American indian potter. In *Ceramics and man*, ed. F. R. Matson, pp. 20-42. Chicago, Aldine.

Litto, G. 1976. *South American folk pottery: traditional techniques from Peru, Ecuador, Bolivia, Venezuela, Chile, Colombia*. New York, Watson Guptill.

Lizot, J. 1974. Contribution à l'étude de la technologie Yanomami: Le modelage de la poterie et l'écorcage des arbres. *Anthropologica* 38:15-33.

Loesch, A. 1954. *The economics of location*. Translated by W. H. Woglam with W. F. Stolper from the second, revised edition, 1944. New Haven, Yale University Press.

Longacre, W. 1970. Archaeology as anthropology: a case study. *Anthropological Papers of the University of Arizona*, No. 17.

Longacre, W. 1974. Kalinga pottery making: the evaluation of a research design. In *Frontiers of anthropology*, ed. M. J. Leaf, pp. 51-67. New York, D. Van Norstrand.

Longacre, W. 1981. Kalinga pottery: an ethnoarchaeological study. in *Pattern of the past: studies in honour of David Clarke*, ed. I. Hodder, G. Isaac and N. Hammond, pp. 49-66. Cambridge, Cambridge University Press.

Mackay, E. 1930. Painted pottery in modern Sind: a survival of an ancient industry. *Journal of the Royal Anthropological Institute of Great Britian and Ireland* 60:127-35.

MacKenzie, C. 1949. *All over the place*. London, Chatto and Windus.

MacNeish, R. S., F. A. Peterson, and K. V. Flannery. 1970. *The prehistory of the Tehuacan Valley*, Vol. 3: Ceramics. Austin, University of Texas Press.

Mager, J., M. Chevion and G. Glaser. 1980. Favism. In *Toxic constituents in plant foodstuffs*, ed. I. R. Liener, pp. 266-94. New York, Academic Press.

Malinowski, B. 1922. *Argonauts of the western Pacific*. London, George Routledge and Sons.

Malinowski, B. 1944. *A scientific theory of culture and other essays*. Chapel Hill, University of North Carolina Press.

Man, E. H. 1894. Nicobar pottery. *Journal of the Royal Anthropological Institute of Great Britian and Ireland* 23:21-7.

Martin, P. S. 1971. The revolution in archaeology. *American Antiquity* 36:1-8.
Maruyama, M. 1963. The second cybernetics: deviation-amplifying mutual causal processes. *American Scientist* 51(2):164-79.
Mason, O. T. 1966. *The origin of invention: a study of industry of primitive people.* Cambridge, Mass., MIT Press (originally published in 1895).
Mathur, K. K. 1967. *Nicobar Islands.* New Delhi, National Book Trust.
Matson, F. R. 1965. Ceramic ecology: an approach to the study of the early cultures of the Near East. In *Ceramics and man,* ed. F. R. Matson, pp. 202-17. Chicago, Aldine.
Matson, F. R. 1972. Ceramic studies. In *The Minnesota Messenia Expedition,* ed. W. A. MacDonald and G. R. Rapp, Jr, pp. 220-4. Minneapolis, The University of Minnesota Press.
Matson, F. R. 1973. The potters of Chalkis. In *Classics and the classical tradition,* ed. E. N. Borza and R. W. Carruba, pp. 117-42. University Park, The Pennsylvania State University Press.
Matson, F. R. 1974. The archaeological present: near eastern village potters at work. *American Journal of Archaeology* 78:345-7.
McBryde, F. W. 1947. *Cultural and historical geography of southwest Guatemala.* Smithsonian Institution, Institute of Social Anthropology Publication No. 4.
Meggers, B. J. 1971. *Amazonia: man and culture in a counterfeit paradise.* Chicago, Aldine.
Menzel, D. 1964. Style and time in the Middle Horizon. *Ñawpa Pacha* 2:1-105.
Menzel, D. 1968. New data on the Huari empire in Middle Horizon Epoch 2A. *Ñawpa Pacha* 6:47-114.
Menzel, D. 1976. *Pottery style and society in ancient Peru.* Berkeley and Los Angeles, University of California Press.
Menzel, D., J. H. Rowe and L. H. Dawson. 1964. *The Paracas pottery of Ica: a study in style and time.* University of California Publications in American Archaeology and Ethnology, Vol. 50.
Miles, S. W. 1957. The sixteenth century Pokom-Maya: a documentary analysis of social structure and archaeological setting. *Transactions of the American Philosophical Society* 47:731-81.
Miles, S. W. 1965. Summary of the preconquest ethnology of the Guatemala-Chiapas Highlands and Pacific slopes. In *Handbook of Middle American Indians,* Vol. 2, ed. G. R. Willey, pp. 276-87. Austin, University of Texas Press.
Miller, G. A., E. Galanter, and K. H. Primbaum. 1960. *Plans and the structure of behavior.* New York, Henry Holt and Company.
Minium, E. W. and R. B. Clarke. 1982. *Elements of statistical reasoning.* New York, John Wiley and Sons.
Mitchell, W. P. 1976. Irrigation and community in the central Peruvian highlands. *American Anthropologist* 78:25-44.
Mitchell, W. P. 1979. Inconsistencia de status social y dimensiones de rango en los Andes Centrales del Perú. *Estudios Andinos* 15:21-31.
Mizuo, H. 1974. Okinawan pottery. *Japan Quarterly* 21:58-67.
Moisley, H. A. and members of the geographical field group. 1962. *Uig, a Hebridean parish.* Glasgow, The University, Department of Geography.
Montgomery, R. D. 1969. Cyanogens. In *Toxic constituents of plant foodstuffs,* ed. I. E. Liener, pp. 143-57. New York, Academic Press.
Montgomery, R. D. 1980. Cyanogens. In *Toxic constituents of plant foodstuffs,* second edition, ed. I. E. Liener, pp. 143-60. New York, Academic Press.
Morgan, L. H. 1963. *Ancient society.* Cleveland, World (originally published in 1877).

Morrill, R. L. 1970. *The spatial organization of society*. Wadsworth, Belmont.

Moseley, M. M., S. G. Pozorski, T. G. Pozorski, R. A. Feldman, E. E. Deeds, J. S. Kus, F. L. Nials, C. R. Ortloff, L. C. Pippin, R. Ravines, G. Barr and A. Narvaez. 1982. *The dynamics of agrarian collapse in coastal Peru*. A report to the National Science Foundation, Division of Behavioral and Neural Sciences, Anthropology Program. Chicago, Field Museum of Natural History.

Murdock, G. P. 1967. *Ethnographic atlas*. Pittsburgh, University of Pittsburgh Press.

Murdock, G. P. and C. Provost. 1973. Factors in the division of labor by sex: a cross-cultural analysis. *Ethnology* 12:203-25.

Murra, J. E. 1972. 'Control vertical' de un máximo de pisos ecológicos en la economía de las sociedades Andinas. In *Visita de la Provincia de Leon de Húanuco en 1562*, Iñigo Ortiz de Zúñiga, Visitador. Documentos para la Historia y Ethnología de Húanuco y la Selva Central, Tomo II, pp. 427-76. Húanuco, Perú, Universidad Nacional Hermilio Valdizan.

Murra, J. E. 1973. Rite and crop in the Inca state. In *Peoples and cultures of native America*, ed. D. R. Gross, pp. 377-89. Garden City, The National History Press. (Revised version of an article published in *Culture and history*, ed. S. Diamond, pp. 393-467, 1960.)

Murray, K. C. 1972. Pottery of the Ibo of Ohuhu-Ngwa. *The Nigerian Field* 37:148-75.

Nash, M. 1961. The social context of economic choice in a small society. *Man* 61:186-91.

Nelen, J. and O. S. Rye. 1976. Electron microprobe analyses of fired glazes. In *Traditional pottery techniques of Pakistan: field and laboratory studies*, Appendix 4, pp. 186-8. Smithsonian Contributions to Anthropology, No. 21.

Netting, R. McC. 1974. Agrarian ecology. In *Annual Review of Anthropology*, ed. B. J. Seigel, A. R. Beals and S. A. Tyler, pp. 21-56. Palo Alto, Annual Reviews.

Newell, H. P. and A. D. Krieger. 1949. *The George C. Davis site, Cherokee County, Texas*. Memoirs of the Society for American Archaeology, No. 5.

Nicholson, W. E. 1931. The potters of Sokoto: -B. Zorumawa: -C. Rumbukawa. *Man* 31:187-90.

Nicholson, W. E. 1934. Bida (Nupe) pottery. *Man* 34:71-3.

Nicklin, K. 1971. Stability and innovation in pottery manufacture. *World Archaeology* 3:13-48,94-8.

Nicklin, K. 1973a. The Ibibio musical pot. *African Arts* 7:50-55, 92.

Nicklin, K. 1973b. Abang isong: the Ibibio ceremonial palm-wine pot. *The Nigerian Field* 38:180-9.

Nicklin, K. 1979. The location of pottery manufacture. *Man* (n. s.) 14:436-8.

Nordenskiöld, E. 1919. *An ethno-geographical analysis of the material culture of two indian tribes in the Gran Chaco*. Comparative Studies No. 1, Göteborg, Erlanders Boktryckeri Artiebolag (reprinted by AMS Press, New York).

Ocholla-Ayayo, A. B. C. 1980. *The Luo culture: a reconstruction of the material culture patterns of a traditional African society*. Wiesbaden, Franz Steiner Verlag GMBH,.

Ochsenschager, E. 1974a. Mud objects from al-Hiba: a study in ancient and modern technology. *Archaeology* 27:162-74.

Ochsenschager, E. L. 1974b. Modern potters at al-Hiba, with some reflections on the excavated early dynastic pottery. In *Ethnoarchaeology*, ed. C. B. Donnan and C. W. Clewlow, Jr, pp. 149-67. Monograph IV, Institute of Archaeology, University of California, Los Angeles.

Ogan, E. 1970. Nasioi pottery-making. *Journal of the Polynesian Society* 79:86-90.

Oliver, D. L. 1967. *A Solomon Island society*. Boston, Beacon Press.

Olivera, L. O., Jefe. 1971. *Boletín del Servicio de Meterología*, Año 1971. Cuzco, Perú, Universidad Nacional del Cuzco, Programa Académico de Ciencias Biológicas.

O'Neale, L. M. 1977. Notes on pottery making in highland Peru. *Ñawpa Pacha* 14 (1976):41-60.

Orlove, B. S. 1974. Urban and rural artisans in southern Peru. *International Journal of Comparative Sociology* 15(3-4):193-211.

Osgood, C. 1940. *Ingalik material culture*. Yale University Publications in Anthropology No. 22.

Oswalt, W. 1953. Recent pottery from the Bering Strait region. *Anthropological Papers of the University of Alaska* 2(1):5-18.

Palau Martí, M. 1957. *Les Dogon*. Paris, Presses Universitaires de France.

Palmer, B. 1968. Manufacture of finger bowls (*vuluvulu*) at Nayawa Village. *Records of the Fiji Museum* 1:72-6.

Palmer, B. and E. Shaw. 1968. Pottery making in Nasama. *Records of the Fiji Museum* 1:80-90.

Papousek, D. A. 1974. Manufactura de alfarería: en Temascalcingo, México, 1967. *América Indígena* 34(4):1009-46.

Parman, S. M. 1972. Sociocultural change in a Scottish crofting township. Ph. D. Dissertation in Anthropology, Rice University. Ann Arbor, University Microfilms Publication 72-26, 459.

Parsons, E. C. 1936. *Mitla: town of souls*. Chicago, University of Chicago Press.

Pastron, A. G. 1974. Preliminary ethnoarchaeological investigations among the Tarahumara. In *Ethnoarchaeology*, ed. C. B. Donnan and C. W. Clewlow, Jr, pp. 93-114. Monograph IV, Institute of Archaeology, University of California, Los Angeles.

Patourel, H. E. J. Le. 1968. Documentary evidence and the medieval pottery industry. *Medieval Archaeology* 12:101-26.

Paullin, C. O. 1932. *Atlas of the historical geography of the United States*. Carnegie Institution of Washington, Publication 401.

Peacock, D. P. S. 1981. Archaeology, ethnology and ceramic production. In *Production and distribution: a ceramic viewpoint*, ed. H. Howard and E. L. Morris, pp. 187-94. BAR International Series 120.

Percival, W. K. 1976. The applicability of Kuhn's paradigms to the history of linguistics. *Language* 52:285-94.

Perlman, F. 1980. Allergens. In *Toxic constituents of plant foodstuffs*, second edition, ed. I. E. Liener, pp. 295-327. New York, Academic Press.

Peterson, S. 1974. *Shoji Hamada: a potter's way and work*. Tokyo, Kodansha International.

Pike, K. 1967. *Language in relation to a unified theory of human behavior*. The Hague, Mouton.

Plog, S. 1980. *Stylistic variation in prehistoric ceramics: design analysis in the American Southwest*. Cambridge, Cambridge University Press.

Pollard, H. P. and S. Gorenstein. 1980. Agrarian potential, population, and the Tarascan State. *Science* 209:274-7.

Price, B. J. 1982. Cultural materialism: a theoretical review. *American Antiquity* 47:709-41.

Proulx, D. A. 1968. *Local differences and time differences in Nazca pottery*. University of California Publications in Anthropology, Vol. 5.

Radcliffe-Brown, A. R. 1933. *The Andaman Islanders*. Cambridge, Cambridge University Press.

Ramírez-Horton, S. E. 1981. La organización económica de la costa norte: un análisis preliminar del período prehispánico tardio. In *Etnohistoria y antropología andina*, ed. A. Castelli, M. Koth de Paredes and M. Mould de Pease, pp. 281-97. Segunda jornada del Museo Nacional de Historia, organizada por el Museo Nacional de Historia y con el auspicio de la Comisión para Intercambio Educativo entre los Estados Unidos e el Perú, llevada a cabo los días 9, 10, 11, y 12 de enero de 1979, Lima, Perú.

Rappaport, R. A. 1971. Ritual, sanctity and cybernetics. *American Anthropologist* 73:59-76.

Ravines, R. H. 1963-4. Alfarería domestica de Huaylacucho, Departamento de Huancavelica. *Folklore Americano*, Año 11-12 (No.11-12):92-6.

Ravines, R. H. 1966. Ccaccasiri-pirurani mankata. *Folklore Americano*, Año 14 (No. 14):210-22.

Raymond, J. S., W. DeBoer and P. G. Roe. 1975. *Cumancaya: a Peruvian ceramic tradition.* Occasional Papers, No. 2, Department of Archaeology, the University of Calgary.

Reese, C. 1974. Women potters in Spain. *Ceramics Monthly* 22:28-33.

Reina, R. E. 1959. Continuidad de la cultura indígena en una communidad Guatemalteca. *Cuadernos del Seminario de Integración Social Guatemalteca,* Primer Serie, No. 4.

Reina, R. E. 1960. *Chinautla, a Guatemalan indian community: a study in the relationship of community culture and national change.* Middle American Research Institute, Tulane University, Publication 24, pp. 55-130.

Reina, R. E. 1963. The potter and the farmer: the fate of two innovators in a Maya village. *Expedition* 5:18-30.

Reina, R. E. 1966. *The law of the saints: a Pokomam pueblo and its community culture.* New York, Bobbs-Merrill.

Reina, R. E. 1969. Eastern Guatemala Highlands: the Pokomames and Chorti. *The Handbook of Middle American Indians* 7:101-32. Austin, University of Texas Press.

Reina, R. and R. M. Hill. 1978. *The traditional pottery of Guatemala.* Austin, University of Texas Press.

Rendón, S. 1950. Modern pottery of Riotenco San Lorenzo, Cuautitlan. *Middle American Research Records* 1(15):251-67.

Reynolds, B. 1968. *Material culture of the peoples of the Gwembe Valley.* New York, Frederick A. Praeger.

Rhodes, D. 1970. *Tamba pottery: the timeless art of a Japanese village.* Tokyo, Kodansha International.

Rice, P. M. 1977. Whiteware pottery production in the Valley of Guatemala: specialization and resource utilization. *Journal of Field Archaeology* 4:221-33.

Rice, P. M. 1978. Ceramic continuity and change in the Valley of Guatemala. In *The ceramics of Kaminaljuyu, Guatemala,* ed. R. K. Wetherington, Monograph Series on Kaminaljuyu, pp. 401-510. University Park, The Pennsylvania State University Press.

Rice, P. M. 1981. Evolution of specialized pottery production: a trial model. *Current Anthropology* 22:219-40.

Ritzenthaler, R. E. 1953. Chippewa pre-occupation with health: change in a traditional attitude resulting from modern health problems. *Milwaukee Public Museum Bulletin* 19(4):175-257.

Rivera, J. 1967. Clima de Ayacucho. *Universidad: Órgano de Extensión Cultural de la Universidad de San Cristobal de Huamanga* 3:15-16,18.

Roark, R. P. 1965. From monumental to proliferous in Nazca pottery. *Ñawpa Pacha* 3:1-92.

Robins, A. H. 1967. *A short history of linguistics.* Bloomington, Indiana University Press.

Robins, A. H. 1975. Some continuities and discontinuities in the history of linguistics. In *History of linguistic thought and contemporary linguistics,* ed. H. Parret, pp. 13-31. Berlin and New York, Walter de Gruyter.

Robles, U. C. 1962. The relation between the Pocomam and Pocomchi languages. *International Journal of American Linguistics* 28:6-8.

Roder, W. 1969. Genesis of the central place system: a Rhodesian example. *Professional Geographer* 21:333-6.

Rogers, M. J. 1936. *Yuman pottery making.* San Diego Museum Papers, No. 2 (reprinted by the Ballena Press, 1973).

Rosman, A. 1966. Social structure and acculturation among the Kanuri of northern Nigeria. Ph. D. Dissertation in Anthropology, Yale University, 1962. Ann Arbor, University Microfilms Publication No. 66-2677.

Roth, K. 1935. Pottery making in Fiji. *Man* 65:217-33.

Rouse, I. G. 1960. The classification of artifacts in archaeology. *American Antiquity* 25:313-23.

Rye, O. S. 1975. Supervivencia de tradición cerámica común a las culturas del Alto Amazonas y de manera especial a las de la zona oriental del Ecuador en Sudamérica, Part 2: Technological analysis of pottery making materials and procedures. *Hombre y Cultura* 2(5):41-62.

Rye, O. S. 1976. Keeping your temper under control: materials and the manufacture of Papuan pottery. *Archaeology and Physical Anthropology in Oceania* 11:106-37.

Rye, O. S. 1977. Pottery manufacturing techniques: X-ray studies. *Archaeometry* 19:205-11.

Rye, O. S. and C. Evans. 1976. *Traditional pottery techniques of Pakistan: field and laboratory studies.* Smithsonian Contributions to Anthropology, No. 21.

Sanders, W. T. 1973. The significance of Pikillaqta in Andean culture history. *Occasional Papers in Anthropology, Department of Anthropology, The Pennsylvania State University*, pp. 379-428.

Saraswati, B. and N. K. Behura. 1966. *Pottery techniques of peasant India.* Anthropological Survey of India Memoir No. 13.

Sarma, P. S. and G. Padmanaban. 1969. Lathrogens. In *Toxic constituents of plant foodstuffs*, ed. I. E. Liener, pp. 267-91. New York, Academic Press.

Scheans, D. J. 1965. The pottery industry of San Nicolas, Ilocos norte. *Journal of East Asiatic Studies* 9:1-28.

Schiffer, M. 1976. *Behavioral Archaeology.* New York, Academic Press.

Schofield, J. F. 1948. *Primitive pottery: an introduction to South African ceramics, prehistoric and protohistoric.* The South African Archaeological Society, Handbook Series, No. 3.

Searle, A. B. and R. W. Grimshaw. 1959. *The chemistry and physics of clays and other ceramic materials*, third edition, revised. New York, Interscience Publishers.

Seligman, C. G. 1910. *The Melanesians of British New Guinea.* Cambridge, Cambridge University Press.

Sharon, D. and C. B. Donnan. 1974. Shamanism in Moche iconography. In *Ethnoarchaeology*, ed. C. B. Donnan and C. W. Clewlow, Jr, pp. 51-92. Monograph IV, Institute of Archaeology, University of California, Los Angeles.

Sharp, L. 1952. Steel axes for stone age Australians. *Human Organization* 11:17-22.

Shepard, A. O. 1952. Ceramic technology. *Carnegie Institution of Washington Yearbook*, No. 51, pp. 263-6.

Shepard, A. O. 1956. *Ceramics for the archaeologist.* Carnegie Institution of Washington, Publication 609.

Shutler, M. E. 1968. Pottery making at Wusi, New Hebrides. *South Pacific Bulletin* 18 (fourth quarter):15-18.

Silver, H. R. 1981. Calculating risks: the socioeconomic foundations of aesthetic innovation in an Ashanti carving community. *Ethnology* 20:101-14.

Simmons, C. S., J. M. Tarano T. and J. H. Pinto Z. 1959. *Classificación de reconocimiento de los suelos de la República de Guatemala*, edición en Español por P. Tirado-Sulsona. Guatemala, Instituto Agropecuario Nacional, Servicio Cooperativo Inter-Americano de Agricultura.

Simmons, M. P. and B. F. Brem. 1979. The analysis and distribution of volcanic ash tempered pottery in the Lowland Maya area. *American Antiquity* 44:79-91.

Skeat, W. W. and C. O. Blagden 1966. *Pagan races of the Malay Peninsula*, Vol. 1. New York, Barnes and Noble (originally published in 1906).

Skinner, G. W. 1964. Marketing and social structure in rural China, Part I. *Journal of Asian Studies* 24:3-43.

Smith, F. J. and W. D. Crano. 1977. Cultural dimensions reconsidered: global and regional analyses of the ethnographic atlas. *American Anthropologist* 79:364-87.

Smith, J. 1967. The potter of Yabob. *Australian Territories* 7:9-13.

Smith, R. E. 1971. *The pottery of Mayapan*. Papers of the Peabody Museum of Archaeology and Ethnology, Vol. 66 (two vols.).

Smith, R. E., G. R. Willey and J. C. Gifford. 1960. The type-variety concept as a basis for the analysis of Maya pottery. *American Antiquity* 25:330-40.

Solheim, W. G., II. 1952a. Pottery manufacturing in the islands of Masbate and Batan, Philippines. *Journal of East Asiatic Studies* 1:49-53.

Solheim, W. G., II. 1952b. Oceanian pottery manufacture. *Journal of East Asiatic Studies* 1:1-39.

Solheim, W. G., II. 1954. Ibanag pottery manufacture in Isabela, Philippines. *Journal of East Asiatic Studies* 3:305-7.

Solheim, W. G., II and T. Shuler. 1959. Further notes on Philippine pottery manufacture: Mountain Province and Panay. *Journal of East Asiatic Studies* 8:1-10.

Spahni, J. C. 1966. *La cerámica popular del Perú*. Lima, Peruano Suiza.

Specht, J. 1968. Preliminary report of excavations on Watom Island. *Journal of the Polynesian Society* 77:117-34.

Specht, J. 1972. The pottery industry of Buka Island, Territory of Papua, New Guinea. *Anthropology and Physical Anthropology in Oceania* 7:125-44.

Spicknall, G. 1975. Some Modern Xinca ceramics. In *Papers on the Xinca of eastern Guatemala*, pp. 32-7. University of Missouri, Museum of Anthropology, Museum Brief No. 19.

Spier, R. F. G. 1967. Work habits, postures and fixtures. In *American historical anthropology: essays in honor of Leslie Spier*, ed. C. L. Riley and W. W. Taylor, pp. 197-220. Carbondale, Illinois, Southern Illinois University Press.

Spooner, B., ed. 1972. *Population growth: anthropological implications*. Cambridge, Mass., MIT Press.

Stanislawski, M. B. and B. B. Stanislawski. 1978. Hopi and Hopi-Tewa ceramic tradition networks. In *The spatial organisation of culture*, ed. I. Hodder, pp. 61-76. London, Gerald Duckworth.

Steadman, P. 1980. *The evolution of designs*. Cambridge, Cambridge University Press.

Stein, W. W. 1961. *Hualcan: life in the highlands of Peru*. Ithaca, Cornell University Press.

Steward, J. 1955. *Theory of culture change*. Urbana, University of Illinois Press.

Stone, D. S. 1949. *The Boruca of Costa Rica*. Peabody Museum of American Archaeology and Ethnology, Vol. 26, No. 2.

Strauss, D. J. and M. Orans. 1975. Mighty shifts: a critical appraisal of solutions to Galton's Problem and a partial solution. *Current Anthropology* 16:573-94.

Tax, S. 1941. *Penny capitalism: a Guatemalan indian economy.* Smithsonian Institution, Institute of Social Anthropology Publication No. 16.

Thomas, D. H. 1974. *Predicting the past: an introduction to anthropological archaeology.* New York, Holt, Rinehart and Winston.

Thomas, N. W. 1910. Pottery-making of the Edo-speaking peoples, Southern Nigeria. *Man* 10:97-8.

Thompson, F. G. 1973. *Harris and Lewis: Outer Hebrides,* revised edition. Newton Abbot, Devon, David and Charles.

Thompson, J. E. 1930. *Ethnology of the Mayas of southern and central British Honduras.* Field Museum of Natural History, Publication 274, Anthropological Series, Vol. 17 no. 2.

Thompson, R. A. 1974. *The winds of tomorrow: social change in a Maya town.* Chicago, University of Chicago Press.

Thompson, R. H. 1958. *Modern Yucatecan Maya pottery making.* Memoirs of the Society for American Archaeology No. 15.

Time Magazine. 1980. 'God I want to live': Mount Saint Helens explodes, spreading death and destruction in the Cascades. 115 (June 2, No. 22):26-35.

Tindale, N. B. and H. K. Bartlett. 1937. Notes on some clay pots from Panaeati Island, south-east of New Guinea. *Royal Society of South Australia Transactions* 61:159-62.

Tosi, J. A. 1960. *Zonas de vida natural en el Perú.* Instituto Interamericano de Ciencias Agricolas de la Organización de Estados Americanos Zona Andina, Boletín Técnico, No. 5. Lima, Organización de Estados Americanos.

Toulmin, S. E. 1961. *Foresight and understanding: an inquiry into the aims of science.* Bloomington, Indiana University Press.

Tschopick, H., Jr. 1947. *Highland communities of central Peru: a regional survey.* Smithsonian Institution, Institute of Social Anthropology Publication No. 5.

Tschopik, H., Jr. 1950. An Andean ceramic tradition in historical perspective. *American Antiquity* 15:196-218.

Tuckson, M. 1966. Pottery in New Guinea. In *Pottery in Australia* 5(1):9-16.

Tuckson, M. and P. May. 1975. Pots, firing and potters in Papua New Guinea. *Australian Natural History* 18(5):168-73.

Tufnell, O. 1961. These were the potters: notes on the craft in southern Arabia. *Leeds Oriental Society* 2:26-36.

Turner, P. R. 1977. Intensive agriculture among the highland Tzeltal. *Ethnology* 16:167-74.

Van Camp, G. R. 1979. *Kumeyaay pottery: paddle and anvil techniques of southern California.* Socorro, New Mexico, Ballena Press.

Van de Velde, P. and H. R. Van de Velde. 1939. *The black pottery of Coyotepec, Oaxaca, Mexico.* Southwest Museum Papers, No. 13.

Van der Leeuw, S. E. 1976. *Studies in the technology of ancient pottery* (two vols.). Amsterdam.

Van der Leeuw, S. E. 1981. Ceramic exchange and manufacture: a 'flow structure' approach. In *Production and distribution: a ceramic viewpoint,* ed. H. Howard and E. L. Morris, pp. 361-86. BAR International Series, No. 120.

Van Etten, C. H. 1969. Goitrogens. In *Toxic constituents of plant foodstuffs,* ed. I. E. Liener, pp. 103-34. New York, Academic Press.

Villa Rojas, A. 1969. The Tzeltal. In *Handbook of Middle American Indians,* Vol. 7, pp. 195-225. Austin, University of Texas Press.

Voyatzoglou, M. 1973. The potters of Thrapsano. *Ceramic Review* 24:13-16.

Voyatzoglou, M. 1974. The jar makers of Thrapsano in Crete. *Expedition* 16:18-24.

Wahlman, M. 1972. Yoruba pottery making techniques. *Baessler-Archiv* 20:313-46.

Ward, R. de C., C. F. Brooks and A. J. Connor. 1972. *The climates of North America*. Handbuch der Klimatologie, Band II. Tiel J. Nendeln, Liechtenstein, Kraus Reprint (originally published in 1936).

Watson, P. J. 1973. The future of archaeology in anthropology: culture history and social science. In *Research and theory in current archaeology*, ed. C. L. Redman, pp. 113-24. New York, John Wiley and Sons.

Watson, V. 1955. Pottery in the eastern highlands of New Guinea. *Southwestern Journal of Anthropology* 11:121-8.

Weber, R. L. 1981. An analysis of Santa Maria urn painting and its cultural implications. *Fieldiana Anthropology*, New Series, No. 2.

Whallon, R., Jr. 1972. A new approach to pottery typology. *American Antiquity* 37:13-33.

Whitaker, I. and E. Whitaker. 1978. *A potter's Mexico*. Albuquerque, University of New Mexico Press.

Whiteford, A. H. 1977. *An Andean city at mid century: a traditional urban society*. Latin American Studies Center Monograph Series No. 14. East Lansing, Michigan State University.

Willett, F. and G. Connah. 1969. Pottery making in the village of Use near Benin City, Nigeria. *Baessler-Archiv* 22:133-49.

Willey, G. R. 1947. Ceramics. In *Handbook of South American Indians*, Vol. V. Smithsonian Institution, Bureau of American Ethnology, Bulletin No. 143 (reprinted by Cooper Square Publishers, 1963).

Willey, G. R. 1971. *An introduction to American archaeology: Volume 2, South America*. Englewood Cliffs, Prentice-Hall.

Willey, G. R. and J. A. Sabloff. 1980. *A history of American archaeology*, second edition. San Francisco, W. H. Freeman.

Williams, H. 1960. Volcanic history of the Guatemalan highlands. *University of California Publications in Geological Sciences* 38:1-72.

Winkler, E. M. 1973. *Stone: properties, durability in man's environment*. New York and Vienna, Springer-Verlag.

Winterhalder, B., R. Larsen and R. B. Thomas. 1974. Dung as an essential resource in a highland Peruvian community. *Human Ecology* 2:89-104.

Witkowski, S. R. and C. H. Brown. 1977. An explanation of color nomenclature universals. *American Anthropologist* 79:50-7.

Wolf, E. 1955. Types of Latin American peasantry: a preliminary discussion. *American Anthropologist* 57:452-71.

Woods, A. 1982. Thin sections and ceramic technology: an introduction. In *Microscopy in archaeological conservation*, ed. M. Corfield and K. Foley. United Kingdom Institute for Conservation Occasional Papers, No. 2.

Yang, M. G. and O. M. Mickelsen. 1969. Cycads. In *Toxic constituents of plant foodstuffs*, ed. I. E. Liener, pp. 159-67. New York, Academic Press.

INDEX

(Page numbers refer to both text and illustrations)